A FOCUSED ISSUE ON IDENTIFYING, BUILDING, AND LINKING COMPETENCES

RESEARCH IN COMPETENCE-BASED MANAGEMENT

Series Editors: Professor Ron Sanchez and
Professor Aimé Heene

Recent Volumes:

RESEARCH IN COMPETENCE-BASED MANAGEMENT
VOLUME 5

A *Focused Issue on* IDENTIFYING, BUILDING, AND LINKING COMPETENCES

EDITED BY

RON SANCHEZ

Copenhagen Business School, Denmark; and
National University of Singapore, Singapore

AIMÉ HEENE

Ghent University, Belgium; and
University of Antwerp Management School, Belgium

United Kingdom – North America – Japan
India – Malaysia – China

Emerald Group Publishing Limited
Howard House, Wagon Lane, Bingley BD16 1WA, UK

First edition 2010

British Library Cataloguing in Publication Data
A catalogue record for this book is available from the British Library

ISBN: 978-1-84950-990-9
ISSN: 1744-2117 (Series)

CONTENTS

**PART II: THE INTELLECTUAL
STRUCTURE OF THE COMPETENCE-BASED
PERSPECTIVE**

LIST OF CONTRIBUTORS

Fran Ackermann — Strathclyde Business School, University of Strathclyde, Glasgow, UK

Jean-Pierre Boissin — CERAG Research Center, Université Pierre Mendès-France (Grenoble II), France

Bénédicte Branchet — CERAG Research Center, Université Pierre Mendès-France (Grenoble II), France

Jean-Claude Castagnos — CERAG Research Center, Université Pierre Mendès-France (Grenoble II), France

Colin Eden — Strathclyde Business School, University of Strathclyde, Glasgow, UK

Jörg Freiling — LEMEX – Chair for Small Business & Entrepreneurship, Universitaet Bremen, Bremen, Germany

Martin Gersch — School of Business & Economics, Freie Universitaet Berlin, Berlin, Germany

Alexander Gerybadze — Department of International Management, University of Hohenheim, Stuttgart, Germany

Christian Goeke — School of Business & Economics, Freie Universitaet Berlin, Berlin, Germany

Gilles Guieu — CRET-LOG Research Center, Université de la Méditerranée (Aix-Marseille II), France

Pekka Huovinen — Department of Structural Engineering and Building Technology, Aalto University, Aalto, Finland

Rudy Moenaert — TiasNimbas Business School, University of Tilburg, Tilburg, Netherlands

Sezi Çevik Onar	Management Faculty, Istanbul Technical University, Istanbul, Turkey
Seçkin Polat	Management Faculty, Istanbul Technical University, Istanbul, Turkey
Frédéric Prévot	Department of Strategy and Environment, Euromed Marseille School of Management, Marseille, France
Adriana Priyono	Emporis GmbH, Frankfurt, Germany
Heike Proff	CAMA – Center for Automotive Management, Universitaet Duisburg-Essen, Duisburg, Germany
Ron Sanchez	Department of Innovation and Organizational Economics, Copenhagen Business School, Frederiksberg, Denmark and National University of Singapore, Singapore
Toni Sfirtsis	TiasNimbas Business School, University of Tilburg, Tilburg, Netherlands
André Slowak	Department of International Management, University of Hohenheim, Stuttgart, Germany
Denis Tejada	INTRADESA, San Salvador, El Salvador

INTRODUCTION: IDENTIFYING, BUILDING, AND LINKING COMPETENCES

Part I of this issue of Research in Competence-Based Management (RCBM) includes eight papers that explore a number of important aspects of identifying, building, and linking competences within and between organizations. Part II includes a special reflection on the intellectual structure of and influences within the competence-based management perspective.

PART I: IDENTIFYING, BUILDING, AND LINKING COMPETENCES

Part I of this issue begins with a paper by Colin Eden and Fran Ackermann on "Competences, distinctive competences, and core competences." Eden and Ackermann draw on their extensive work with top management teams in workshops focused on identifying the competences of an organization. They describe an interactive process of engagement with managers through which an organization's competences are identified, some of which are further judged to be "distinctive competences" of the organization. Analysis of the interrelationships among a firm's identified competences then leads to the discovery of a pattern of competence interactions in which some competences appear to be at the "core" of the organizations distinctive competences. The paper presents an interesting perspective on how the capabilities and competences of a firm are often interrelated in ways that invite special attention and development by managers. Further, the paper explains the systems methodology that the authors have developed for use with managers to help identify and assess an organization's competences.

In their paper "Managing the interaction of exploration and exploitation: Ambidexterity as a high-order dynamic capability," Toni Sfirtsis and Rudy Moenaert address the ways in which developing organizational ambidexterity requires achieving a balance between exploration and exploitation. They specifically address the ways in which barriers to resource reconfiguration may constrain a firm's combinative capabilities and suggest how under those conditions a firm's combinative capabilities take on the character of "balancing routines."

Sezi Çevik Onar and Seçkin Polat's paper "Factors affecting the relation between strategic options and the competence building process: An empirical examination" examines the ways in which competence building processes may create important strategic options for a firm when market and technology conditions are uncertain. They construct a model suggesting the ways in which mergers and acquisitions may be used as a vehicle to acquire or build new competences. They then analyze mergers and acquisitions undertaken through the Istanbul stock exchange to identify the competences the mergers and acquisitions brought to firms. They then analyze changes in the market value of acquiring or merged firms to determine the value of the strategic options that acquiring or extending competences created for the acquiring and merging firms. From this they draw some conclusions about effective versus ineffective practices in building new competences capable of creating valuable strategic options.

In their paper "The coevolution of alliances and industries: How industry transformation influences alliance formation and vice versa," Christian Goeke, Martin Gersch, and Jörg Freiling examine the important role of alliances during periods of industry transformation. Taking the case of the transformation of the German Health Care industry during 2004–2007, they identify and elaborate three motivations for alliance formation during periods of transformation: (i) "gap-closing alliances" intended to close perceived resource and competence gaps; (ii) alliances intended to act as "option networks" that bring firms new strategic options during periods of uncertain change; and (iii) "steering alliances" intended to achieve a critical mass capable of exerting influence on the evolving industry environment.

The paper "The role of distributed competences for standard-setting communities: The case of industrial automation" by Alexander Gerybadze and André Slowak extends the study of industry alliances into the domain of standards-setting processes. Taking the open-systems view of organizations, the authors study the ways in which firms in the industrial automation industry try to bundle together complementary assets from proprietary and open technologies to achieve integration of knowledge that crosses firm and even industry boundaries. Their study suggests the importance of learning how to link together the "distributed competences" within an industry in order to define new standards that enable the industry to advance its technological capabilities and market development.

In her paper "Challenges for differentiators combining modularization and competence renewal," Heike Proff assesses the impacts of modularization on the distribution of competences within the vertical structure of an industry. Taking the automotive industry as the context for analysis, Proff suggests that as modularization of product designs enables greater outsourcing of component development from OEMs to specialized suppliers, competences are effectively being transferred as well, resulting in new firm boundaries for both parties. Proff also argues that such transfers of competences affect the future distributions of profits within an industry.

In his study "Recursive advancement of competence-based business management and its conceptual modeling," Pekka Huovinen elaborates the open-systems view of organizations by extending Stafford Beer's viable system model of the firm. Huovinen proposes use of a "recursive template" composed of three competence- and process-based systems within firms that can serve as a framework for managing competences within a firm. Each system is characterized as having its own systemic competences and flexibilities. This recursive systems view suggests important approaches not only to managing competence building and leveraging in firms, but to further theoretical development of the open-systems view of firms that is a cornerstone of the competence perspective.

In their paper "An expanded view of "Management Processes" in the systems view of organizations," Adriana Priyono, Denis Tejada, and Ron Sanchez elaborate the concept of "Management Processes" in the open-system model of organization. They identify specific kinds of activities that must be undertaken in the management processes that mediate between a firm's Strategic Logic and its current resources and processes, and they suggest how the identified activities provide linkages to related activities and useful frameworks in marketing, operations, human resources, and other functional areas of management.

PART II: THE INTELLECTUAL STRUCTURE OF THE COMPETENCE-BASED PERSPECTIVE

In their paper "The intellectual structure of the competence-based management field: A bibliometric analysis," Frédéric Prévot, Benedicte Branchet, Jean-Pierre Boissin, Jean-Claude Castagnos, and Gilles Guieu provide a retrospective look at the intellectual structure and evolution of the competence-based management perspective. The authors trace a network of 7,958 citations in 185 competence publications by 213 authors between 1994 and 2008 to identify the authors that have become key nodes in the web of competence citations. They also identify the most frequently cited competence papers and categorize the cited papers according to their theoretical or empirical emphasis, their use of qualitative or quantitative methods, and their keywords. From this analysis emerges an informative picture of the evolving organization and emerging influences within the competence-based management perspective as a field of study and research.

Ron Sanchez
Aimé Heene
Editors

PART I
IDENTIFYING, BUILDING, AND LINKING COMPETENCES

COMPETENCES, DISTINCTIVE COMPETENCES, AND CORE COMPETENCES

Colin Eden and Fran Ackermann

ABSTRACT

In order to elaborate the concept of resources (a key component of the well-established resource-based theory of the firm) this paper concentrates on exploring and elaborating the associated concept of competences, in particular distinctive and core competences. This exploration includes an examination of the extant literature, alongside and in parallel with, an extensive body of action research undertaken over 15 years and with 44 top management teams engaged in strategy making. As such the concepts are scrutinized both in terms of their theoretical underpinnings as well as their impact on practice. The research reinforces the view that distinctiveness emerges most powerfully from the identification (or creation) of unique bundles or combinations of competences and that effective and meaningful core competences can be identified from understanding and refining the links between competences and organizational goals. The resultant conceptualization of the systemic competence/goals structure emerges from the interaction of theory and practice.

A Focused Issue on Identifying, Building, and Linking Competences
Research in Competence-Based Management, Volume 5, 3–33
ISSN: 1744-2117/doi:10.1108/S1744-2117(2010)0000005004

INTRODUCTION

Within the resourcebased view (RBV) of competitiveness there is ambiguity about what constitutes a resource. Indeed many of the concepts in this field are regarded as ambiguous and open to multiple interpretations (Foss & Knudsen, 2003; Hoopes, Madsen, & Walker, 2003; Priem & Butler, 2001; Rugman & Verbeke, 2002). This contrasts with the more highly developed assertions about the categories of resources – expressed originally by Barney (1991, 2001) as valuable/rare/imperfectly imitable/nonsubstitutable (VRIN). One consequence of this opacity is the suggestion that the imprecise nature of the various concepts within the field constrains their usefulness for strategic management (Nanda, 1996). Some also argue that this difficulty with the inherent vagueness of terms is what makes repeatable empirical research problematic (Hoopes et al., 2003). These criticisms of the RBV make it less useful than it might be to both scholars and practitioners. This paper thus concentrates on understanding the practical nature of competence-based management (CBM), and in particular of distinctive competences as one important type of resource as a means to achieving competitive advantage. This focus seeks to reduce the degree of vagueness about what makes competences distinctive and also what might make them core to the success of a business. The emphasis in the research reported here reflects the more credible European developments of RBV into a CBM perspective (Sanchez, Heene, & Howard, 1996; Sanchez & Heene, 2004).

In this paper we suggest that (i) the most likely form of resource distinctiveness arises through the identification of a unique *pattern of competences* and (ii) that core competences arise by analyzing the *network of relationships* between competences and the distinctive business goals or purpose of the organization. Core competences are central to (or at the core of) the network relationships between competences and organizational pur- pose (goals). The research reported in this paper considers the characteristics of competences, distinctive competences, and core competences by exploring their use in the context of strategy making practice among top management teams (TMTs). In so doing we aim to elaborate theory through its exploitation in practice, and so also explore the implications of the theory for practice.

BACKGROUND

Many researchers argue that attention to *distinctive* competences and core competences (Hamel, 1994; Hamel & Heene, 1994; Prahalad & Hamel, 1990;

Sanchez, 2002; Schoemaker, 1992; Selznik, 1957) is significant in explaining, and so managing, the success of an organization. For example, organizations with strategies based on core versus noncore competences are expected to survive recession better than others and emerge stronger as economic recovery develops (Bogner & Thomas, 1994).

Selznik (1957) and Penrose (1959) are among the first to identify and label a distinctive competence as a particularly valuable resource for organizations. They believe that a key role for organizational leaders is to identify, invest in, and protect such competences and the resources that underlie them. The RBV and CBM model, of the firm (Barney, 1986, 1991; Peteraf, 1993; Rumelt, 1984; Sanchez & Heene, 2004; Wernerfelt, 1984) focuses on the crucial importance of competences, assets, and resources for organizational survival, growth, and overall effectiveness. One of the key insights of the RBV is that "scarce, valuable, and imperfectly imitable resources are the only factors capable of creating sustained performance differences among competing firms, and that these resources should figure prominently in strategy making" (Kraatz & Zajac, 2001, p. 632). Distinctive competences are regarded as one such resource. Thus, a necessary part of strategy making for any management team in any type of organization – not-for-profit as well as for-profit – is to reflect upon organizational competences that are distinctive. For example, Collis (1991, p. 51) argues that "the resources the firm possesses must still be evaluated against those held by competitors, because only a competitively unique and superior competence can be a source of economic value."

The need to understand how the concepts are used in *the practice of strategic management* influences the nature of the research in this paper. The application of the concepts by real strategy making teams across many organizations is an appropriate vehicle for such an exploration. In the same way Lewin (1951, p. 169) argues that "nothing is as practical as a good theory"; this research aims to find out whether these concepts conform to good theory. The research did not divorce theory development from the utility of the theories to practitioners; instead theory development is taken to occur through engaging practitioners in attempts to operationalize often vague, but attractive, concepts.

The paper begins with a discussion of the research design. Subsequently, the paper is structured to introduce the development of the concepts step by step. Thus the paper explores what a distinctive competence is, and how distinctive competences arise from "patterns" of competences. This leads to the exploration of the practical implications of the concept of "core" competences, focusing upon a need to examine the relationships between the distinctive competence patterns and the business goals of the organization. The paper concludes with a review of the elaborated concepts, a discussion about how this work relates to the RBV, and possible future research.

RESEARCH DESIGN

General concerns about practical relevance have been identified in relation to strategy research (Chakravarthy & Doz, 1992; Gopinath & Hoffman, 1995; Jarzabkowski, Balogun, & Seidl, 2007), even though strategy research claims relevance to practice (Bettis, 1991; Pettigrew, Thomas, & Whittington, 2002). Acknowledging this disquiet, the general basis of this paper is to develop the concepts in relation to strategy making and in particular explore theory within the context of practice. As such we have been more concerned with the significance of organizational experiences than with theory development *in the abstract* (Hambrick, 2007). As Huff (2000) argues in her 1999 presidential speech to the Academy of Management, an important role for management research is to develop appropriate concepts, conduct comparative studies across contexts, and develop more general frameworks, with *these frameworks being validated in use* (our emphasis). Thus a "Research Oriented Action Research" format has been followed, but within the tradition of extending theories from extensive, multiple, case study research (Eden & Huxham, 2006; Eisenhardt, 1989a). Action research is not without problems – for example, explicit interference from the investigator, difficulties of replication, emotional involvement from researchers (Champion & Stowell, 2003; Huxham & Hibbert, 2006).

To test the concepts of distinctive and core competence the research was undertaken with those who have substantial power to make and implement strategy – the TMT. As such the research on the application of the concepts was set within a wider involvement with each of the TMTs – that of developing an overall strategy but from a standpoint of exploring competitive advantage. The action research program typically involved a strategy making engagement over several 1–2 day sessions with the TMT of each of 44 organizations, and the complete research program spanned a period of 15 years. The research initiative started with a project located in Shell group planning in 1990 where there was a recognized difficulty in operationalizing the concept of distinctive competences. It then continued with other multinational organizations as well as within SMEs and public or not-for-profit organizations. These organizations comprised: 9 not-for-profit and 35 for-profit organizations of which 4 were multinational. Inevitably the sample is biased – they are all interventions where the CEO was attracted to our approach to strategy making and was prepared to have academics working with their top management colleagues as researchers as well as facilitators. Thus the organizations cannot be regarded as representative of any particular set of industries, size or type. Nevertheless opportunities were filtered in order to allow a wide range of organizations to be involved. The size of the TMT ranged from 5 to 14 managers. Conducting the research as an action research program, where the intervention is dominated by research aims, rather than the completion of a consultancy project, provides access to data that would otherwise not be available to researchers. Thus, the authors are "researchers *qua* interventionists, as distinct from interventionists *qua* researchers" (Eden & Huxham, p. 395).

Although there was no absolute control over the stream of contexts applying to each team, similar characteristics emerging from the different contexts were sought. For example, there was no evidence of the nature of the data being particularly specific to public versus private, or any other context. Views were sought from as many team members as became engaged in conversation about the impact of the concepts in use. The research data is, to some extent, possibly biased by those with "strong" views. The researchers are of different ages, and of different gender, and these features were exploited in order to gain triangulation. For example, the nature of the delivery of comments to each researcher varied and sometimes revealed additional views, sometimes conflicting views, and most often similar views expressed differently. Because of the nature of data delivery the data collection from conversation was dependent on notes recorded from short-term memory.

The focus of the overall approach to strategy making was process driven, where the methods for the analysis of competitive advantage were developed through qualitative interactive models ("transitional objects" [de Geus, 1988; Winnicott, 1953]). These models facilitated and represented strategic conversations within the TMT, rather than being the output of the analysis of a "back-room" support team. Thus, the research deliberately focused upon direct engagement with members of the TMT, both at meetings of the team, and as individual members of the team. The transitional object – a continuously developing cause map (Eden & Ackermann, 2001; Huff & Jenkins, 2001; Huff, 1990) – was also fundamental to the recording of data used by the TMT in real time and was subsequently an important part of the research data set.

After each intervention a research review considered how the TMT had related to the concepts of a competence, distinctive competence, and core competence. Had the concepts been understood? Did they make sense? Were they capable of being operationalized in the context of the known organization? Did they influence strategy agreements? The research followed a "fine-grained methodology" (Harrigan, 1983). The review involved a combination (where possible) of sharing facilitator observations and notes (typically there were two facilitators working with the group), examining the cause map – the changing "transitional object" that captured the data generated by the TMT as the meeting progressed, and asking the participants themselves through unstructured conversations determined by local circumstances and influenced by the participants being elites. In addition, a data log tracking each contribution provided time series indications of how the assertions of competence and their causal relationships changed during the meeting.

The significant advantage of designing the research as action research for this stream of cases was that the researchers were working "behind the scenes" and given access to sensitive information and to the team members "real" experience of working with the concepts. Care was taken to document as much "relevant" data as possible and be reflective about the meaning of the data (Huxham & Vangen, 2003). It has been noted that data from the study of senior management teams is important in managerial research (Starbuck & Mezias, 1996). But, gaining access to elites and getting close to their views on strategy making and the concepts embedded in the strategy making process is notoriously problematic (Norburn, 1989) with a few exceptions (Eisenhardt, 1989b; Eisenhardt & Schoonhoven, 1990; Pettigrew & McNulty, 1995). Access difficulties have been and remain a source of constraint on studies of elites (Pettigrew, 1992, p. 164).

As with "pure" case study research, "the method relies on continuous comparison of data and theory, beginning with data collection" (Eisenhardt, 1989a). After the data collection from each intervention, the data was analyzed to search for patterns. Thus the comparisons made across multiple case studies sought to develop conceptual rather than statistical generalization beyond specific local conditions (Tsoukas, 1989). Theory built from case studies, is situated in and developed by the recognition of patterns of constructs and relationships within and across the cases (Doktor, Tung, & Glinow, 1991; Eisenhardt & Graebner, 2007). Through an iterative process, this was done until "saturation" (in the language of Glaser & Strauss, 1967, p. 61, 111) of the emergent characteristics was reached. Subsequently, the concepts were redefined to produce sharper (and more useful) concepts. Also, after each intervention, potential changes to the nature of the concepts were debated, often resulting in a reexamination and reinterpretation of the literature. In addition, new developments in the literature influenced the interpretation of the concepts.

DISTINCTIVE *COMPETENCES* AND COMPETENCE *OUTCOMES*

Confusions

There are two specific confusions about the nature of distinctive competences, both within the literature and emergent from working with managers in practice: what is a competence? and what is meant by distinctive? A further confusion is the lack of clarity between distinctive competence outcomes (i.e., the outcomes from the competences) and the competences themselves. It can be argued that the discussion of the concepts and examples in the literature tend to focus on distinctive competence outcomes (e.g., "reputation") rather than on the distinctive competences that create or sustain them. Alternatively, sometimes the focus is directly on the saleable commodity, as if it were the competence. Both competences and outcomes are acknowledged and valued in an example presented by Collins and Porras (1995). They report that when David Packard (cofounder of Hewlett-Packard) was asked which product decisions he was most proud of, he answered entirely in terms of *organizational* achievements (competences and competence outcomes). Packard argued that developing an engineering team culture, designing a pay-as-you-go policy to encourage fiscal discipline, creating a profit-sharing scheme that stimulated cooperation, and constructing the "HP Way" philosophy of management were the achievements. Cooperation and developing an engineering culture are competence outcomes. They are outcomes not competences because it would be difficult for others to easily identify the competences required to create these outcomes, whereas the ability to create a profit-sharing scheme that *will stimulate* cooperation within HP is a competence, and one that is possibly distinctive. Similarly, as Hall (1992) commented: "Jaguar cars enjoys the differentiation achieved by the reputation of the Jaguar name; the distinctive competence which the company enjoys, however, is the ability to build a special type, a quality car. This ability is founded on the skill and experience, or know-how, of the employees" (p. 139). This is an example of a product as the outcome of competences, where the competences that deliver the outcome are expressed in a way that enables them to be protected, and sustained, or exploited.

Our own data consistently records the same hierarchy – see Fig. 2 for an example of a part of some early discussion within a TMT.

Outcomes or Competences?

Distinguishing competences from competence outcomes is important. When managers discuss distinctive competences our research indicates that they usually start by reporting the outcomes of competences. TMTs find it extremely difficult to identify *distinctive* competences, but easy to identify distinctive competence outcomes and distinctive assets that might be exploited by competences and so deliver distinctive competence outcomes. A distinguishing characteristic of a distinctive competence outcome is that it *cannot be managed directly*; rather it is the competences that deliver the outcomes that can be managed. For example, "reputation for on-time delivery" is a competence outcome not a competence. It is the particular portfolio of competences that enable the reputation to be gained that can be managed strategically. Similarly, low cost production is often argued to be a competence, whereas it is a competence outcome that may not be distinctive unless it can be sustained through the continued exploitation of distinctive competences.

During the research reported here, it became increasingly clear that four helpful, but not precise, guidelines distinguish distinctive competences, distinctive competence outcomes, and distinctive assets. A distinctive competence, as a strategically useful resource, is: (i) amenable to being strategically managed in a relatively unambiguous way; (ii) an ability to do something, and so the phrase "ability to…" can be inserted at the beginning of the stated competence. Whereas, (iii) distinctive competence outcomes more directly support a goal (e.g., "significantly low levels of waste"), or something the customer values ("consistent quality") – an outcome the customer appreciates directly. Competence outcomes are more externally focused. Finally, (iv) a distinctive asset is typically an obvious resource, often history, that can be exploited by competences (e.g., "extensive, and better, knowledge of customers"). Thus, the conceptual separation of distinctive competence outcome and distinctive competence implies a hierarchy that shows chains of assumed causality from manageable competences to the competence outcome (see Fig. 1 illustrating the possible mini-hierarchy identified above by David Packard). The hierarchy illustrates that competences become increasingly manageable the further down the

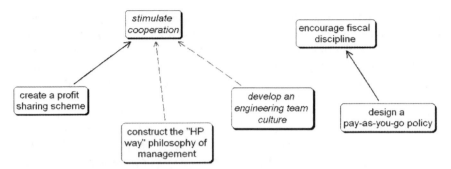

Fig. 1. David Packard's View: An Illustration of Linking Competences and Outcomes. *Note:* The statements in italics are likely competence outcomes, the remainder are likely competences or distinctive competences. Causal links that are solid are directly stated, possible links are dotted arrows.

chain of causality they are from directly impacting the goals and customer values – as it becomes clearer what the activity is and who is doing it.

It is not surprising, that Priem and Butler (2001) noted that "simply advising practitioners to obtain rare and valuable resources in order to achieve competitive advantage and, further, that those resources should be hard to imitate and non-substitutable for sustainable advantage, does not meet the operational validity criterion" (p. 31). However, by starting with distinctive competence outcomes it is possible for TMTs to move on naturally to discussing how these are realized. In this typology "rare and valuable resources" are distinctive assets that can be exploited, and distinctive competences are those that exploit and are properties of organization which can be managed. Distinctive competence outcomes are not resources but the outcomes of the management of resources.

Distinctiveness?

Although the literature is apparently very clear about the characteristics of distinctiveness, this research indicated considerable difficulties in using these characteristics in practice. Distinctiveness is a relative concept (Collis & Montgomery, 1995), and it is also dependent on the timescale over which a competence is expected to remain distinctive. Creating a sustainable strategic future over a 5-year period makes different demands to that for 20 years. Throughout the entire research effort we never experienced a situation where a management team was able to identify any *individual* competences that met absolutely the characteristics of distinctiveness. They were able to identify those competences that were more distinctive in relation to each other and the competition, and subsequently rate all the candidates on a scale of relative distinctiveness. Indeed, the process of developing a detailed picture of distinctiveness through debating whether (i) they are competence outcomes or not and (ii) they are distinctive or not, leads to the meaning and therefore wording of the competence or competence outcome being tightened and made more specific, and therefore becomes a significant part of the strategic conversation. The meaning of any one statement was generally uniquely defined by the supporting competences and supported outcomes.

DISTINCTIVE COMPETENCES AS A DISTINCTIVE *PATTERN* OF COMPETENCES

An Emergent Network of Competences

Earlier we reflected on the existence of a hierarchical map or network (Figs. 1 and 2) that showed chains of assumed causality from manageable competences to competence outcomes to discover what competences drive competence outcomes. Embedded in the network are causal patterns comprising unique portfolios, or bundles of competences. On some

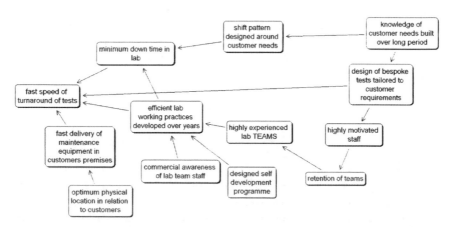

Fig. 2.   An Example of Some Early Discussion of Distinctiveness Within a TMT.

occasions a cycle of causal links arises showing reinforcing feedback where competences are self-sustaining. The patterns indicate how it might be possible to position the organization so that it is able to build, integrate, and reconfigure organizational resources and competences (Adner & Helfat, 2003; Teece, Pisano, & Shuen, 1997).

The notion of seeking out unique bundles has been suggested by many, but the implications and means of doing so have been under-explored. Day (1994), for example, suggests that "capabilities are the *complex bundles* of skills and accumulated knowledge, exercised through organizational processes that enable firms to coordinate activities and make use of their assets" (p. 38, our emphasis). "Strategic advantage for firms is often based on bundles of related resources" (Barney, 1991). As has been argued, a competitor should find it difficult to overcome distinctiveness that is grounded in a complex *pattern* of internal coordination and learning – suggesting elements of causal ambiguity (Prahalad & Hamel, 1990). "One explanation may be that the strength of some resources is dependent on *interactions or combinations with other resources* and therefore no single resource – intangible or otherwise – becomes the most important to firm performance" (Galbreath & Galvin, 2004).

It is the way in which one competence supports or sustains another, and that, in turn, supports another, which can be distinctive. The process of causally linking competences and distinctive competences as an emerging network or pattern develops a "cause map" of competences. By capturing this *network of competences*, as a cause map, portfolios of competences can be revealed which in themselves give rise to distinctiveness. For example where each of the individual competences is held by other organizations, but the whole – the "complex bundle" of competences working together as a system – is unique and therefore distinctive.

Fig. 3 shows the developing network shown in Fig. 1. Here the TMT have started the process of categorizing statements as either a distinctive competence outcome (DCO), distinctive competence (DC), and distinctive asset (DA). They have also begun the process of tightening the wording of their statements and, during this process, have discussed how a distinctive asset might be a distinctive competence by making history a part of the future ("highly experienced lab TEAM" becomes "ability to manage and retain highly experienced lab TEAMS" – note the insertion of the phrase "ability to").

Fig. 4 shows a small extract from an emerging cause map from the TMT of a multinational corporation as a first response to the request to identify distinctive competences. The map shows how the first step in eliciting

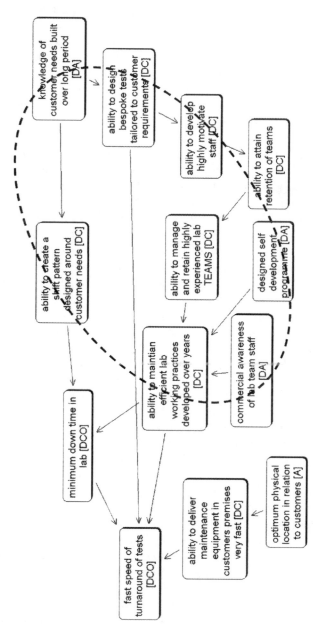

Fig. 3. The Developing Wording and Pattern of Distinctiveness (from Fig. 2). Note the changed wording (in particular the asset of a highly experienced lab teams becomes a competence), and the coding of all statements. At this stage the TMT realized that those marked DC were not particularly distinctive, but when taken as a bundle (in the cluster marked) were highly distinctive. The network continued to be developed and tightened by the TMT.

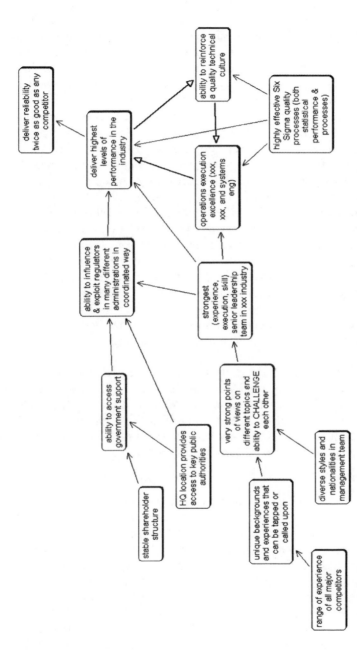

Fig. 4. A Small Extract from the First Steps in Developing a Cause Map of Competences Developed (in this case) by the Top Management Team of a Multinational Corporation. The assertions shown in this example belong to the TMT, and the map is shown exactly as it was displayed while the team discussed and changed the map.

distinctive competences produces a mixture of distinctive assets at the bottom of the hierarchy, possible distinctive competences, and distinctive competence outcomes – many of which are stated broadly and imprecisely. Thus, the statement at the top of the network or pattern ("deliver reliability twice as good as any competitor") was accepted by the team to be an obvious competence outcome, but, moving down the hierarchy, the statements supporting this outcome show competences that are increasingly capable of being managed. Indeed, the bottom of one causal chain of statements reveals what the TMT took to be distinctive *tangible assets* ("stable shareholder structure") rather than distinctive competences. The figure also shows a self-sustaining feedback *loop* including "high level" competence outcomes (illustrated by bold arrows): where "deliver highest levels of performance in the industry," supports the "ability to reinforce a quality technical culture," which supports "operations execution excellence," which reinforces "delivering highest levels of performance in the industry."

As the TMT continued discussing the map they gradually tightened the wording of statements, and thus became clearer about what it meant to have "an ability to...." They also became concerned about the distinctiveness of parts of the network as a bundle. It was the particular pattern of assets, competences, and outcomes that was distinctive, rather than individual competences.

It is invariably the case that a portfolio of competences and a portfolio of relationships between them represent significant distinctiveness. This does not mean that feedback always occurs but when it does, it is a significant and sustainable form of distinctiveness. Specifically the pattern of relationships that represent the dynamic of continuing sustenance of the competences may be a powerful form of distinctiveness.

Virtuous Cycles of Competences

As patterns are made explicit and displayed (through a visual representation of the cause map – the transitional object) some hitherto unforeseen powerful potential distinctive competences – unique patterns – arise. Moreover, a reinforcing feedback *loop of competences* often makes the feedback loop, as a whole, a distinctive competence rather than the competences themselves. It is the pattern that is unique. Similarly, a feedback *loop with at least one distinctive competence* in it is important because the self-sustaining loop sustains the distinctive competence. This is because *loops with the ability to resource the distinctive competences* makes the distinctive competences more powerful. A design (for strategy) may elicit "not only static capabilities; it launched 'virtuous circles' that turn asymmetries into *ever-growing* capabilities" (Miller, 2003, p. 24). Feedback loops of distinctive competences are particularly important because they reveal the dynamics of self-sustaining competences. Thus, a distinctive competence that is likely to be significant incorporates the sustaining *relationships* as well as the distinctive competence itself. Finally, a *patterning of competences*, for example a *portfolio*, is often important. As noted above, the *pattern* is the distinctive competence because nobody else could achieve the pattern even if they had the competences. "Imitation is made difficult, therefore, because rarely does a firm with a sustained competitive advantage possess only one key resource" (Pringle & Kroll, 1997, p. 87).

Causal Ambiguity

This research supports the view that "many asymmetries go unnoticed because they are buried within an organization and are therefore *subtle and causally ambiguous*" (Miller, 2003, p. 967). Similarly it shows that the process of elicitation, causal linking, and categorization (as competence or outcome) enables the codification of some of the "uncodified" knowledge. This codification process partly resolves difficulties TMTs experience in discovering distinctive competences. For example, it may help overcome situations where "managers themselves do not know why their dynamic capabilities are successful. For example, the CEO of a major biotech firm told one of the authors 'we have the best research process in the industry but we don't know why'" (Eisenhardt & Martin, 2000, p. 1114). Reducing the causal ambiguity for those within the organization allows for more effective strategic management without reducing the causal ambiguity for competitors. This potentially counters the view that "firms owning the resources have no informational advantage over other firms and little ability to leverage these resources further since there is uncertainty regarding their dimensions and/or their value" (Peteraf, 1993, p. 187).

This research implies that invariably *distinctive* competences are usually the *combination of particular unique patterns of interrelated competences*, where it is the patterns that are especially distinctive (Amit & Schoemaker, 1993). Moreover, when a pattern is self-sustaining (a virtuous cycle of distinctive competences) then the pattern is of particular importance.

THE NATURE OF A CORE COMPETENCE (AND CORE *DISTINCTIVE* COMPETENCE)

Core to What?

The definition of a core competence depends on answering the question: "core to what?" Firstly, as we noted above, others have commented and our experience supports, that for many managers the answer is given in relation to competence outcomes rather than competences. Secondly, if managers are asked to elaborate their notion of "coreness" then they refer to a loose and intuitive understanding of importance rather than a precise conceptual or analytical understanding. What is more, "evaluating a company's competences is not the same as determining the right competences for the company's future competitive position. Similarly, building consensus on the firm's competences is important, but does not guarantee that the firm's managers will correctly identify the competences that will be most important for the future" (King, Fowler, & Zeithaml, 2001, p. 102). Setting the distinctive competences within the context of the business goals of the organization is, conceptually and analytically, a way of addressing this issue and so determining core distinctive competences.

The strategic future of an organization, or division, or business unit, or department, whether private, public, or not-for-profit, depends on its ability to *exploit competences in* relation to *its business goals*. The security and stability of an organization's future – achieving the business goals – depends on the distinctiveness of the competences that deliver these goals and on their sustainability. Thus distinctiveness can also be seen as being determined by the nature of the business goals *system* (Ackermann, Eden, & Brown, 2005, pp. 77–78) – these goals provide the benchmark against which distinctiveness can be assessed. For example, an organization with a goal of being number one in a domestic market place would be comparing itself to other players in that market place and therefore viewing distinctiveness according to those competitors. However, if the organization wished to be a world player then the number of competitors increases making distinctiveness more challenging.

To be clear, business goals are the specific and distinctive goals that deliver customer value in the context of not-for-profit, public, or private organizations. These business goals, in turn, deliver the generic goals of profit, profitability, shareholder value, or mandate, etc. Distinctive business goals are those that differentiate "the business we are in" from the general requirements (goals) of conducting business (increase turnover, reduce costs, etc.). There are usually a number of these goals and they influence one another – producing a goals system. Thus, core competences are those that are core, are central, to achieving the system of business goals. The research suggests that TMTs are able to appreciate analytically the centrality, or "coreness," of distinctive competences as evidenced, in part, through particular distinctive competences (or patterns of competences) supporting a large number of the business goals (and possibly through a number of causal routes – a measure of robustness). "Coreness" is thus a feature or emergent property of the network which links competences to goals. However, the other part of determining "coreness" relies upon a TMT making judgments about the strength of the links as well as relative robustness. This elaborated conceptualization is illustrated in Fig. 5a – where competences are shown to deliver competence outcomes which in turn support business goals that deliver customer value and so realize generic goals. Fig. 5b shows the addition of distinctiveness and "threshold competences – those that provide the legitimacy to operate in the industry" (Johnson, Scholes, & Whittington,

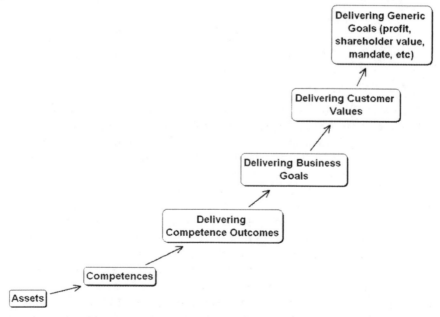

Fig. 5a. The Basic Structure of the Relationship between Competences and Goals.

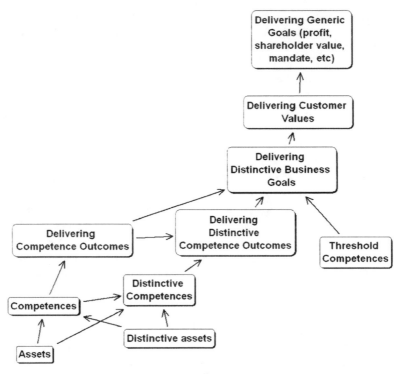

Fig. 5b. The Distinctive/Differentiated Strategy Model.

2005, pp. 119–120). The exploration of this structure enabled TMTs to identify the most critical resources controlled by the firm (see Fig. 5c), and thereby increase the likelihood that they will be used to gain sustained strategic advantage (Barney, 2001). Core competences must be able to disproportionately contribute to the customer-perceived value (Hamel, 1994) through the nature of their link to business goals (i.e., having a far greater number of supporting links to goals than other competences).

Exploring this linkage between competences (distinctive or not) and business goals enables a validation of: (i) the utility of the competences, (ii) distinctiveness relative to specified goals, (iii) the distinctiveness of patterns of competences and distinctive competences, and (iv) the goals as being realistic even if aspirational. Invariably TMTs identified what they thought were core competences that turned out to be of little importance in delivering business goals – these were often a part of the legacy of the organization. If the customer or the business does not currently value the

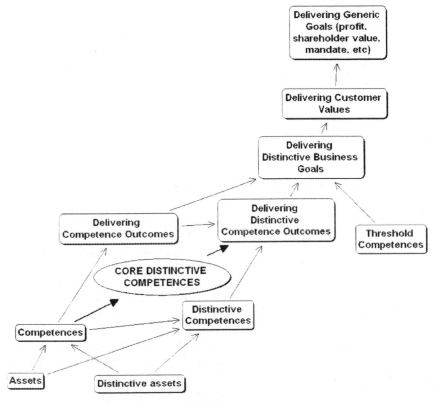

Fig. 5c. Identifying Core Competences.

consequences of any distinctive competences then there is no competitive advantage. But, if the customer can be persuaded to value the outcomes of a distinctive competence (through particular strategies) then it may create competitive advantage. However, it is important to note that if strategy is developed from customer values first, rather than from seeking to exploit distinctive competences, then it is possible that the exploitation of a distinctive competence might be missed. "Firms should focus their analysis mainly on their 'unique' skills and resources rather than on the competitive environment" (Dierickx & Cool, 1989, p. 1504).

The above notion of core competence varies from that suggested by Prahalad and Hamel (1990) because it argues that (i) core *distinctive* competences provide competitive advantage, (ii) core competences are *discovered* from an analysis of the relationship of competences to goals, and

(iii) the discovery of distinctive patterns suggests the exploitation of competences through the *modification or addition of goals*. Thus, the discovery of distinctiveness provides the basis for competitively growing the business in different directions through the exploitation of distinctiveness. In practice this is how many of our TMTs established a growth strategy that avoided growth by acquisition. If the question "what are your core competences" can be answered at the outset of an exploration of distinctiveness then the organization will be locked into an existing strategic future.

Discovery and Refinement of "Coreness"

The conceptualization of core competences in relation to the business goals expressed in this way has elaborated, "put flesh on," the vague concept of "coreness" and has, without exception, made sense in practice to TMTs. As one CEO admitted: "I always use the language of core competences, but really didn't understand what they really were; now I do!" Typically the exploration of the causal links between distinctive competences, competence outcomes, business goals, and customer values presented above led to some competences that managers were proud of being seen to be isolated from other competences, and playing no role in the support of those which were now seen to be distinctive. Sometimes distinctive patterns of competences, or individual distinctive competences, were disconnected from business goals. Consequently, either business goals were changed so that the distinctive competences were exploited, or the energy that was going into sustaining so-called core competences became strategic slack available for use elsewhere. Similarly, some business goals were revealed as having no support from any distinctive competences, and so new competences had to be developed (or existing competences refined to support the goals – thus creating new links) or the goals modified. *This cyclical process gradually revealed and refined those distinctive competences that were core*. If there are no distinctive competences within the network then the competences that are most core to the network are *core competences* that are still worthy of identification, but do not provide significant competitive advantage.

It is reasonable to believe that future corporate success can only *reliably* be based on existing strengths rather than those the organization has yet to acquire. "By identifying key asymmetries [distinctive competences], managers are able to make them a high priority, fund them and turn them into valuable resources or capabilities" (Miller, 2003, p. 968) and so make them *core* distinctive competences by modifying business goals. Core capabilities, by definition, cannot be purchased off the shelf but require strategic vision, development time, and sustained investment (Schoemaker, 1992). As such, for the organization to remain viable, capitalization of existing capabilities (rather than some anticipated or visionary competences) is important. This view implies strategy, viability, and exploitation and so the need to be able to capitalize upon competences and their strategic management. The protection and maintenance of *core distinctive* competences became an obvious aspect of strategic management for the TMTs.

ISSUES IN SUSTAINING CORE DISTINCTIVE COMPETENCES

To argue that core distinctive competences must be sustained and maintained and so strategically managed is to state the obvious. Most capabilities become obsolete unless they are continually renewed and periodically reinvented (Miller, 2003). Inimitability is at the heart of value creation because it limits competition. If the resource is inimitable, then any profit stream it generates is more likely to be sustainable. But, inimitability rarely, if ever, can last forever. Competitors eventually will find ways to copy most valuable resources in a manner that can, at least, deliver a replicated distinctive competence *outcome*. Strategic management must, therefore, be expected to retain differentiation for as long as possible by building strategies around distinctive competences. As Miller (2003) argues, "asymmetries are unlikely to give rise to sustainable capabilities unless they become a *priority*: unless managers take the trouble to embed them within the organization" (p. 968). By identifying key asymmetries – core distinctive competences – managers are able to make them a high priority, fund them, and more effectively sustain and exploit them.

However our research indicates that TMTs rarely find that determining the best ways of sustaining core distinctive competences is easy. Often their sustenance depends on being able to release imprisoned and/or under-leveraged competences and avoid unwittingly surrendering core competences through investment cuts or outsourcing (Prahalad & Hamel, 1990, p. 88). A core distinctive competence comprising only a few elements is much easier to understand and imitate than one that relies on the subtle alignment of myriad elements (Coyne, 1986, p. 47).

The research reported here has consistently found that protecting distinctiveness as patterns is usually easier than protecting "single" distinctive competences. "Superior *combinations* of inputs can be more economically identified and formed from resources already used in the organization than by obtaining new resources (and knowledge of them) from the outside" (Priem & Butler, 2001, p. 36, our emphasis). At the same time recognition of these competences' longevity is important – as it is to some extent dependent on their integration with the goals (and therefore sustenance) and the corporate direction and environmental conditions staying relatively stable. Therefore, core *distinctive* competences, by definition, cannot be purchased off the shelf but require strategic vision, development time, and sustained investment (Amit & Schoemaker, 1993).

This research suggests that the only reasonable chance of *developing* (and even sustaining) distinctiveness is by putting strategies in place to create new links (patterns) between existing competences, in particular the creation of new self-sustaining feedback loops. In some respects this can be seen as being related to dynamic capabilities – organizational and strategic routines by which firms integrate, build, and reconfigure organizational assets to address swiftly changing environments (Teece et al., 1997; Eisenhardt & Martin, 2000). Miller (2003) calls for firms to build simple unharnessed strengths into complex exploitable ones – patterns of relationships – and to ensure that any virtuous cycles can be identified and/or developed to grow ever-growing capabilities. This is precisely what TMTs are able to do once they have a picture of their own network of competences.

"Superior rents are not likely to derive from specialized inimitable resources or routines, but rather from the ability to destroy and rebuild them over time" (Fiol, 2001, p. 692). However, while there is always a danger of strategic inertia arising from protecting and developing core distinctive competences, it is the case that many TMTs have not even got as far as understanding and reflecting upon their competence resources. Until they become better at understanding their own business there is little chance of them asking themselves about other considerations that must follow such understandings!

CONCLUDING DISCUSSION

In this research we have encountered difficulties in applying the concepts of distinctive competences and core competences in organizational settings. This is not an untypical experience, for example, identifying "core

competence has too often become a 'feel good' exercise that no one fails"
(Collis & Montgomery, 1995, p. 123) and "true core competences are hard
to define precisely and are often discovered retrospectively. That is, as you
experiment, you define your competences by simply describing your
successes and failures." Dan Simpson, Director of Strategy and Planning,
The Clorox Corporation (quoted in Coyne, Hall, & Clifford, 1997, p. 42).
Other experts also have had difficulty: "We talked to [core competence
experts] and asked them to help us identify our core competences. But after
having them work with our senior management, leading them through some
group exercises, we really had a mess on our hands. We could not define
what was core as opposed to non-core, and what was a competence as
opposed to some process or offering we just did well." Paula Cholmondeley,
VP, Business Development and Global Sourcing, Owens-Corning Fiberglass
(quoted in Coyne et al., 1997, p. 42). Nevertheless, the notion of core and
distinctive competences is intuitively very powerful and, in our experience
from this research, at least conceptually makes sense to TMTs. The research
reported here has sought to elaborate the concepts of distinctive
competences, distinctiveness, and "coreness."

With respect to distinctive *competences*, we conclude that there is
confusion between competences and competence outcomes. Competence
outcomes are not competences. Competences are manageable statements
and can usually be prefaced by the phrase "an ability to," competences
causally deliver competence outcomes. Competence outcomes are causally
closer to what customer can directly appreciate. Additionally, there is a
hierarchy of chains of assumed causality from manageable competences to a
competence outcome.

Distinctive competences are most often a distinctive *pattern* of competences. These patterns emerge from a network of causally linked
competences and competence outcomes. Embedded in the network are
patterns comprising unique portfolios, or bundles of competences. Virtuous
cycles of competences show a potentially self-sustaining distinctive
competence, where the feedback loop as a whole is distinctive.

"Coreness" arises as an emergent property of the network which links
distinctive competences to business goals. The core distinctive competences
are those that are at the core of this network by, in general, supporting the
greatest number of business goals.

Core distinctive competences must be maintained and, preferably,
sustained; otherwise they can dissolve away, gradually be duplicated, or
no longer be fully relevant to a particular market. Distinctiveness as a
pattern is usually easier to protect than "single" distinctive competences.

Thus, distinctive competences and their linkages must be explicitly understood and appreciated so that as necessary they can be protected
(sometimes, but rarely, through legal barriers), enhanced (by adding or
strengthening), changed (by dropping those that no longer help to create
customer value), or refreshed. None of this is easy; awareness of the
potential failure of distinctive competences arises not so much from a study
of strengths and weaknesses, but from being aware of the competences in the
first place, how they relate to one another, and how they support the
business goals. *Developing* (and even sustaining) distinctiveness is more
likely to derive from new links (patterns) between existing competences, in
particular the creation of new self-sustaining feedback loops.

This paper has focused on differentiation through *distinctive* competences.
Needless to say, TMTs realize, often in a stark way, that a common error is
to assume that being the best at a particular skill offsets other
disadvantages, or can offset a lack of threshold competences. The fact that
a company has discovered core *distinctive* competences does not erase a
scale or scope disadvantage, or compensate for inferiority in other areas. As
many have argued, for a competence-led strategy to win, the core distinctive
competence must be more powerful than other strategic levers relevant to
the industry, such as structural advantage or access to cheap resources
(Coyne et al., 1997).

Needless to say, we have concentrated on the use of concepts in practice
and so have considered the way in which the concepts relate to each other
rather than seeking tight definitions of each concept. However, in appendix
we set out our definitions for working with each of the concepts. We show
the more precise definitions introduced by Sanchez (2008) for comparison. It
is noticeable that his definitions focus on for-profit organizations and so
focus on products as the outcomes whereas the conceptualization of core
competences introduced in this paper focuses on the relationship between
competences and business goals in a manner that deliberately allows for the
practical use of the concepts in a not-for-profit organization (where some of
our research was conducted).

THE RESEARCH IN CONTEXT

As suggested in the introduction this research is set within the context of the
RBV of competitiveness. Competences are an important resource and
therefore can be viewed through the VRIN (now VRIO) lens to determine
their competitive advantage. Therefore identifying and managing them is an

important managerial activity. A further and complementary school of writing discusses the capabilities of an organization (another resource form). Capabilities are taken to refer to a firm's capacity to deploy *resources*, usually in combinations, using organizational processes, to effect the servicing of business goals (Amit & Schoemaker, 1993). Others, for example Sanchez and Heene (2004) and Sanchez (2008), are keen to define these terms precisely. However, we would argue, as others have argued (Bogner, Thomas, & McGee, 1999; Day, 1994), that the two concepts (capabilities and competences) can be used interchangeably. Indeed, the difference between capabilities, competences, and resources is never very clear and this research suggests that it need not be.

The elaboration of both distinctiveness and "coreness" is also illustrated through a range of other strategy literature. For example, Porter (1980) argued that *competences* must be capable either of differentiating the organization's products (rather than the organization) from those of others (the competences thus must be *distinctive*), or the organization must produce the products at low cost – but not both. This would correlate with our elaboration of distinctiveness – but at a fairly generic level.

The notion of a *core* competence captured attention in 1990 with the publication of the 1990 (Prahalad & Hamel, 1990) article and subsequent book (Hamel & Prahalad, 1994). For these authors success largely depended on the organization's ability to identify, cultivate, and exploit core competences. Core competences are seen by these researchers as a portfolio of *integrated*, complementary skills and technologies. In contrast to Porter (1980) core competences are not only about products but about a range of products and services – the business of the organization. World-class organizational leadership is taken to follow from the design and development of "core products" (Bogner et al., 1999; Prahalad & Hamel, 1990). This view, while not being contradictory to our development, does not provide a key indication of what constitutes "core" and therefore while providing useful concepts benefits from the future elaboration presented in this paper.

FUTURE RESEARCH?

This research program has, in passing, revealed the significance of dynamics – both controlling and self-sustaining feedback – for understanding the changing nature of distinctiveness and competitive advantage. Although the literature in the field mentions this aspect (Miller, 2003), it is underdeveloped. Seeing a resource base as stocks and flows (Amit & Schoemaker, 1993; Dierickx & Cool, 1989) may allow the base to be usefully examined through a system dynamics model (Warren, 2002) that can simulate the growth and decline of distinctiveness and particularly of distinctive patterns that are feedback cycles. Thus a fruitful area for future research is exploring these aspects from the standpoint of the strategic manager.

Similarly, the literature is overwhelmed with characteristics of resources that elaborate the four broad categories expressed by Barney as VRIN – valuable/rare/imperfectly imitable/nonsubstitutability or more recently VRIO – valuable/rare/imitable/organization (Dierickx & Cool, 1989; Galbreath & Galvin, 2004; Peteraf, 1993). To what extent do these categories helpfully relate to the data presented by real managers? To what extent are they well described or defined so that they are usable in practice to help strategy managers be more exhaustive in their search for distinctiveness? How might the categories suggest strategic action that might develop distinctiveness? These are questions for future research.

However, in addition, this research has entailed using a very particular research methodology – research-oriented action research (RO-AR) – and it is appropriate to reflect on its potential in future research into CBM. As we noted in our discussion of research design, action research is not without its dangers. But equally other research methodologies often result in the study of data about organizations rather than the study of organizations *and their managers*. As Eden and Huxham argue, "reliable data about organizational life is predominantly qualitative, *situational, and is collected as the opportunity arises*. Traditional tests of validity, therefore, cannot be used when data is collected in this manner. Thus, systematic method, as well as critical reflection and triangulation, becomes particularly important" (2006, p. 399, our emphasis). The work reported here is the result of seeking to understand managers who are fully engaged in discussions that mattered to their own personal future as well as that of the organization (at least as they saw it). They did not behave in ways that many scholars would wish – they were imprecise, emotional, committed, and wanted theory that was exceedingly practical. Their understanding of their own world was often not at all evidence based and utilized beliefs that outsiders might question, but they were highly intelligent and successful managers seeking to manage an uncertain world where they would rightly argue that evidence about the past was not necessarily relevant to managing the future. RO-AR is an appropriate methodology for getting closer to the impact of concepts on managerial practice.

Eden and Huxham suggest that action research is challenging because "(i) the uncertainty and lack of control creates anxiety for anyone other than confident and experienced researchers and (ii) doing the action in *RO-AR* demands experience and understanding of methods for consultancy and intervention." They "generally advise new researchers not to use *RO-AR* unless they are already experienced consultants or managers" (2006, p. 403). Our experiences in this research would support these views and so suggest that future research might be successful when undertaken by scholars who are comfortable meeting these challenges.

REFERENCES

Ackermann, F., Eden, C., & Brown, I. (2005). *The practice of making strategy*. London: Sage.

Adner, R., & Helfat, C. R. (2003). Corporate effects and dynamic managerial capabilities. *Strategic Management Journal, 24,* 1011–1025.

Amit, R., & Schoemaker, P. J. (1993). Strategic assets and organizational rent. *Strategic Management Journal, 14,* 33–46.

Barney, J. B. (1986). Organizational culture: Can it be a source of sustained competitive advantage? *Academy of Management Review, 11,* 656–665.

Barney, J. B. (1991). Firm resources and sustained competitive advantage. *Journal of Management, 17,* 99–120.

Barney, J. B. (2001). Is the resource based "view" a useful perspective for strategic management research. *Academy of Management Review, 26,* 41–56.

Bettis, R. (1991). Strategic management and the straightjacket: An editorial essay. *Organization Science, 2,* 315–319.

Bogner, W. C., & Thomas, H. (1994). Core competence and competitor advantage: A model and illustrative evidence from the pharmaceutical industry. In: G. Hamel & A. Heene (Eds), *Competence based competition* (pp. 111–143). Chichester: Wiley.

Bogner, W. C., Thomas, H., & McGee, J. (1999). Competence and competitive advantage: Towards a dynamic model. *British Journal of Management, 10,* 275–290.

Chakravarthy, B. S., & Doz, Y. (1992). Strategy process research: Focusing on corporate self-renewal. *Strategic Management Journal, 13*(Special Issue), 5–14.

Champion, D., & Stowell, F. A. (2003). Validating action research field studies: PEArL. *Systemic Practice and Action Research, 16.*

Collins, J. C., & Porras, J. I. (1995). *Built to last: Successful habits of visionary companies.* London: Century.

Collis, D. J. (1991). A resource based analysis of global competition: The case of the bearings industry. *Strategic Management Journal, 12,* 49–68.

Collis, D. J., & Montgomery, C. A. (1995). Competing on resources: Strategy in the 1990s. *Harvard Business Review, July–Aug,* 118–128.

Coyne, K. P. (1986). Sustainable competitive advantage – What it is and what it isn't. *Business Horizons, Jan/Feb,* 54–61.

Coyne, K. P., Hall, S. J. D., & Clifford, P. G. (1997). Is your core competence a mirage? *The McKinsey Quarterly,* 40–54.

Daft, L. R. (1983). *Organization theory and design*. St. Paul, MN: West Publishing Co.

Day, G. S. (1994). The capabilities of market-driven organizations. *Journal of Marketing*, *58*, 37–52.

de Geus, A. (1988). Planning as learning. *Harvard Business Review*, *March–April*, 70–74.

Dierickx, I., & Cool, K. (1989). Asset stock accumulation and sustainability of competitive advantage. *Management Science*, *35*, 1504–1511.

Doktor, R., Tung, R. L., & Glinow, M. A. (1991). Future directions for management theory development. *Academy of Management Review*, *16*, 362–365.

Eden, C., & Ackermann, F. (2001). A mapping framework for strategy making. In: A. Huff & M. Jenkins (Eds), *Mapping strategy* (pp. 173–195). London: Wiley.

Eden, C., & Huxham, C. (2006). Researching organizations using action research. In: W. Nord (Ed.), *Handbook of organization studies* (pp. 388–408). Beverly Hills, CA: Sage.

Eisenhardt, K. M. (1989a). Building theories from case study research. *Academy of Management Review*, *14*, 532–550.

Eisenhardt, K. M. (1989b). Making fast strategic decisions in high velocity environments. *Academy of Management Journal*, *32*, 543–576.

Eisenhardt, K. M., & Graebner, M. E. (2007). Theory building from cases: Opportunities and challenges. *Academy of Management Journal*, *50*, 25–32.

Eisenhardt, K. M., & Martin, J. A. (2000). Dynamic capabilities: What are they? *Strategic Management Journal*, *21*, 1105–1121.

Eisenhardt, K. M., & Schoonhoven, C. B. (1990). Organizational growth-linking founding team, strategy, environment, and growth among United States semiconductor ventures, 1978–1988. *Administrative Science Quarterly*, *35*, 504–529.

Fiol, C. M. (2001). Revisiting an identity-based view of sustainable competitive advantage. *Journal of Management*, *27*, 691–699.

Foss, N. J., & Knudsen, T. (2003). The resource-based tangle towards a sustainable explanation of competitive advantage. *Managerial & Decision Economics*, *24*, 291–307.

Galbreath, J., & Galvin, P. (2004). Testing the resource-based view: How important are intangible resources to performance? *Proceedings of the Academy of Management conference*, New Orleans.

Glaser, B. G., & Strauss, A. L. (1967). *The discovery of grounded theory*. Chicago, IL: Aldine.

Gopinath, C., & Hoffman, R. C. (1995). The relevance of strategy research: Practitioner and academic viewpoints. *Journal of Management Studies*, *32*, 575–594.

Hall, R. (1992). The strategic analysis of intangible resources. *Strategic Management Journal*, *13*, 135–143.

Hambrick, D. C. (2007). The field of management's devotion to theory: Too much of a good thing? *Academy of Management Journal*, *50*, 1346–1352.

Hamel, G. (1994). The concept of core competence. In: G. Hamel & A. Heene (Eds), *Competence based competition* (pp. 11–33). Chichester: Wiley.

Hamel, G., & Heene, A. (1994). *Competence-based competition*. London: Wiley.

Hamel, G., & Prahalad, C. K. (1994). *Competing for the future*. Harvard, MA: Harvard Business School Press.

Harrigan, K. R. (1983). Research methodologies for contingency approaches to business strategy. *Academy of Management Review*, *8*, 398–405.

Hoopes, D. G., Madsen, T. L., & Walker, G. (2003). Guest editors' introduction to the special issue: Why is there a resource-based view? Toward a theory of competitive advantage. *Strategic Management Journal*, *24*, 889–902.

Huff, A., & Jenkins, M. (Eds). (2001). *Mapping strategy*. London: Wiley.

Huff, A. S. (2000). Changes in organisational knowledge production: 1999 presidential address. *Academy of Management Review, 25*, 288–293.

Huff, A. S. (Ed.) (1990). *Mapping strategic thought.* New York: Wiley.

Huxham, C., & Hibbert, P. (2006). From items of data to usable management theory using the interpretive clustering approach. Presented to the Academy of Management Conference, Atlanta.

Huxham, C., & Vangen, S. (2003). Researching organizational practice through action research: Case studies and design choices. *Organizational Research Methods, 6*, 383–403.

Jarzabkowski, P., Balogun, J., & Seidl, D. (2007). Strategizing: The challenges of a practice perspective. *Human Relations, 60*, 5–27.

Johnson, G., Scholes, K., & Whittington, R. (2005). *Exploring corporate strategy: Text and cases* (7th ed.). Harlow, Essex: Prentice Hall.

King, A. W., Fowler, S. W., & Zeithaml, C. P. (2001). Managing organizational competencies for competitive advantage: The middle-management edge. *Academy of Management Executive, 15*, 95–106.

Kraatz, M. S., & Zajac, E. J. (2001). How organizational resources affect strategic change and performance in turbulent environments: Theory and evidence. *Organization Science, 12*, 632–657.

Lewin, K. (1951). *Field theory in social science: Selected theoretical papers.* New York: Harper & Row.

Miller, D. (2003). An asymmetry-based view of advantage: Towards an attainable sustainability. *Strategic Management Journal, 24*, 961–976.

Nanda, A. (1996). Resources, capabilities and competencies. In: B. Moingeon & A. Edmondson (Eds), *Organizational learning and competitive advantage.* London: Sage.

Norburn, D. (1989). The chief executive: A breed apart. *Strategic Management Journal, 10*, 1–15.

Penrose, E. T. (1959). *The theory of growth of the firm.* London: Basil Blackwell.

Peteraf, M. A. (1993). The cornerstones of competitive advantage: A resource-based view. *Strategic Management Journal, 124*, 179–191.

Pettigrew, A., & McNulty, T. (1995). Power and influence in and around the boardroom. *Human Relations, 48*, 845–873.

Pettigrew, A., Thomas, H., & Whittington, R. (2002). Strategic management: The strengths and limitations of a field. In: *Handbook of strategy and management* (pp. 3–30). London: Sage.

Pettigrew, A. M. (1992). On studying managerial elites. *Strategic Management Journal, 13*, 163–182.

Porter, M. E. (1980). *Competitive strategy: Techniques for analysing industries and competitors.* New York: Free Press.

Prahalad, C. K., & Hamel, G. (1990). The core competences of the corporation. *Harvard Business Review, May–June*, 79–91.

Priem, R. L., & Butler, J. E. (2001). Is the resource-based "view" a useful perspective for strategic management research? *Academy of Management Review, 26*, 22–40.

Pringle, C. D., & Kroll, M. J. (1997). Why Trafalgar was won before it was fought: Lessons from resource-based theory. *Academy of Management Executive, 11*, 73–89.

Rugman, A. M., & Verbeke, A. (2002). Edith Penrose's contribution to the resource-based view of strategic management. *Strategic Management Journal, 23*, 769–780.

Rumelt, R. P. (1984). *Towards a strategic theory of the firm.* Englewood Cliffs, NJ: Prentice-Hall.

Sanchez, R. (2002). Understanding competence-based management, identifying and managing five modes of competence. *Journal of Business Research, 57*, 518–532.

Sanchez, R. (2008). *A focused issue on fundamental issues in competence theory development (research in competence-based management): 4.* Bingley, UK: Emerald Group Publishing Limited.

Sanchez, R., & Heene, A. (2004). *The new strategic management: Organizations, competition and competence.* London: Wiley.

Sanchez, R., Heene, A., & Howard, H. (Eds) (1996). *Dynamics of competence-based competition: Theory and practice in the new strategic management.* Technology, Innovation, Entrepreneurship and Competitive Strategy Series. Oxford: Pergamon.

Schoemaker, P. J. H. (1992). How to link strategic vision to core capabilities. *Sloan Management Review, 34*, 67–81.

Selznik, P. (1957). *Leadership in administration: A sociological interpretation.* Evanston, IL: Row Peterson.

Starbuck, W. H., & Mezias, J. M. (1996). Opening Pandora's box: Studying the accuracy of managers' perceptions. *Journal of Organizational Behavior, 17*, 99–117.

Teece, D. J., Pisano, G., & Shuen, A. (1997). Dynamic capabilities and strategic management. *Strategic Management Journal, 18*, 509–533.

Tsoukas, H. (1989). The validity of idiographic research explanations. *Academy of Management Review, 14*, 551–561.

Warren, K. D. (2002). *Competitive strategy dynamics.* Chichester: Wiley.

Wernerfelt, B. (1984). A resource based view of the firm. *Strategic Management Journal, 5*, 171–180.

Winnicott, D. W. (1953). Transitional objects and transitional phenomena: A study of the first not-me possession. *The International Journal of Psych-Analysis, XXXIV*(Part 2), 89–97.

APPENDIX

Competence: could be seen as an *activity* (hence being able to put the words "an ability to" at the beginning) that can be *managed*.

Pattern of competences: an identified system of linked competences which might include a portfolio supporting a single or multiple outcomes or self-sustaining feedback loop.

Bundle of competences: combinations – the specific relationship between them may not be clear – for example, the bundle could be a set of competences that are not necessarily linked.

System of competences: where the whole set of competences is greater than the sum of the parts – for example, a feedback loop creates dynamic change in the whole that would not exist without all of the competences in the set or without their being linked in a specific manner.

Resources: can be seen as a broad overarching term encompassing everything. For example, Barney (1991) notes "...firm resources include all assets, capabilities, organizational processes, firm attributes, information, knowledge, etc.; controlled by a firm that enable the firm to conceive of and implement strategies that improve its efficiency and effectiveness" (Daft, 1983).

Asset: can either be a tangible or nontangible entity that may (and probably should) support competences. Typically assets are historically generated – possibly through serendipity. The path of history may be unique and so the asset is path dependent. It is not a competence that can be managed. Sometimes a historical asset may be reconceived as a competence that is managed into the future. When a historical asset is claimed to be a part of a self-sustaining feedback loop then it must be reconceived as manageable into the future (the past cannot be a dynamic variable). An asset can be exploited by competences to deliver business goals.

Compare to: Sanchez (2008) – A Scientific Critique of RBV in Strategy Theory (p. 46):

> *Assets* are anything tangible or intangible that *could be useful* to a firm in developing and realizing products (hardware, software, or services) to create economic value in its product markets. Assets may be firm specific (internal to the firm) or firm-addressable (able to be accessed by the firm in resource factor markets).
>
> *Resources* are assets that a firm can actually access and use in developing and realizing products to create value in its product markets.
>
> *Capabilities* are repeatable patterns of action that are created through a firm's management processes for coordinating its resources in processes for value creation.

MANAGING THE INTERACTION OF EXPLORATION AND EXPLOITATION: AMBIDEXTERITY AS A HIGH-ORDER DYNAMIC CAPABILITY[☆]

Toni Sfirtsis and Rudy Moenaert

ABSTRACT

The dynamic capabilities perspective focuses on the ability of an organization to develop its resource base in order to meet environmental expectations. Therefore, it is closely interrelated to the issue of managing the interaction of exploration and exploitation. The competence of continuously optimizing the interaction of exploration and exploitation has been referred to as organizational ambidexterity. *Managing this interaction implies resolving a firm's permanent struggle to overcome the barriers related to the right configuration between exploration and exploitation.*

[☆]Paper presented at the 8th International Conference on Competence-Based Management, 'Perspectives on Management Theory, Research, Practice and Education,' Copenhagen, 1–3 October 2008.

A Focused Issue on Identifying, Building, and Linking Competences
Research in Competence-Based Management, Volume 5, 35–57
ISSN: 1744-2117/doi:10.1108/S1744-2117(2010)0000005005

By incorporating the concept of combinative capabilities *as balancing routines into the conceptualization of ambidexterity we distinguish structural, interaction, and socialization capabilities that are deployed in overcoming these barriers to resource (re)configuration.*

Drawing on knowledge management and barriers to resource configuration we expect that the way organizations deploy combinative capabilities to manage the interaction between exploration and exploitation depends on the observed barriers to resource (re)configuration. By combining the constructs of barriers to resource reconfiguration, ambidexterity, and combinative capabilities we intend to gain more insight in the way organizations manage the actual interaction between exploration and exploitation. Our paper will introduce a set of propositions indicating the relationship between ambidexterity, barriers to resource (re)configuration, and combinative capabilities as balancing routines.

INTRODUCTION

The current business environment is confronted with a high amplitude and pace of change. Shortening life cycles, rapid technological change, increased globalization of markets, and sharpened competition challenge firms to respond more flexibly and rapidly. Achieving and sustaining a competitive advantage in a dynamic business environment with accelerated pace of change is, both from a researcher and a managerial point of view, a fundamental question in the field of strategic management.

Successful organizations survive in highly dynamic business environments through a process of continuous adaptation. Central to this adaptation processes is the notion of a firm's ability to exploit existing assets and positions in a profitable way, while simultaneously exploring new technologies and markets; and configuring and reconfiguring organizational resources to capture existing as well as new opportunities (March, 1991; Teece, 2006).

Exploitation is associated with refining and extending existing competences. Key to exploitation is that it is possible to secure comfortable position in the marketplace by committing sufficient organizational resources to ensure the current viability of the firm. Thus, the emphasis is on operational efficiency, achieved by engaging in similar activities more efficiently (Porter, 1985). So the returns from exploitation are typically positive, proximate, and predictable.

On the contrary, the outcome of exploration activities, in the short term, is difficult to measure (March, 1991). The organizational returns from exploration can be uncertain, distant, and often negative: "the distance in time and space between the locus of learning and the locus of realization of returns is generally greater in the case of exploration than in the case of exploitation, as is the uncertainty" (March, 1991; Auh & Menguc, 2005).

Investing exclusively on exploration or exploitation could threat over time the aspired competitive advantage. However, in the current highly dynamic environment most of the organizations have a focus or a preference for short-term returns and exploitation activities.

Too great a reliance on exploration without complementary levels of exploitation may lead to an organizational "failure trap," placing a continuous pressure on the organization's resources with no immediate financial reward in sight (Levinthal & March, 1993). However, an excessive reliance on exploitation without supporting levels of exploration may drive the firm into a "success trap" where the more certain short-term returns will lead the organization to overlook the distant and uncertain, albeit potentially profitable, outcomes associated with exploration (Levinthal & March, 1993; Auh & Menguc, 2005). Consequently, a strategy of exploitation without exploration leads to obsolescence and a strategy of exploration without exploitation leads to elimination.

However, while March's propositions (1991) and O'Reilly and Tushman's normative prescriptions (2004) on balancing exploitation and exploration are intuitively appealing, there is limited empirical evidence that supports these perspectives. He and Wong (2004) deserve credit for being among the first to empirically test the ambidexterity hypothesis and its effects on performance. Scholars have begun to shift their focus from a trade-off (either/or) to a paradox (both/and) perspective (Gresov & Drazin, 1997; Bouchikhi, 1998; Morgeson & Hofmann, 1999; Earley & Gibson, 2002; Lewis, 2000). We expect that ambidexterity will have a positive and significant effect on organizational performance (Tushman & O'Reilly, 1996; He & Wong, 2004; Gibson & Birkinshaw, 2004). Firms that manage the tensions of exploration and exploitation by designing appropriate organizational architectures (Tushman & O'Reilly, 1996), or engaging in design of cross-functional subsystems to overcome disruptions (Christensen, 1997) and competency traps (Levitt & March, 1988), or creating an organizational context where "alignment" and "adaptability" are simultaneously realized will achieve a higher performance in the industry, even compared to firms that may pursue solely and successfully exploitation or exploitation. So our first proposition is:

P1. The higher the level of ambidexterity in an organization or SBU, the higher the level of performance.

Overlooking the extensive research on managing simultaneously exploration and exploitation, there seems to be agreement on the fact that organizations need to balance exploration and exploitation to gain sustainable competitive advantage. Levinthal and March (1993, p. 105) state it as follows: "The basic problem confronting an organization is to engage in sufficient exploitation to ensure its current viability and, at the same time, to devote enough energy to exploration to ensure its future viability."

What is not clear is the way organizations design and manage the *actual interaction* between exploration and exploitation. Elaborating on the concept of dynamic capabilities and ambidexterity we will try to enlarge our understanding of managing the interaction between exploration and exploitation.

THEORETICAL PERSPECTIVES

Ambidexterity as Balancing Exploration and Exploitation

There is a widespread agreement on the fact that long-term survival depends on the ability of an organization to balance exploration and exploitation. In various management literatures like organizational learning (e.g., Crossan & Bedrow, 2003; Holmqvist, 2004; Levinthal & March, 1993; March, 1991), strategic management (e.g., Floyd & Lane, 2000; McGrath, 2001; Volberda, Baden-Fuller, & van den Bosch, 2001; Burgelman, 1991), organizational design (e.g., Rivking & Siggelkow, 2003; Sheremata, 2000; Adler, Goldoftas, & Levine, 1999; Volberda, 1996), technological innovation (Benner & Tushman, 2003; Nerkar, 2003; Tushman & O'Reilly, 1996; Duncan, 1976) and knowledge literature (e.g., Grant & Baden-Fuller, 2004; Zack, 1999; Van den Bosch et al., 1999; Kogut & Zander, 1992) the posed arguments for balancing exploration and exploitation are well established and accepted.

This ability to balance exploration and exploitation simultaneously has been defined as ambidexterity. Previous literatures have argued that successful organizations are ambidextrous-aligned and efficient in managing today's demands, while also being adaptable to changes in the environment (Duncan, 1976; Gibson & Birkinshaw, 2004; He & Wong, 2004; Tushman & O'Reilly, 1996). Since the introduction of the term "ambidextrous organization" by Duncan (1976), the concept has been used to describe a variety of distinctions in organizational behavior and outcomes. It has increasingly been used to refer to an organization's ability to do two different things at the same time – for example, exploitation and exploration, efficiency and flexibility, change and preservation, or alignment and adaptability (Gibson & Birkinshaw, 2004). Duncan (1976) referred to the ability of organizations to design dual structures that facilitate the initiating stage and implementation stage of the innovation process. From a structural point of view ambidexterity has been defined as the "ability to simultaneously pursue both incremental and discontinuous innovation and change" (Tushman & O'Reilly, 1996) through an organizational design or form containing not only separate structural subunits for exploration and exploitation, but also different competences, systems, incentives, processes, and cultures for each unit (Benner & Tushman, 2003). The behavioral view defines ambidexterity as the organization's or business unit's behavioral capacity to simultaneously pursue alignment and adaptability. Alignment refers to the coherence among all the patterns of activities in the organization or business unit. Adaptability refers to the capacity to reconfigure activities in the business unit quickly to meet changing demands in the task environment. So besides the structural ambidexterity, a supportive organizational context is needed to enable the meta-capabilities of alignment and adaptability to flourish simultaneously (Gibson & Birkinshaw, 2004). The realized view defines ambidexterity in terms of the organization's exploitation and exploration attainments. This view focuses explicitly on the organization's actual exploration and exploitation performance; for example, ambidextrous organizations successfully pursue both incremental and discontinuous innovations (Benner & Tushman, 2003; Smith & Tushman, 2005). Although there are a lot of valuable contributions, both researchers and managers still struggle to understand how organizations may manage and organize simultaneously exploration and exploitation and how to find the right configuration between exploration and exploitation activities.

Ambidexterity as Managing Paradoxes

Duncan (1976) argues that for long-term success organizations need to consider dual structures. In his view, ambidexterity occurs sequentially as organizations switch structures as innovations evolve. The innovation process is leading in the adjustment of their structures: organic structures serve exploration, while subsequent mechanistic structures serve exploitation. However, market complexity and rapid change compel organizations to pursue exploration and exploitation simultaneously. According to Tushman and O'Reilly (2007), ambidexterity, in this conceptualization, entails not only separate structural subunits for exploration and exploitation but also different competences, systems, incentives, processes, and cultures – each internally aligned. These separate units are held together by a common strategic intent, an overarching set of values, and targeted structural linking mechanisms to leverage shared assets (Tushman & O'Reilly, 2007).

Many researchers believe that ambidexterity can be organized and managed on the same organizational level, i.e., unit, team, or individual (Adler & Borys, 1996; Gibson & Birkinshaw, 2004; McDonough & Leifer, 1983). In this perspective Gibson and Birkinshaw (2004) developed the concept of *contextual ambidexterity*, which implies the behavioral capacity to simultaneously demonstrate alignment and adaptability in an entire business unit. Alignment refers to the coherence among all the patterns of activities in the business unit, i.e., they are working together toward the same goals. Adaptability refers to the capacity to reconfigure activities in the business unit quickly to meet changing demands in the task environment. So besides structural ambidexterity, a supportive organizational context is needed to enable the meta-capabilities of alignment and adaptability to simultaneously flourish (Gibson & Birkinshaw, 2004). Obviously then, managing ambidexterity requires different competences, incentives, and cultures, hence increasing the chances for conflict, disagreement, and difficult coordination. Overall there is broad recognition that the challenges of managing ambidexterity as two paradoxical frames of exploration and exploitation create stresses, and it requires from management cognitive flexibility and complexity to manage these paradoxes.

Managing this paradox can be seen as a developmental transformation, reflecting the kind of organizational change resulting from the interaction of opposites (Markova, 1987). Developmental transformation combines a process in which a desirable future state is expected to result from the change process, and a dialectical process in the sense that such a trajectory reflects ongoing interactions between opposing tendencies (exploration vs. exploitation) that will result into a new synthesis (Van den Ven & Poole, 1995). In order to ensure developmental change, implying a juxtaposition of two dialectical processes is required: one that emphasizes on stability and order through negative feedback mechanisms and another that emphasizes radical change and chaos through positive feedback (Buckley, 1968; Maruyama, 1963).

We miss, at present, a clear articulation of those capabilities that govern the successful interaction/integration of exploration and exploitation activities over time. This process of continuously managing tensions/ contradictions in the interaction between exploration and exploitation shows similarities to the management of paradoxes (Weick, 1982; Lewis, 2000;

Poole & Van de Ven, 1989; Volberda, 1996, 1998). Poole and Van de Ven (1989) and Volberda (1998) have argued that organizations that are confronted with the issues of balancing exploration and exploitation can choose from four different coop-strategies:

1. *Accept* the paradox of exploration and exploitation and learn to live with it.
2. *Structuring* the paradox of exploration and exploitation by clarifying levels of reference and connections among them.
3. *Prioritize* the paradox of exploration and exploitation by taking into account the role of time and separate exploration and exploitation over time.
4. *Solve* the paradox of exploration and exploitation by introducing new ambidexterity concepts or a new perspective.

By *accepting* the tensions between exploration and exploitation, organizations can either come to a compromise (Murnighan & Conlon, 1991) or decide to outsource one based on the belief that two contradicting learning modes cannot be combined in one and the same domain, i.e., unit, team, or individual (Baden-Fuller & Volberda, 1997). *Resolving* the paradox through structuring or prioritizing, implies three ways of handling ambidexterity. First, resolving can be accomplished by means of organizational partitioning, i.e., explorative and exploitative activities differ per hierarchical level in terms of present competences in order to cope with different paces of change, time frames, or information needs (Floyd & Lane, 2000; Volberda et al., 2001). Second, organizational partitioning may also be based on discipline or location. In this approach, explorative and exploitative activities are organized in different organizational units (Benner & Tushman, 2003; Tushman & O'Reilly, 1996). Third, an organization may periodically change the focus of innovation (Duncan, 1976; Tushman & Anderson, 1986).

Solving the paradox is associated with terms such as combining, configuring and synthesizing the contradicting learning modes, independent of hierarchical level, function, or domain.

Thus, structural (structuring and prioritizing) and contextual ambidexterity are two complementary ways of managing the interaction between exploration and exploitation. Based on the recent focus on paradoxical approach to management, as opposed to an "either/or" focus (Lewis, 2000), structural ambidexterity without an adequate organizational context, i.e., the systems, processes, and beliefs that shape individual-level behaviors in an organization, can't flourish. According to Crossan, Lane, and White (1999) exploitative and explorative learning takes place at the individual level, the group level and the organizational level. Crossan et al. (1999) argued that organizational learning through all the levels is linked by social and psychological processes: intuiting (at individual level), interpreting (at individual level and between individual and group level), and integrating (at group level). So structural ambidexterity cannot flourish without an organizational context encouraging individuals and groups to make their own choices as to how they divide their time between alignment and adaptability-oriented activities, i.e., exploration and exploitation activities (Gibson & Birkinshaw, 2004). So we pose:

P2. Organizations/SBUs with a coping strategy of solving will realize higher performance than organizations with a coping strategy of accepting or structuring/prioritizing.

Ambidexterity as High-Order Dynamic Capability

Based on the above, we conclude that the core ideas of ambidexterity refer to an organization's capability to manage contradicting learning mechanisms.

Managing these contradictions and tensions simultaneously, i.e., between efficiency in the short term and effectiveness in the long term is common to the dynamic capabilities approach and March's (1991) proposition of balancing exploration and exploitation.

Embedding the notion of ambidexterity in the dynamic capabilities framework (Teece, Pisano, & Shuen, 1997, Eisenhardt & Martin, 2000; Zollo & Winter, 2002; Zahra, Sapienza, & Davidsson, 2006; Wang & Ahmed, 2007) broadens our understanding of how organizations manage these contradicting learning mechanisms and tensions.

Dynamic capabilities have been conceptualized as the firm's ability to "integrate, build, and reconfigure internal and external competences to address rapidly changing environments" (Teece et al., 1997, p. 516). Dynamic capabilities are also "organizational and strategic routines by which firms achieve new resource configurations as market emerge, collide, split, evolve and die" (Eisenhardt & Martin, 2000). Zollo and Winter (2002) define a dynamic capability as "a learned and stable pattern of collective activity through which the organization systematically generates and modifies its operating routines in pursuit of improved effectiveness," and they argue that dynamic capabilities exist "even in environments subject to lower rates of change." Common in these three different conceptualizations is the central paradox within the dynamic capabilities approach and in organizational life: optimization and replication versus innovation and adaptation. Dynamic capabilities relate to a firm's ability to integrate, build, and reconfigure internal and external competences to address rapidly changing environments (Teece et al., 1997; Eisenhardt & Martin, 2000; Zollo & Winter, 2002; Winter, 2003).

This is common to March's proposition of balancing exploration and exploitation.

But much of the research exploring how dynamic capabilities might enable firms to balance exploration and exploitation is preliminary and conceptual and is primarily focused on the organizational context of managing ambidexterity. What is sharply missing, however, is a clear articulation of those capabilities that manage the actual interaction/integration of exploration and exploitation over time, i.e., the process of continuous resource reconfiguration.

Organizations need to use and to coordinate their processes (optimization, replication). Concurrently, organizations need to adapt existing capabilities (routines) and resources as well as develop new opportunities (innovation, adaptation). In this perspective, the distinction is made between dynamic capabilities, which are described as being learned and stable patterns – and therefore represent high-order routines – and operating routines, which are modified by those high-order routines (Zollo & Winter, 2002).

The operative core of organizations is based on first-order (Collis, 1994), zero-level (Winter, 2003), or substantive (Zahra et al., 2006) capabilities. These routine-based capabilities are the foundation of a firm's activity (e.g., production processes, marketing, and sales). A changing environment necessitates a constant development of operative routines. Consequently, organizations develop (first-order) dynamic capabilities that provide knowledge to change operative routines. First-order dynamic capabilities (Zollo & Winter, 2002) govern modifications of operative routines. On a higher level (second or high order), dynamic capabilities govern the change of (first-order) dynamic capabilities and operative routines (Collis, 1994; Zollo & Winter, 2002; Winter, 2003; Zahra et al., 2006; Wang & Ahmed, 2007). High-order dynamic capabilities influence high-order organizational learning and determine the corridor of the organization's development. So if second-order dynamic capabilities imply experience accumulation, knowledge transfer and generation (Zollo & Winter, 2002), high-order change will be realized. Moreover, on the level of first-order dynamic capabilities, conflicts on resource allocation, values, and norms may arise from the fact that the intensity and direction of these change routines are antagonistic, as some of them follow an exploration while others follow an exploitation logic (Wang & Ahmed, 2007, p. 37).

In conclusion, organizations learn to balance contradictory logics through experience accumulation both on the level of operative routines and on the level of change routines. However, the dynamic capabilities literature is silent in regard to the question of how diverse and opposed (first-order) dynamic capabilities are balanced.

Ambidexterity: Managing the Interaction between
Exploration and Exploitation

As posited earlier, ambidexterity may be defined as a high-order dynamic capability that governs the continuous optimization of the interaction between exploration and exploitation (first-order dynamic capabilities). Managing this interaction implies the resolution of the firm's permanent struggle to overcome the barriers related to the right resource configuration between exploration and exploitation (March, 1991; Argote, 1999).

Such coping with contradictory learning modes (exploration/exploitation) through the reconfiguration of resources is common to the concept of "absorptive capacity (Cohen & Levinthal, 1990) and combinative capabilities" (Kogut & Zander, 1992; Grant, 1996; Iansiti & Khanna, 1995).

Absorptive capacity refers to a firm's ability to identify, assimilate, and exploit knowledge to commercial ends (Cohen & Levinthal, 1990). Zahra and George (2002) define absorptive capacity as "as set of organizational routines and processes by which firms acquire, assimilate, transform, and exploit knowledge to produce a dynamic organizational capability." This is common to the tripartite taxonomy of Teece (2006) who defines sensing, seizing, and reconfiguration as a process to develop dynamic capabilities. Kogut and Zander (1992) defined combinative capabilities as the intersection of the capability of an organization to exploit its knowledge and the unexplored potential of the technology.

Generally, combinative capabilities can be defined as an organization's ability to make efficient use of its resources by combining internal resources or internal and external resources to create new resource configurations that are rare, valuable, hardly imitable, and nonsubstitutable. Koruna (2004) concludes that to achieve successful and valuable resource reconfigurations, organizations have to circumvent the barriers to resource reconfiguration.

So combinative capabilities can be seen as balancing routines, i.e., high-order change routines (Zollo & Winter, 2002). We conceive a balancing routine as the main high-order dynamic capability of ambidextrous organizations that is responsible for the governance of ambidexterity, i.e., optimizing the interaction between exploration and exploitation in time through continuous solving of the barriers to resource reconfiguration.

Although developed separately and for different purposes, absorptive capacity and combinative capabilities refer to the receptivity of an organization to external sources of knowledge or technologies. We contend that absorptive capacity and synthesizing capabilities can be used as a proxy for high-order dynamic capabilities. First, just as dynamic capabilities, absorptive capacity and combinative capability have been positively associated with organizational change and innovation (e.g., Tsai, 2001; Szulanski, 1996; Cohen & Levinthal, 1990; Zahra & George, 2002). Second, Zahra and George (2002) equated explicitly "we recognize absorptive capacity as a dynamic capability that influences the nature and sustainability of a firm's competitive advantage." Third, similar to existing views on dynamic capabilities, is absorptive capacity/combinative capabilities embedded within the organizational processes and routines (i.e., organizational mechanisms) that can be seen as common features of synthesizing capabilities.

We define three types of combinative capabilities: structural capabilities, interaction capabilities, and socialization capabilities.

Structural capabilities' primarily goal is to formalize and centralize the interaction between exploration and exploitation. The interaction between exploration and exploitation is structured through a high degree of programmed behavior in advance of their execution and provide memory for handling routine situations (Galbraith, 1977; March & Simon, 1958; Van den Bosch et al., 1999). *Formalization* is defined as the degree to which rules, procedures, instructions, and communications are formalized and written down. Formalization acts as a frame of reference that constrains exploration efforts and directs attentions toward restricted aspects of an external environment (Weick, 1979). On the other hand, organizations pursue *routinization* to develop sequences of tasks that require relatively little attention (Galunic & Rodan, 1998) and to ensure that inputs are transformed into outputs (Perrow, 1967). So routinization limits the search for new external opportunities and constrains exploration efforts. So routinization provides efficient structures for collective action and decreases time and effort spent on decision making and implementation (Cohen & Bacdayan, 1994).

Thus, the deployment of structural capabilities for enabling ambidexterity is more positively related to exploitation activities than exploration activities. Further, the deployment of structural capabilities aims to manage ambidexterity based on ex ante rules and procedures and so implies the structural ambidexterity form.

Hence, we assume:

P3. Structural capabilities will be negatively related to organizational ambidexterity.

Interaction capabilities enhance knowledge exchange across disciplinary and hierarchical boundaries (Henderson & Cockburn, 1994; Teece et al., 1997). These interaction capabilities evolve in time through education and job rotation, the use of natural interfaces (natural liaison devices), and enhancing the participation in decision making (Galbraith, 1977; Henderson & Cockburn, 1994; Van Den Bosch et al., 1999).

Organizations use *cross-functional interfaces* such as liaison personnel, taskforces, and teams to enable the interaction between exploration and exploitation (Gupta & Govindarajan, 2000). These interfaces enable lateral forms in communication that deepen information and knowledge flows and mutual understanding across functional boundaries and lines of authority. They promote nonroutine and reciprocal information processing (Egelhoff, 1991) and so enhance the common understanding about issues concerning the tensions/contradictions of the interaction between exploration and exploitation.

Participation in decision making refers to the extent to which subordinates take part in higher level decision-making processes (Hage & Aiken, 1967). A higher participation degree enhances the acceptance of divergent perspectives on different issues, contradictions etc., resulting in possible innovative initiatives but it decreases the successful implementation of taken decisions.

We define *job rotation* as the lateral transfer of employees between jobs (Campion, Cheraskin, & Stevens, 1994). This lateral transfer enhances the redundancy as well as diversity of backgrounds, to increase problem-solving skills, and to develop organizational contacts (Cohen & Levinthal, 1990; McGrath, 2001). We assume that interaction capabilities will have a high potential for exploration and a low potential for exploitation. But the primary focus is on the interaction between exploration and exploitation activities.

Based on the above arguments we assume:

P4. Interaction capabilities will be positively related to organizational ambidexterity.

Socialization capabilities are deployed to develop an organizational context with strong values and norms. This is established through interpersonal relationships which lead to the contribution of common codes of communication and dominant values (Henderson & Cockburn, 1994; Teece et al., 1997). We distinguish two organizational mechanisms: socialization tactics and connectedness. *Socialization tactics* refer to the way organizations offer newcomers specific information and encourage them to interpret and respond to situations in a predictable way (Jones, 1986). Primary aim is to realize a high level of concurrence and conformance among the organization members (Ashfort & Saks, 1996; Jones, 1986). Socialization tactics enhance the combination of exploration and exploitation through "facilitating bisociation" among unit members (Zahra & George, 2002). On the other hand, the enhancement of commitment and compliance within exploitation of newly developed/acquired innovations (i.e., knowledge, concepts, products etc.) through a strong value system (strong norms and beliefs) will stimulate the exploitation processes, or otherwise stated.

Connectedness (the density of linkages) could be seen as a governance mechanism that facilitates the exchange of knowledge, information, experience etc. (Jaworski & Kohli, 1993). A high level of connectedness implies dense network(s) which are advantageous to the development of trust and cooperation but increase the redundancy of information and results in a diminished access to divergent perspectives (Nahapiet & Ghoshal, 1998; Sethi, Smith, & Park, 2001). Connectedness encourages also the communication and improves the efficiency of knowledge exchange throughout units (Galunic & Rodan, 1998).

Clearly, socialization capabilities are path dependent and can create mental prisons that prevent organizational members from seeing important new opportunities or changes and seizing them adequately. So we assume that the deployment of socialization capabilities will be more positively related to exploitation activities than exploration activities.

Due to the clear path dependency of socialization we assume that:

P5. Socialization capabilities will be negatively related to organizational ambidexterity.

P6. The higher the interactive effect of structural, interaction, and socialization capabilities, the higher the level of ambidexterity and thus the positive effect on performance.

Table 1. Assumptions Regarding Impact of Synthesizing Capabilities
on Exploration, Exploitation and Ambidexterity.

	Combinative Capabilities		
	Structural capabilities	Interaction capabilities	Socialization capabilities
Exploration	Low	High	Low
Exploitation	High	High	High
Impact on organizational ambidexterity	Moderate	Positive	Negative

To summarize, Table 1 illustrates our arguments on the deployment effect
of combinative capabilities and shows the impact these capabilities will have
on exploration, exploitation, and ambidexterity.

Overcoming Barriers to Resource Reconfiguration

Central to the definition of organizational ambidexterity as high-order
dynamic capability (balancing routine) is the concept of resource
reconfiguration. Many researchers have proposed that resource recombina-
tion or reconfiguration is an important source for innovation (Gilfillan,
1935; Usher, 1954; Schumpeter, 1934; Prahalad & Hamel, 1990). In a
Schumpeterian way, innovation can be defined as the reconceptualization of
an existing system in order to use the resources from which it is built in novel
and potentially rent-generating ways (Henderson & Clark, 1990; Kogut &
Zander, 1992; Grant, 1996). Penrose (1959) pointed out that a firm's ability
to reconfigure the resources inside its boundaries represents a major
competitive advantage. Galunic and Rodan (1998) revealed insight in the
process of resource reconfiguration within firms and partially explained why
firms face difficulties in achieving systematic reconfiguration of resources.

In their study on the success of Japanese firms against US and European
competitors, Prahalad and Hamel (1990) emphasized the importance of
resource (re)configuration by deploying their resources in a creative and
efficient way (Bierly & Chakrabarti, 2001). In this way they created new and
more capabilities and achieved sustainable competitive advantages. To do
so the Japanese organizations had to overcome specific barriers to resource
reconfiguration (Koruna, 2004). We distinguish the following categories of

barriers to resource reconfiguration related to managing the interaction between exploration and exploitation:Knowledge-based barriers

1. *Tacitness of knowledge.* Tacitness generally describes the extent to which knowledge in the organization is or is not codifiable. Because of strict relatedness to individuals, knowledge is difficult to detect and sharing will be a time-consuming and costly process. It will thus be more difficult for someone to identify this potential resource and imagine how it may be used in novel ways, so the potential of new configurations of resources will decline (Galunic & Rodan, 1998; Teece, 1980).
2. *Dispersion of knowledge.* Most of the organizations are often not aware of the available knowledge (i.e., on individual level or knowledge that resides in systems of interaction). Organizations need to achieve transparency regarding the resources they possess (O'Dell & Grayson, 1998). Thus, dispersion of knowledge will influence its detection and movement and hence the probability of (re)configuration (Galunic & Rodan, 1998).
3. *Context specificity.* The context in which knowledge is developed is also important to its flow. One of the primary difficulties in the process of resource reconfiguration is identifying the context in which such configurations are valuable (Hargadon, 1998). Knowledge can be highly customized to one particular use, thus increasing the context specificity, but the likelihood of resource reconfiguration will be diminished the more the context-specific knowledge is involved.

Cognitive barriers

4. *Diverging mental models.* Different experience curves, perspectives and attitudes don't facilitate the communication and interaction between different units or individuals or even contradicting learning modes. So the probability of new resource configuration will decline based on the fact that "over time disciplines increasingly divide rather than combine" (Brown & Duguid, 1998).
5. *Language.* Based on diverging mental models, each organizational unit, group, or discipline tends to develop its own internal language and definitions regarding organizational issues. This results in the development and institutionalization of different sublanguages, so complicating the interaction inside organizations.
6. *Cognitive flexibility.* Cognitive flexibility is closely related with diverging mental models and the path dependency of developed knowledge and assumptions about the interaction between exploration and exploitation.

Sanchez (2004) defined two types of cognitive flexibility: cognitive flexibility to imagine alternative strategic logics and to imagine alternative management processes. Thus, cognitive flexibility is the ability of an organization and its management to define alternative strategic logics for using resources in processes for creating value in markets and thereby achieving the organization's goals (cf. Mahoney & Sanchez, 1997). Hence, the lower the cognitive flexibility, the lower the potential to create new resource configurations.

Organizational barriers

7. *Intra-organizational boundaries*. There is common agreement on the fact that organizational structure can be a barrier to resource configuration because of different stakes, contradicting logics of management, focus, delivered value, specialization etc. So, the higher the extent of structuring, the lower the potential to resource reconfiguration.

8. *Status*. In organizations there are continuous disputes regarding the hierarchical position of individuals, disciplines, or units. The higher the intensity and frequency of these disputes and the lower the transparency about positions, the lower the potential to new resource reconfigurations.

9. *Specialization*. With increased division of labor and specialization organizational members loose the ability to see the interdependencies between different disciplines and to communicate beyond the boundaries of their unit or discipline. This makes the process of resource reconfiguration costly and complex.

10. *Clear objectives/assumptions regarding the interaction between exploration and exploitation*. In most of the organizations there is a lack of clearly defined objectives or assumptions about the way the organization enables and governs the interaction between exploration and exploitation. Individuals, units, and disciplines don't have clear guidelines concerning their role and contribution in the optimization of the resource reconfiguration process. Thus, the more diffuse the objectives and assumptions the lower the potential to resource reconfiguration.

Thus, we can state that organizations will differ in deploying the defined combinative capabilities to overcome the perceived barriers to resource reconfiguration. Based on the above we pose the following:

P7. Socialization capabilities and interaction capabilities will be more deployed in overcoming knowledge-based and cognitive barriers.

P8. Structural capabilities will be more deployed in overcoming organizational barriers.

DISCUSSION

Strategic management literatures, organizational change and organizational learning literatures have increasingly discussed the need for firms to balance exploration and exploitation simultaneously (Eisenhardt & Martin, 2000; Levinthal & March, 1993; Teece et al., 1997).

This study departs from the need to increase our understanding of how organizations manage and organize exploration and exploitation simultaneously through the deployment of dynamic capabilities in order to realize ambidexterity. More specifically, the purpose of this study is to enhance conceptually and empirically validated understanding of how organizations manage the actual interaction between exploration and exploitation (ambidexterity) by overcoming the perceived barriers to resource reconfiguration through the deployment of dynamic capabilities.

Our intent was to review current perspectives on ambidexterity and further specify the organizational ambidexterity construct and develop a more encompassing model of managing the actual interaction between exploration and exploitation. To that end, we first reviewed extant research using a framework where ambidexterity has been explored from different perspectives. We then elaborated upon a coherent, multilevel model that not only discerns the key definition of organizational ambidexterity, but also specifies the shaping influences of the perceived barriers to resource reconfiguration on organizational ambidexterity and the way the different combinative capabilities are deployed to manage the interaction between exploration and exploitation as a continuous process of resource (re)configuration.

FURTHER RESEARCH

With further investigating and testing, forthcoming research based on the conceptual framework presented here on managing the interaction between exploration and exploitation will contribute to the existing literature in several ways (Fig. 1).

First, recent literatures on organizational ambidexterity have primarily focused on the contextual and structural aspects of balancing two

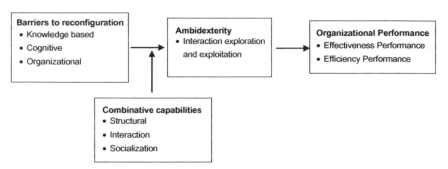

Fig. 1. Conceptual Framework.

contradicting learning mechanisms like exploration and exploitation. Empirical results indicate that organizations adopt structures or develop a type of culture or context to enable exploration and exploitation simultaneously (Tushman & O'Reilly, 1996; Gibson & Birkinshaw, 2004; Benner & Tushman, 2003; March, 1991). However, no insights, till now, have been gained into how the interaction between exploration and exploitation can be managed and what the effects are on organizational performance.

By drawing on the research of dynamic capabilities, this study will contribute to and extend our understanding of organizational ambidexterity by conceptually and empirically investigating the organizational processes of managing the actual "interaction" between exploration and exploitation.

Second, this study will contribute conceptually and empirically to research of related management fields by defining the management of the interaction between exploration and exploitation as a continuous process of solving the barriers to resource reconfiguration through the deployment of combinative capabilities as balancing routines (Kogut & Zander, 1992; Teece et al., 1997; Van den Bosch et al., 1999; Grant, 1996; Iansiti & Khanna, 1995; Zollo & Winter, 2002; Argote, 1999).

Hence, we conceptually identify and will empirically examine how common features of combinative capabilities have an impact on the way organizations solve the barriers to resource reconfiguration to realize organizational ambidexterity. By linking these three constructs, this study reveals how organizations manage this interaction and which combinative capabilities are deployed to overcome the barriers to research reconfiguration.

Third, this study will contribute to and empirically validate the further conceptualization of organizational ambidexterity and its impact on performance (Ghemawat, Ricart, & Costa, 1993; Adler et al., 1999; Benner & Tushman, 2003; Gibson & Birkinshaw, 2004; Leana & Barry,

2000; McGrath, 2001; Rivkin & Siggelkow, 2003; Sheremata, 2000). By making the distinction between effectiveness performance and efficiency performance, current literature and management practice could benefit from a further insight in the way exploration, exploitation, and their interaction have an impact on performance. For the first time, these relationships will empirically be validated by an extensive cross-sectional empirical study.

Fourth, this research will contribute to organizational learning literature by empirically investigating how barriers to resource reconfiguration affect the interaction between exploration and exploitation. Till now, no insights however have been gained into how these barriers affect the actual interaction between two opposing learning mechanisms. By defining the management of the interaction as high-order learning, we reveal how barriers to resource reconfiguration matter and examine the linkage between barriers to resource reconfiguration, specific organizational mechanisms as common features of combinative capabilities and organizational ambidexterity. To date, reliable and valid measures for these constructs are still lacking. Strategic management, organizational learning and organization theory literature will benefit from reliable and valid scales for the developed and presented key constructs.

Finally, this study may particularly contribute to management practice regarding the issue of how firms manage and organize the interaction between exploration and exploitation (e.g., Duncan, 1976; Gibson & Birkinshaw, 2004; Levinthal & March, 1993; Tushman & O'Reilly, 1996) through broadening their insight into which barriers are observed in this process of managing this interaction and which combinative capabilities should be deployed to overcome these barriers based on their strategic orientation in maximizing organizational performance.

CONCLUSION

The challenge of organizational ambidexterity is a crucial one for managers and scholars. However, even as research accumulates, organizational ambidexterity still remains a construct that has a lot to gain from further theorization and conceptualization. Even though we have drawn upon theories from various disciplines and traditions to integrate and extend current understanding about organizational ambidexterity, much remains to be understood. Thus, further dialogue on organizational ambidexterity promises to be interesting and valuable for both researchers and practitioners.

REFERENCES

Adler, P. S., & Borys, B. (1996). Two types of bureaucracy: Enabling and coercive. *Administrative Science Quarterly, 41*, 61.

Adler, P. S., Goldoftas, B., & Levine, D. I. (1999). Flexibility versus efficiency? A case study of changeovers in the Toyota production system. *Organization Science, 10*(1), 43–68.

Argote, L. (1999). *Organizational learning. Creating, retaining and transferring knowledge.* Norwell, MA: Kluwer Academic Publishers.

Ashfort, B. E., & Saks, A. M. (1996). Socialization tactics: Longitudinal effects on newcomer adjustment. *Academy of Management Review, 21*, 149–178.

Auh, S., & Menguc, B. (2005). Balancing exploration and exploitation: The moderating role of competitive intensity. *Journal of Business Research, 58*(12), 1652–1661.

Baden-Fuller, C., & Volberda, H. (1997). Strategic renewal international studies. *Management and Organisations, 2*, 95–120.

Benner, M., & Tushman, M. (2003). Exploitation, exploration, and process management: The productivity dilemma revisited. *Academy of Management Review, 29*, 238–256.

Bierly, P. E., & Chakrabarti, A. (2001). Dynamic knowledge strategies and industry fusion. *International Journal of Manufacturing Technology and Management, 3*(2), 31–48.

Bouchikhi, H. (1998). Living with and building on complexity: A constructivist perspective on organizations. *Organization, 5*(2), 217–232.

Brown, J. S., & Duguid, P. (1998). Organizing knowledge. *California Management Review, 40*(1), 90–111.

Buckley, W. (1968). *Modern systems research for the behavioral scientist: A sourcebook.* Chicago. IL: Aldine Publishing Company.

Burgelman, R. A. (1991). Intraorganizational ecology of strategy making and organizational adaptation: Theory and field research. *Organization Science, 2*(3), 239–262.

Campion, M., Cheraskin, L., & Stevens, M. (1994). Career-related antecedents and outcomes of job rotation. *Academy of Management Journal, 37*(6), 1518–1542.

Christensen, C. M. (1997). *The innovator's dilemma: When new technologies cause great firms to fail.* Boston, MA: Harvard Business School Press.

Cohen, M. D., & Bacdayan, P. (1994). Organizational routines are stored as procedural memory: Evidence from a laboratory study. *Organization Science, 5*(4), 554–568.

Cohen, W. M., & Levinthal, D. A. (1990). Absorptive capacity: A new perspective on learning and innovation. *Administrative Science Quarterly, 35*(September), 128–152.

Collis, D. J. (1994). Research note: How valuable are organizational capabilities? *Strategic Management Journal, 15*(Winter Special Issue), 143–152.

Crossan, M., & Bedrow, I. (2003). Organizational learning and strategic renewal. *Strategic Management Journal, 24*(11), 1087–1105.

Crossan, M., Lane, H., & White, R. (1999). An organizational learning framework: From intuition to institution. *Academy of Management Review, 24*, 522–537.

Duncan, R. (1976). The ambidextrous organization: designing dual structures for innovation. In: Kilmann, R., Pondy, L., & Slevin, D. (Eds) *The management of organization design* (Vol. I, 167–188). New York: North-Holland.

Earley, P. C., & Gibson, C. B. (2002). *Multinational teams: New perspectives.* Mahwah, NJ: Lawrence Erlbaum Associates.

Egelhoff, W. G. (1991). Information-processing theory and the multinational enterprise. *Journal of International Business Studies, 22*, 341–368.

Eisenhardt, KM., & Martin, J. A. (2000). Dynamic capabilities: What are they? *Strategic Management Journal, 21*, 1105–1121.

Floyd, S. W., & Lane, P. J. (2000). Strategizing throughout the organization: Managing role conflict in strategic renewal. *Academy of Management Review, 25*, 154–177.

Galbraith, J. R. (1977). *Organisation design*. Reading, MA: Addison-Wesley.

Galunic, D. C., & Rodan, S. (1998). Resource recombinations in the firm: Knowledge structures and the potential for schumpeterian innovation. *Strategic Management Journal, 19*(12), 1193–1201.

Ghemawat, P., Ricart, J. E., & Costa, I. (1993). The organizational tension between static and dynamic efficiency. *Strategic Management Journal, 14*(special issue Winter), 59–73.

Gibson, C. B., & Birkinshaw, J. (2004). The antecedents, consequences, and mediating role of organizational ambidexterity. *Academy of Management Journal, 47*, 209–226.

Gilfillan, S. C. (1935). *Inventing the ship*. Chicago, IL: Follett Publishing Co.

Grant, R. M. (1996). Toward a knowledge-based theory of the firm. *Strategic Management Journal, 17*, 109–122.

Grant, R. M., & Baden-Fuller, C. (2004). A knowledge accessing theory of strategic alliances. *Journal of Management Studies, 41*(1), 61–84.

Gresov, C., & Drazin, R. (1997). Equifinality: Functional equivalence in organization design. *Academy of Management Review, 22*, 403–428.

Gupta, A. K., & Govindarajan, V. (2000). Knowledge flows within multinational corporations. *Strategic Management Journal, 21*, 473–496.

Hage, J., & Aiken, M. (1967). Relationship of centralization to other structural properties. *Administrative Science Quarterly, 12*(1), 72–92.

Hargadon, A. B. (1998). *Knowledge brokers: A field study of organizational learning and innovation*. San Diego, CA: Academy of Management Proceedings.

He, Z., & Wong, P. (2004). Exploration vs. exploitation: An empirical test of the ambidexterity hypothesis. *Organization Science, 15*, 481–494.

Henderson, R., & Clark, K. (1990). Architectural innovation: The reconfiguration of existing product technologies and the failure of established firms. *Administrative Science Quarterly, 35*(1), 9–30.

Henderson, R., & Cockburn, I. (1994). Measuring competence? Exploring firm effects in pharmaceutical research. *Strategic Management Journal, 15*, 63–84.

Holmqvist, M. (2004). Experiential learning processes. *Organization Science, 15*(1), 70–81.

Iansiti, M., & Khanna, T. (1995). Technological evolution, system architecture and the obsolescence of firm capabilities. *Industrial and Corporate Change, 4*, 333–361.

Jaworski, B., & Kohli, A. (1993). Market orientation: Antecedents and consequences. *Journal of Marketing, 52*(July), 53–70.

Jones, G. R. (1986). Socialization tactics, self-efficacy, and newcomers' adjustments to organizations. *Academy of Management, 29*(2), 262.

Kogut, B., & Zander, U. (1992). Knowledge of the firm, combinative capabilities, and the replication of technology. *Organization Science, 3*, 383–397.

Koruna, S. (2004). Leveraging knowledge assets: Combinative capabilities – Theory and practice. *R&D Management, 34*(5), 505–516.

Leana, C. R., & Barry, B. (2000). Stability and change as simultaneous experiences in organizational life. *Academy of Management Review, 25*(4), 753–759.

Levinthal, D. A., & March, J. G. (1993). The myopia of learning. *Strategic Management Journal, 14*(8), 95–112.

Levitt, B., & March, J. G. (1988). Organizational learning. *Annual Review of Sociology, 14*, 319–340.

Lewis, M. W. (2000). Exploring paradox: Toward a more comprehensive guide. *Academy of Management Review, 25*, 760–776.

Mahoney, J. T., & Sanchez, R. (1997). Competence theory building: Reconnecting management research and management practice. In: *Competence-based strategic management.* Chicester: Wiley.

March, J. G. (1991). Exploration and exploitation in organizational learning. *Organization Science, 2*, 71–87.

March, J. G., & Simon, H. A. (1958). *Organizations.* Cambridge MA: Blackwell.

Markova, I. (1987). On the interaction of opposites in psychological processes. *Journal for the Theory of Social Behaviour, 17*(3), 279–299.

Maruyama, M. (1963). The second cybernetics: Deviation-amplifying mutual causal processes. *American Scientist, 5*(2), 164–179.

McDonough, E., & Leifer, R. (1983). Using simultaneous structures to cope with uncertainty. *Academy of Management Journal, 26*, 727–736.

McGrath, R. G. (2001). Exploratory learning, innovative capacity, and managerial oversight. *Academy of Management Journal, 44*, 118–131.

Morgeson, F. P., & Hofmann, D. A. (1999). The structure and function of collective constructs: Implications for research and theory development. *Academy of Management Review, 24*, 249–265.

Murnighan, J. K., & Conlon, D. E. (1991). The dynamics of intense work groups: A study of British string quartets. *Administrative Science Quarterly, 36*(2), 165–186.

Nahapiet, J., & Ghoshal, S. (1998). Social capital, intellectual capital, and the organizational advantage. *Academy of Management Review, 23*(2), 242–266.

Nerkar, A. (2003). Old is gold? the value of temporal exploration in the creation of new knowledge. *Management Science, 49*(2), 211–229.

O'Dell, C., & Grayson, C. J. (1998). If only we knew what we know: Identification and transfer of internal best practices. *California Management Review, 40*(3), 154–174.

Penrose, E. T. (1959). *The theory of the growth of the firm.* New York: Wiley.

Perrow, C. (1967). A framework for the comparative analysis of organizations. *American Sociological Review, 32*, 194–208.

Poole, M., & Van de Ven, A. (1989). Using paradox to build management and organization theory. *Academy of Management Review, 14*, 562–578.

Porter, M. E. (1985). *Competitive advantage.* New York: Free Press.

Prahalad, C. K., & Hamel, G. (1990). The core competence of the corporation. *Harvard Business Review, 68*(3), 79–91.

Rivkin, J. W., & Siggelkow, N. (2003). Balancing search and stability: Interdependencies among elements of organizational design. *Management Science, 49*(3), 290–311.

Sanchez, R. (2004). Understanding competence-based management: Identifying and managing five modes of competence. *Journal of Business Research, 57*(5), 518–532.

Schumpeter, J. A. (1934). *The theory of economic development.* Cambridge MA: Harvard University Press.

Sethi, R., Smith, D., & Park, C. W. (2001). Cross-functional product development teams, creativity, and the innovativeness of new consumer products. *Journal of Marketing Research, 38*(1), 73–85.

Sheremata, W. A. (2000). Centrifugal and centripetal forces in radical new product development under time pressure. *Academy of Management Review, 25*(2), 389–408.

Smith, W., & Tushman, M. (2005). Managing strategic contradictions: A top management model for managing strategic innovations. *Organization Science, 16*, 522–536.

Szulanski, G. (1996). Exploring internal stickiness: Impediments to the transfer of best practice within the firm. *Strategic Management Journal, 17*(special issue Winter), 27–43.

Teece, D. J. (1980). The diffusion of an administrative innovation. *Management Science, 26*(5), 464–470.

Teece, D. J. (2006). Reflections on "Profiting from Innovation". *Research Policy, 35*(8), 1131–1146.

Teece, D. J., Pisano, G., & Shuen, A. (1997). Dynamic capabilities and strategic management. *Strategic Management Journal, 18*(7), 509–533.

Tsai, W. (2001). Knowledge transfer in intraorganizational networks: Effects of network position and absorptive capacity on business unit innovation and performance. *Academy of Management Journal, 44*(5), 996–1004.

Tushman, M., & O'Reilly, C. (1996). Ambidextrous organizations: Managing evolutionary and revolutionary change. *California Management Review, 38*, 8–30.

Tushman, M., & O'Reilly, C. (2007). *Ambidexterity as a dynamic capability: Resolving the innovator's dilemma.* Working Paper No. 07-088. Harvard Business School.

Tushman, M. L., & Anderson, P. (1986). Technological discontinuities and organizational environments. *Administrative Science Quarterly, 31*(3), 439–465.

Usher, A. P. (1954). *A history of mechanical inventions.* Cambridge, MA: Harvard University Press.

Van den Bosch, F. A. J., et al. (1999). Coevolution of firm absorptive capacity and knowledge environment: Organizational forms and combinative capabilities. *Organization Science, 10*(5), 551–568.

Van den Ven, A. H., & Poole, M. S. (1995). Explaining development and change in organizations. *The Academy of Management Review, 20*(3), 510–540.

Volberda, H. W. (1996). Toward the flexible form: How to remain vital in hypercompetitive environments. *Organization Science, 7*(4), 359–374.

Volberda, H. W. (1998). *Building the flexible firm: How to remain competitive.* Oxford: Oxford University Press.

Volberda, H. W., Baden-Fuller, C., & van den Bosch, F. A. J. (2001). Mastering strategic renewal: Mobilising renewal journeys in multi-unit firms. *Long Range Planning, 34*(2), 159–178.

Wang, C. L., & Ahmed, P. K. (2007). Dynamic capabilities: A review and research agenda. *International Journal of Management Reviews, 9*, 31–51.

Weick, K. E. (1979). *The social psychology of organizing* (2nd ed.). New York: McGraw Hill.

Weick, K. E. (1982). Management of organizational change among loosely coupled elements. In: P. S. Goodman, et al. (Eds), *Change in organizations: New perspectives in theory, research and practice* (pp. 375–408). San Francisco, CA: Jossey-Bass.

Winter, S. G. (2003). Understanding dynamic capabilities. *Strategic Management Journal, 24*, 991–995.

Zack, M. H. (1999). Managing codified knowledge. *Sloan Management Review, 40*(4), 45–58.

Zahra, S. A., & George, G. (2002). Absorptive capacity: A review, reconceptualization, and extension. *Academy of Management Review, 27*(2), 185–203.

Zahra, S. A., Sapienza, H. J., & Davidsson, P. (2006). Entrepreneurship and dynamic capabilities: A review, model and research agenda. *Journal of Management Studies, 43*, 917–955.

Zollo, M., & Winter, S. G. (2002). Deliberate learning and the evolution of dynamic capabilities. *Organization Science, 13*, 339–351.

THE FACTORS AFFECTING THE RELATIONSHIP BETWEEN STRATEGIC OPTIONS AND THE COMPETENCE BUILDING PROCESS: AN EMPIRICAL EXAMINATION

Sezi Çevik Onar and Seçkin Polat

ABSTRACT

The objectives of this study are to reveal the relationship between strategic options and competence building processes and to investigate the effect of environmental and firm-related factors on competence building. Competence building is defined as the qualitative change in firms' existing assets and capabilities; exercising strategic options may trigger this process. In this study an empirical model is developed and tested using structural equation modeling techniques. Many researchers have examined the relationship between strategic options and competence building theoretically, and this study aims to support these theoretical efforts with empirical research.

A Focused Issue on Identifying, Building, and Linking Competences
Research in Competence-Based Management, Volume 5, 59–77
ISSN: 1744-2117/doi:10.1108/S1744-2117(2010)0000005006

INTRODUCTION

Recent developments such as the removal of cross border barriers in Europe, product market globalization, new technology developments, and changes in organizational forms have increased the level of competition among firms. This increased competition has caused high levels of uncertainty in firms' environments (Englahardt & Simmons, 2002), as the management practices appropriate for stable environments may not be suitable for the new dynamic environments. In order to respond to this dynamic and uncertain environment, managers and researchers have focused on an organization's strategic flexibility (Ford, Lander, & Voyer, 2002; Kulatilaka & Perotti, 1998). According to the strategic options view, strategic flexibility is defined as the "condition of having strategic options that are created through combined effects of an organization's coordination flexibility in acquiring and using flexible resources" (Sanchez, 1993). Thus the main property of strategic flexibility is the ability to access the required resources and capabilities when they are needed (Sanchez, 1997). According to this definition, in order to have strategic flexibility, firms need to have strategic options, and the main task of managers is to define, develop, acquire, and coordinate the resources and competences that will optimize the value of a firm's strategic options portfolio. The importance of strategic options is reflected in a growing body of research (Amram & Kulatilaka, 1998; Dixit & Pindyck, 1994; Kogut & Kulatilaka, 2001; McGrath, 1997; Trigeorgis, 1996).

In order to optimize a firm's strategic options portfolio, managers should focus on the firm's competence building and competence leveraging processes. Sanchez, Heene, and Thomas (1996, p. 8) define competence building as "any process by which a firm achieves qualitative changes to its existing stocks of assets and capabilities, including new abilities to coordinate and deploy new or existing assets and capabilities in ways that help the firm achieve its goals." Competence leveraging is defined as "the process by which the firm exercises its existing strategic options to create and market products" (Sanchez & Heene, 1997). By exercising the options created (utilizing the firm's resources and competences), firms may build new competences, and these new competences may in turn create new strategic options (Sanchez & Heene, 1997).

Competence building is the qualitative change in firms' existing assets and capabilities, and exercising strategic options triggers this process. Both environmental factors (Folta & O'Brien, 2008; Kogut, 1991; Vassolo, Anand, & ve Folta, 2004; Folta & O'Brien, 2004) and firm-related factors (Trevino & Grosse, 2002; Kumar & Nti, 1998; Allen & Pantzalis, 1996;

Reuer & Leiblein, 2000) have crucial roles in this process. Several researchers have emphasized the relationships among resources, capabilities, and strategic options (Kogut & Kulatilaka, 2001; Bernardo & Chowdhry, 2002; Pandza, Horsburgh, Gorton, & Polajnar, 2003; Kyläheiko & Sandström, 2007; Maritan & Alessandri, 2007; Hubler & Meschi, 2000; Meschi & Cremer, 1997). But the effect of strategic options on the competence building process and the factors affecting this process have been largely unexamined.

The objective of this study is to reveal the relationship between strategic options and competence building processes and also to investigate the effect of environmental and firm-related factors on competence building. In the next section, we present a literature review on the relationship between competence building and real options and the factors affecting this relationship. Then we establish a model showing this relationship and test the model via structural equation modeling techniques. In the final section, we present our conclusions and suggestions for further research.

LITERATURE REVIEW

There has been much recent research relating to strategic options and capabilities. Kogut and Kulatilaka (2001) define capabilities as real options which bring future opportunities. Bernardo and Chowdhry (2002) claim that with real investment decisions, firms learn information about the different types of resources they have, and therefore firms should consider this learning process while exercising their strategic options. Pandza et al. (2003) consider real options thinking as an appropriate heuristic for capability development. Kyläheiko and Sandström (2007) developed a framework for managing dynamic capabilities by using strategic options. Maritan and Alessandri (2007) also consider capabilities as real options. They reveal that industry-based returns and firm-specific returns are the components of returns on capability investment. Most of these studies are conceptual; there is little empirical evidence for these conceptual models. While a few studies have evaluated the performance of competence building processes (Hubler & Meschi, 2000; Meschi & Cremer, 1997), the main objective of these studies is to reveal the effect of competence building on firms' performance. But the effect of strategic options on competence building processes is not evaluated in these studies.

In order to evaluate the effect of strategic options on a competence building process, it is necessary to first evaluate the performance of the competence building process by measuring the qualitative change in a firm's existing assets and capabilities. There is not a standard approach to evaluating capabilities. Some researchers define functional capabilities (such as general management, production, marketing, and sales, etc.) and evaluate the level of these capabilities (Meyer & Utterback, 1993; Hafeez, Zhang, & Malak, 2002; Carmeli & Tishler, 2004).

According to McGrath, Ferrier, and Mendelow (2004), the link between a firm's real options, the factors that are affecting these options, and a firm's performance is largely unexamined. Several researchers have focused on the factors affecting the value of a strategic option that a firm is holding. For instance, by combining transaction cost theory and real options theory, Sanchez (2003) created a theoretical framework to explain the value created by a firm's strategy under uncertainty. In his study on the effect of market growth on acquisitions, Kogut (1991) claims that joint ventures create real options to expand, and the results of the study support the interpretation of joint ventures as options to expand. Reuer and Leiblein (2000) analyzed the value of international investments they expected to enhance corporate flexibility and reduce risk. The results indicate that these investments do not reduce downside risk and therefore do not bring the flexibility they were expected to bring. Tong and Reuer (2006) analyzed the firm and industry influences on the value of growth options. The results indicate that the industry effects are important, but the firm effect is more dominant on the growth option value. McGrath and Nerkar (2004) utilized real option reasoning in analyzing R&D investment strategies and claim that scope of opportunity, prior experience, and competitive effects have an effect on the value created by these options. Vassolo et al. (2004) consider equity alliances as real options. The termination of these alliances, whether by acquisition or divesture, is regarded as an exercise decision and the researchers focused on the factors affecting this decision. O'Brien, Folta, and Johnson (2003) investigated the effects of uncertainty and irreversibility on entrepreneurial entry with a real options perspective. The results of the study show that high uncertainty deters the entry decision and irreversibility has a moderating effect on this decision.

These studies indicate that there is a relationship between firms' strategic options and their competence building process and several factors are affecting this relationship. The factors affecting this relationship can be classified as environmental factors and firm-related factors. Different studies focus on different factors and measure these factors differently. Table 1 summarizes these factors in the literature.

Table 1. Factors Affecting Strategic Options.

Factor	Measurement style	Related studies
1. Environmental Factors		
Industry uncertainty	Monthly standard deviation on returns of an industry index	Vassolo et al. (2004), and Folta and Ferrier (2000)
	The annual demand variance	Folta and O'Brien (2004), and Campa (1993)
	Conditional variance of industry's gross product generated from generalized autoregressive conditional heteroskedasticity	O'Brien et al. (2003)
	Conditional variance of industry's stock index generated from generalized autoregressive conditional heteroskedasticity	Folta and O'Brien (2008)
	Technological uncertainty Standard deviation of the log of weekly returns for each industry index	Folta (1998)
	Perceptional uncertainty measured via questionnaires	Miller (1993), and Werner, Brouthers, and Brouthers (1996)
Industry generosity	Industry return based on the target industry index	Vassolo et al. (2004)
	Industry's systematic risk, covariance between the total return for value weighted returns in the industry and the total market return	O'Brien et al. (2003), and Folta and O'Brien (2007), and Reuer and Leiblein (2000)
	Industry market to book ratio, median market to book ratio of all firms in the target industry	Folta and O'Brien (2007)
	Growth in the total gross product of the region	Folta (1998)
	Total weekly returns of the selected firms in the industry	O'Brien et al. (2003), and Kogut (1991)
Irreversibility Fixed assets	Ratio of property, plant, and equipment to total assets for the median firm in each industry	O'Brien et al. (2003)
Intangible assets	Ratio of intangible assets to total assets for the median firm in each industry	O'Brien et al. (2003)

Table 1. (Continued)

1. Environmental Factors

Factor	Measurement style	Related studies
Inverse leverage ratio	Inverse of the leverage for the median firm in each industry	Titman and Wessels (1988), Shleifer and Vishny (1992), and Gompers (1995)
Region concentration	Percentage of all employees working in a given industry who worked in the same region	O'Brien et al. (2003)
Industry capital intensity	Industry's median level of capital expenditures divided by median sales	Folta and O'Brien (2008)
Industry size	Sum of assets across all business segments in the industry	O'Brien et al. (2003)
	Total expected demand in the industry	O'Brien et al. (2003)
Industry concentration	Concentration ratio of the 4 digit SIC level	Kogut (1991)
	Four firm concentration ratio	Folta and O'Brien (2007)
Industry type	Dummy variable coded based on the industry	Tong and Reuer (2008), O'Brien et al. (2003), Folta (1998), and Kogut (1991)
Industry intensity for advertisement	The median ratio of total advertising to total sales	O'Brien et al. (2003)
Industry intensity for Research and Development (R&D)	The median ratio of total R&D to total sales	O'Brien et al. (2003), Folta (1998), and Folta and O'Brien (2008)
Industry merger waves	The total number of acquisitions in the target industry	Folta and O'Brien (2008)
Number of rivals	The number of rival firms in the industry	Folta (1998)
Interest	Risk-free interest rate	Vassolo et al. (2004), and Folta (1998)

2. Firm-Related Factors

Firm's performance	Total operating profit divided by total sales	O'Brien et al. (2003)
	Return on assets, operating profit divided by assets	Folta and O'Brien (2008)
	Accounts receivable divided by sales	Reuer and Leiblein (2000)
	Inventory divided by sales	Reuer and Leiblein (2000)
	Selling, general and administrative expenses divided by sales	Reuer and Leiblein (2000)

Formalization	The existence of formal coordination mechanisms measured via questionnaires	Fryxell et al. (2002)
Degree of decentralization	The degree of decentralization measured via questionnaires	Hurry et al. (1992)
Firm size	Logarithmic transaction of sales	Laamanen (1999), Vassolo et al. (2004), Reuer and Leiblein (2000)
	Logarithmic total firm assets	Folta and O'Brien (2004)
Firm's diversification level	Sum of squared shares of the firm's business segments	Folta and O'Brien (2004, 2007)
Firm's research and development (R&D) intensity	Firm's R&D expense divided by assets	Folta and O'Brien (2008)
Firm's concentration	Sum of the squared market shares of all business segments competing in that industry	O'Brien et al. (2003)
Founder's properties	Formal education of firm's primary founder	O'Brien et al. (2003)
	Age of the entrepreneur	O'Brien et al. (2003)
	Dummy variable; coded 1 if the entrepreneur was male	O'Brien et al. (2003)
Chief executive officer (CEO) duality	Dummy variable; coded 1 if CEO is also chairman of the board	Folta and O'Brien (2008)
Inside ownership	Percent of stock owned by insiders, equity joint ventures formed abroad or with a foreign partner	Folta and O'Brien (2008)
Number of large block holders	The number of block holders owing at least 5%	Folta and O'Brien (2008)
Prior experience	Number of technologies	Vassolo et al. (2004)
	The count of all total acquisitions that the focal firm made in 3 years prior to the focal year	Folta and O'Brien (2008)
	Distance between target industry and the firm's industry	Reuer and Leiblein (2000) and Folta and O'Brien (2004, 2008)
	Dummy variable; coded 1 if the partners are from the same industry	Folta (1998)
	The common technological domains among partners	Vassolo et al. (2004)
Multinationality	Dummy variable; coded 1 if the involved two firms are from the same country	Folta (1998)
	The number of countries in which a firm had foreign subsidiaries	Reuer and Leiblein (2000)

Table 2.   Strategic Decisions Considered as Strategic Options.

Type of the Exercised Strategic Option	Studies
Equity alliances	Folta and Miller (2002), Vassolo et al. (2004), and Folta (1998)
Market entry	Folta, Johnson, and O'Brien (2006), Folta and O'Brien (2004), O'Brien et al. (2003), Miller and Folta (2002), Dixit (1989), and Campa (1993)
Joint ventures	Cuypers and Martin (2007), Reuer and Tong (2005), Kumar (2005), Reuer and Leiblein (2000), Chi (2000), Chi and McGuire (1996), Kogut (1991), Folta (1998), and Hurry et al. (1992)
Acquisitions	Folta and O'Brien (2007), Folta and O'Brien (2008), Laamanen (1999), and Trigeorgis (1993)

All of these studies focus on the value created using strategic options, but they do not explain the relationship between competence building and strategic options. There is a need to understand the factors that affect the relationship and the effectiveness of exercising strategic options and competence building. Yet analyzing all kinds of strategic options would be beyond the scope of this discussion. We focus here on strategic decisions that are generally accepted in the literature to be competence building triggers and therefore can be considered as strategic options: equity alliances, market entry, joint ventures, and acquisitions. For instance, company acquisitions may be regarded as options to acquire a new technology or business area (Laamanen, 1999; Folta & O'Brien, 2008; Trigeorgis, 1993), increasing a firm's capabilities such as technological capability. Table 2 summarizes the strategic decisions considered as strategic options. These decisions are mainly based on external growth (Hubler & Meschi, 2000).

HYPOTHESES

Based on Sanchez and Heene (1997), the relationship between competence building and leveraging is illustrated in Fig. 1. This study focuses on the relationship between exercising a strategic option and the competence building process. The dotted area in Fig. 1 illustrates this focus. The factors affecting the competence building process through the exercising of strategic options are classified as internal (firm-related) factors and external (environmental) factors.

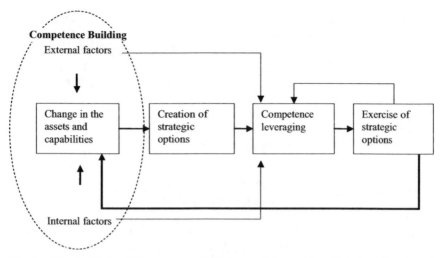

Fig. 1.   Firm's Circle of Competence Building and Leveraging (Based on Sanchez & Heene, 1997).

Environmental Factors

According to this model, environmental factors affect the competence building process through the exercising of strategic options. Several studies have shown that environmental factors have a significant effect on firm structure (Baum & Doyle, 1988; Sumantra & Nitin, 1993; Oxley, 1999). Two of the most commonly used environmental factors are uncertainty and generosity; both may affect a firm's internal structure. As a result, these environmental factors may affect the competence building process both directly and indirectly through a firm's internal factors.

Uncertainty is an important aspect of a firm's environment. Since the logic of options theory is based on uncertainty, the effect of uncertainty on the value created through strategic options is of vital importance. Greater variance of the potential outcome of an asset's value implies higher option value. As a result, more uncertainty may increase the expected upside gains. Uncertainty therefore may increase the value of strategic options and trigger competence building processes (Folta & O'Brien, 2008; Vassolo et al., 2004; Folta & O'Brien, 2004; O'Brien et al., 2003; McGrath & McMillan, 2000; McGrath, 1999; Folta, 1998; Campa, 1990).

Generosity is another characteristic of a firm's environment and is indicated by growth of the industry, demand in the industry, and opportunities in the industry. More generous environments offer more valuable opportunities; therefore the value of the strategic options created in these industries may be higher (O'Brien et al., 2003; Reuer & Leiblein, 2000). Firms targeting higher growth industries may have more valuable growth options and the capability levels of the firms may be higher (Folta & O'Brien, 2004).

Hypothesis. Environmental factors affect the competence building process through the exercising of strategic options.

Firm-Related Factors

In addition to environmental factors, firm-related factors are also thought to have an effect on competence building processes. (See Table 1 for a list of these firm-related factors.) In this study, a firm's financial performance and degree of centralization and formalization are selected as indicators for firm-related factors. Firms with better financial performances have more resources to create strategic options (O'Brien et al., 2003; Folta & O'Brien, 2008; Reuer & Leiblein, 2000). Therefore higher financial performance may lead to better management of competence building processes. Decentralized firms may create learning mechanisms through strategic options; therefore they may be better able to capture value from exercising options (Hurry, Miller, & Bowman, 1992). Fryxell, Dooley, and Vryza (2002) showed that formal control mechanisms affect the performance of joint ventures. Existence of formal control mechanisms may decrease the flexibility of a firm and lower the performance of competence building processes.

Hypothesis. Firm-related factors affect the competence building process through the exercising of strategic options.

According to the literature there is a strong relationship between competence building and strategic options (Kyläheiko & Sandström, 2007; Maritan & Alessandri, 2007; Pandza et al., 2003; Bernardo & Chowdhry, 2002; Kogut & Kulatilaka, 2001; Hubler & Meschi, 2000; Meschi & Cremer, 1997). By exercising the options created, firms may build new competences, and these new competences may in turn create new strategic options (Sanchez & Heene, 1997).

Hypothesis. A better managed strategic option portfolio will improve the capabilities of a firm.

METHODOLOGY

This study tries to reveal the effect of external and internal factors and option exercising decisions on the competence building process. In order to achieve this goal, first the decisions made by 104 firms quoted on the Istanbul Stock Exchange (IMKB) are evaluated. Since the performance of competence building processes is defined as the qualitative change in firms' existing assets and capabilities, the capability levels of a company will represent the performance of competence building processes. In this study, we will focus on 13 functional capabilities and use questionnaire data from the 104 firms to measure the level of these capabilities. A questionnaire was completed by either the general manager or the human resources manager of each firm. In order to evaluate capability levels, respondents are asked to evaluate the level of functional capabilities in their firms (namely management, production, marketing and sales, logistics, information technologies, finance and accounting, human resources, after sales services, procurement, research and development, technology management, innovativeness, and customer relations) (Meyer & Utterback, 1993; Hafeez et al., 2002; Carmeli & Tishler, 2004). The respondents are asked to evaluate their firms' functional capabilities on a 1 to 7 Likert scale with 1 indicating very low and 7 indicating very high.

Then the relationship between strategic options and the competence building process is revealed through structural equation modeling. Because of computational concerns, only some of the factors defined in the literature are used. Factors were selected based on their utilization frequency. This paper focuses on the competence building achieved by strategic decisions such as equity alliances, market entry, joint ventures, and acquisitions. These decisions create new strategic options for the firm, and some of these options are then exercised. For instance, a joint venture decision can result in an acquisition decision. A firm gains the strategic option to acquire an entire company with the joint venture decision, and if the option is profitable the firm may choose to exercise it. According to the strategic options literature, the objective of managers is to create the optimal strategic options portfolio for the firm (Sanchez, 2004). In order to create an optimal strategic options portfolio, firms need to have strategic options which can be exercised in the future. This idea is in line with studies focused on the sequence of options exercised (Cuypers & Martin, 2007; Reuer & Tong, 2005; Kumar, 2005; Folta & Miller, 2002; Reuer & Leiblein, 2000; Chi & McGuire, 1996; Kogut, 1991; Folta, 1998). All of the strategic decisions made by these 104 firms between 1998 and 2007 are analyzed based on whether any of the strategic options created through these strategic decisions were exercised or not. The average number of decisions which result from exercising an option is considered to be the strategic option performance.

In order to evaluate environmental effects, the most commonly used environmental factors of uncertainty and generosity are used. Our hypothesis that environmental factors affect the competence building process through the exercising of strategic options will be measured by investigating these two environmental characteristics. In order to evaluate the level of uncertainty, the respondents are asked to define the level of uncertainty in the following dimensions of their firms: resources, demand, competitors, technology, and politics at three periods between 1998 and 2007 with a 1 to 7 Likert scale (1 indicating very low, 7 indicating very high). Then the average of these measures was calculated in order to define the average uncertainty level of each dimension. The process for measuring the level of environmental generosity followed a similar approach. Respondents were asked to evaluate the generosity of their firm's environment in the same dimensions (resources, demand, competitors, technology, and politics) at three periods between 1998 and 2007, and the average generosity of each dimension was evaluated.

Studies trying to evaluate the value created though strategic options usually consider a firm's performance. In this study we also consider a firm's performance. A firm's performance is a consequence of its capabilities, but a firm's previous performance may also affect the development of its capabilities. Again a 1 to 7 Likert scale is utilized to measure firm performance. Since decentralized firms may create learning mechanisms through strategic options, the level of decentralization is evaluated with a 1 to 7 Likert scale (1 indicating very low, 7 indicating very high). In addition, degree of formalization and centralization are other firm-related aspects that may affect competence building and are also measured on a 1 to 7 Likert scale (1 indicating very low level of, 7 indicating very high). By evaluating these factors, the validity of the hypothesis that firm-related factors affect the competence building process through the exercising of strategic options will be evaluated.

Analysis

In this study, structural equation modeling is utilized to investigate the relationship between competence building and strategic options. Structural equation modeling is a way of investigating theoretical relationships that combines principles of factor analysis and multiple regression analysis. Hair, Anderson, Tatham, and Black (1999) claim that the software packages utilized to evaluate structural equation models create robust results. The structural equation model in this study is evaluated using the software package LISREL 8.54 (Jöreskog & Sörbom, 1993).

Fig. 2 summarizes the structure equation model of the competence building process. MANA refers to general management capability, PROD refers to production capability, LOGIS refers to logistics capability, IT refers to information technologies capability, FINAN refers to finance capability, HR refers to human resources capability, MARKETIN refers to marketing and sales capability, AFTERSAL refers to after sales capability, PROCURE refers to after procurement capability, RD refers to research and development capability, TECHNOLO refers to technology management capability, INNOVATI refers to after innovativeness capability, and CUSTOMER refers to customer relations management capability. These capabilities form the latent variable capability which is labeled as "Capabil."

Resource, demand, competitor, technology, and political uncertainties are represented in as URESOR, UDEMAND, UCOMPET, UTECHNO, and UPOLITIC, respectively. These uncertainties form the latent variable uncertainty which is labeled as "Unc." Growth of the industry, demand in the industry, and opportunities in the industry are represented respectively as GROWTH, DEMAND, and OPPORT. These uncertainties form the latent variable generosity which is labeled as "Gen."

"Firm" refers to firm-related factors and is a combination of firm performance (PERFORMA), firm formalization level (FORMAL), and firm centralization level (CENTRAL). OPTION is the variable which measures strategic option performance.

The model indicates a good fit. The χ^2 ratio to degrees of freedom is less than 2 which indicates a good fit ($\chi^2 = 140.53$, df $= 269$). The other parameters also indicate good fit. The normed fit index (NFI) is 0.97. NFI is a ratio of the difference in the χ^2 value for the fitted model and the null model divided by the χ^2 value for the null model. A model with perfect fit would produce an NFI of 1 (Hair et al., 1999). In this model the NFI value is 0.97 and thus shows that the model fits well. Goodness of fit index (GFI) is 0.90 representing a good fit. Root mean square error of approximation (RMSEA) is 0.0; it should be smaller than 0.1 to show a good fit. In addition, all the relationships in the model are significant and positive except formalization. Formalization does not have a significant impact on competence building and may be removed from the model, but since the model fit indices are very good, it may also remain in the model. Fig. 2

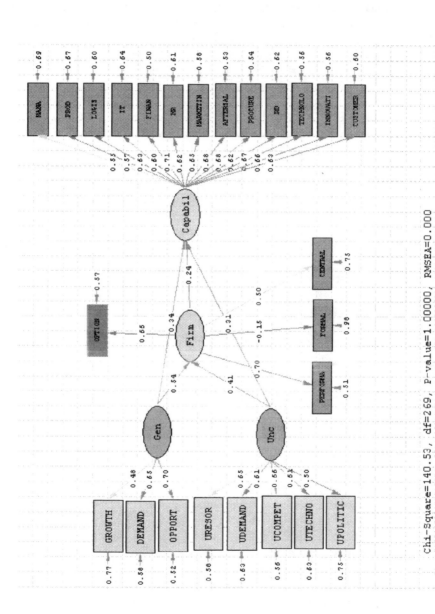

chi-Square=140.53, df=269, P-value=1.00000, RMSEA=0.000

Fig. 2. The Structure Equation Model of the Competence Building Process with Standardized Coefficients.

shows the standardized coefficients; all the coefficients except formalization are positive which shows a positive relationship between variables.

The model indicates that uncertainty and generosity have a direct and indirect positive effect on capability levels; a firm's capability levels will be higher in environments with higher levels of generosity and uncertainty. Therefore environmental factors affect the competence building process through the exercising of strategic options. The performance of the firm and level of decentralization also have a positive effect on capability level. Although the degree of formalization has a negative effect on capability level, this effect is weak. Based on these findings we can say that the firm-related factors affect the competence building process through the exercising of strategic options.

The model shows that strategic option performance increases a firm's capability level. Based on the results we can say that a better managed strategic options portfolio can improve the capabilities of a firm.

CONCLUSION

This study shows that there is a significant relationship between a firm's strategic option exercising decisions and the competence building process. The firms which create more exercisable (more valuable) strategic decisions have higher capabilities. Many researchers have examined this relationship between strategic options and competence building theoretically. This study supports these theoretical efforts with empirical research. In order to have higher capabilities, managers must consider the strategic options portfolio created through strategic decisions. The study also focuses on the factors that affect the competence building process which may be triggered by exercising strategic options. Environmental and firm-specific effects are investigated. Environmental factors are grouped into two categories, uncertainty and generosity. Uncertainty and generosity positively affect the latent environment factor, and the environment factor positively affects the capability level. The positive significant relationship between capability level and uncertainty shows that uncertainty in the environment positively affects the competence building process. In uncertain environments firms try to develop higher capabilities in order to adapt to the changes. Environmental generosity also improves a firm's capability level. If there are opportunities for growth in their environment, firms can improve their capability levels more easily. A firm's performance is directly affected by and also positively affects the capability level. There is a virtuous circle between firms' performance and their capability levels. Managers should include environmental and firm-related factors in their strategic decision-making processes. They should also consider the strategic options that are involved in their strategic decisions.

For further research the number of firms can be increased and the model can be tested in other countries. Also, because of computational concerns only some of the external and internal factors affecting the competence building process were selected for this study. In further research the effect of other factors which are not considered here can be evaluated.

REFERENCES

Allen, L., & Pantzalis, C. (1996). Valuation of the operating flexibility of multinational corporations. *Journal of International Business Studies, 27*(4), 633–653.

Amram, M., & Kulatilaka, N. (1998). *Real options: Managing strategic investment in an uncertain world.* Boston, MA: Harvard Business School Press.

Baum, C. F., & Doyle, J. M. (1988). Dynamic adjustment of firms' capital structures in a varying-risk environment. *Journal of Economic Dynamics and Control, 12*(1), 127–133.

Bernardo, A. E., & Chowdhry, B. (2002). Resources, real options, and corporate strategy. *Journal of Financial Economics, 63*, 211–234.

Campa, J. M. (1990). Exchange rates and economic recovery in the 1930s: An extension to Latin America. *The Journal of Economic History, 50*(3), 677–682.

Campa, J. M. (1993). Entry by foreign firms in the United States under exchange-rate uncertainty. *Review of Economics and Statistics, 75*, 614–622.

Carmeli, A., & Tishler, A. (2004). Resources, capabilities, and the performance of industrial firms: A multivariate analysis. *Managerial and Decision Economics, 25*(6–7), 299–315.

Chi, T. (2000). Option to acquire or divest a joint venture. *Strategic Management Journal, 21*(6), 665–687.

Chi, T., & McGuire, D. J. (1996). Collaborative ventures and value of learning: Integrating the transaction cost and strategic option perspectives on the choice of market entry modes. *Journal of International Business Studies, 27*(2), 285–307.

Cuypers, I. R., & Martin, X. (2007). Joint ventures and real options: An integrated perspective. In: J. Reuer & T. Tong (Eds), *Advances in Strategic Management* (Vol. 24, pp. 103–144). Amsterdam: Elsevier.

Dixit, A. K. (1989). Entry and exit decisions under uncertainty. *Journal of Political Economy, 97*, 620–638.

Dixit, A. K., & Pindyck, R. S. (1994). *Investment under uncertainty.* Princeton, NJ: Princeton University Press.

Englahardt, C. S., & Simmons, P. R. (2002). Organizational flexibility for a changing word. *Leadership and Organizational Development Journal, 23*(3), 113–121.

Folta, T. B. (1998). Governance and uncertainty: The tradeoff between administrative control and commitment. *Strategic Management Journal, 19*(11), 1007–1029.

Folta, T. B., & Ferrier, W. (2000). The effect of national culture on partner buyouts in cross-border biotechnology alliances. *Journal of High Technology Management Research, 11*(2), 175–198.

Folta, T. B., Johnson, D. R., & O'Brien, J. (2006). Uncertainty, irreversibility, and the likelihood of entry: An empirical assessment of the option to defer. *Journal of Economic Behavior & Organization, 61*(3), 432–452.

Folta, T. B., & Miller, K. D. (2002). Real options in equity partnerships. *Strategic Management Journal, 23*(1), 77–88.

Folta, T. B., & O'Brien, J. P. (2004). Entry in the presence of dueling options. *Strategic Management Journal, 25*(2), 121–138.

Folta, T. B., & O'Brien, J. P. (2007). Market versus managerial valuations of real options. In: J. Reuer & T. Tong (Eds), *Advances in strategic management* (Vol. 24, pp. 199–224). Amsterdam: Elsevier.

Folta, T. B., & O'Brien, J. P. (2008). Determinants of firm-specific thresholds in acquisition decisions. *Managerial and Decision Economics, 29*(2/3), 209–225.

Ford, D. N., Lander, D. M., & Voyer, J. J. (2002). A real options approach to valuing strategic flexibility in uncertain construction projects. *Construction Management and Economics, 20*, 343–351.

Fryxell, G. E., Dooley, R. S., & Vryza, M. (2002). After the ink dries: The interaction of trust and control in US-based international joint ventures. *Journal of Management Studies, 39*(6), 865–886.

Gompers, P. A. (1995). Optimal investment, monitoring, and the staging of venture capital. *Journal of Finance, 50*(5), 1461–1489.

Hafeez, K., Zhang, Y., & Malak, N. (2002). Determining key capabilities of a firm using analytic hierarchy process. *International Journal of Production Economics, 76*(1), 39–51.

Hair, J. F., Anderson, R. E., Tatham, R. L., & Black, W. C. (1999). *Multivariate data analysis*. New York: Prentice-Hall.

Hubler, J., & Meschi, P. X. (2000). Takeovers and alliances as competence building decisions: A stock market-based view. *Advances in Applied Business Strategy, 6*(C), 125–146.

Hurry, D., Miller, A. T., & Bowman, E. H. (1992). Calls on highğtechnology: Japanese exploration of venture capital investments in the United States. *Strategic Management Journal, 13*(2), 85–101.

Jöreskog, K. G., & Sörbom, D. (1993). *LISREL 8 user's reference guide*. Chicago, IL: SSI.

Kogut, B. (1991). Joint ventures and the option to expand and acquire. *Management Science, 37*(1), 19–33.

Kogut, B., & Kulatilaka, N. (2001). Capabilities as real options. *Organization Science, 12*(6), 744–758.

Kulatilaka, N., & Perotti, E. C. (1998). Strategic growth options. *Management Science, 44*(8), 1021–1031.

Kumar, M. V. S. (2005). The value from acquiring and divesting a joint venture: A real options approach. *Strategic Management Journal, 26*, 321–331.

Kumar, R., & Nti, K. O. (1998). Differential learning and interaction in alliance dynamics: A process and outcome discrepancy model. *Organizational Science, 9*, 356–367.

Kyläheiko, K., & Sandström, J. (2007). Strategic options based framework for management of dynamic capabilities in manufacturing firms. *Journal of Manufacturing Technology Management, 18*(8), 966–984.

Laamanen, T. (1999). Option nature of company acquisitions motivated by competence acquisition. *Small Business Economics*, *12*(2), 149–169.

Maritan, C., & Alessandri, T. (2007). Capabilities, real options, and the resource allocation process. *Advances in Strategic Management*, *24*, 307–332.

McGrath, R. G. (1997). A real options logic for initiating technology positioning investments. *Academy of Management Review*, *22*(4), 974–996.

McGrath, R. G. (1999). Falling forward: Real options reasoning and entrepreneurial failure. *Academy of Management Review*, *24*, 13–30.

McGrath, R. G., Ferrier, W. J., & Mendelow, A. L. (2004). Real options as engines of choice and heterogeneity. *Academy of Management Review*, *29*(1), 86–101.

McGrath, R. G., & McMillan, I. (2000). *The entrepreneurial mindset: Strategies for continuously creating opportunity in an age of uncertainty*. Boston, MA: Harvard Business School Press.

McGrath, R. G., & Nerkar, A. (2004). Real option reasoning and a new look at the R&D investment strategies of pharmaceutical firms. *Strategic Management Journal*, *25*, 1–21.

Meschi, P. X., & Cremer, E. (1997). Integrating corporate strategy and competence building process: A case study. In: R. Sanchez & A. Heene (Eds), *Competence based strategic management*. Chichester: Wiley.

Meyer, M. H., & Utterback, J. M. (1993). The product family and the dynamics of core capability. *Sloan Management Review*, *34*(3), 29–38.

Miller, K. D. (1993). Industry and country effects on managers' perceptions of environmental uncertainty. *Journal of International Business Studies*, *24*(4), 693–714.

Miller, K. D., & Folta, T. B. (2002). Option value and entry timing. *Strategic Management Journal*, *23*, 655–665.

O'Brien, J. P., Folta, T. B., & Johnson, D. R. (2003). A real options perspective on enterpreneural entry in the face of uncertainty. *Managerial and Decision Economics*, *24*, 515–533.

Oxley, J. E. (1999). Institutional environment and the mechanisms of governance: The impact of intellectual property protection on the structure of inter-firm alliances. *Journal of Economic Behavior & Organization*, *38*(3), 283–309.

Pandza, K., Horsburgh, S., Gorton, K., & Polajnar, A. (2003). A real options approach to managing resources and capabilities. *International Journal of Operations & Production Management*, *23*(9), 1010–1032.

Reuer, J. J., & Leiblein, M. J. (2000). Downside risk implications of multinationality and international joint ventures. *Academy of Management Journal*, *43*, 203–214.

Reuer, J. J., & Tong, W. T. (2005). Real options in international joint ventures. *Journal of Management*, *31*(3), 403–423.

Sanchez, R. (1993). Strategic flexibility, firm organization, and managerial work in dynamic markets: A strategic options perspective. *Advances in Strategic Management*, *9*, 251–291.

Sanchez, R. (1997). Preparing for uncertain future. *International Studies of Management & Organization*, *27*(2), 71–94.

Sanchez, R. (2003). Integrating transaction costs theory and real options theory. *Managerial and Decision Economics*, *24*, 267–282.

Sanchez, R. (2004). Understanding competence-based management: Identifying and managing five modes of competence. *Journal of Business Research*, *57*, 518–532.

Sanchez, R., & Heene, A. (1997). Reinventing strategic management: New theory and practice for competence-based competition. *European Management Journal*, *15*(3), 303–317.

Sanchez, R., Heene, A., & Thomas, H. (Eds). (1996). *Dynamics of competence based competition: Theory and practice in the new strategic management.* Oxford: Elsevier Pergamon Press.

Shleifer, A., & Vishny, R. W. (1992). Liquidation values and debt capacity: A market equilibrium approach. *Journal of Finance, 47*(4), 1343–1366.

Sumantra, G., & Nitin, N. (1993). Horses for courses: Organizational forms for multinational corporations. *Sloan Management Review, 34*(2), 23–35.

Titman, S., & Wessels, R. (1988). The determinants of capital structure choice. *Journal of Finance, 43*(1), 1–19.

Tong, W. T., & Reuer, J. J. (2006). Firm and industry influences on the value of growth options. *Strategic Organization, 4*(1), 71–95.

Trevino, L. J., & Grosse, R. (2002). An analysis of firm-specific resources and foreign direct investment in the United States. *International Business Review, 11*, 431–452.

Trigeorgis, L. (1993). Real options and interactions with financial flexibility. *Financial Management, 22*, 202–204.

Trigeorgis, L. (1996). *Managerial flexibility and strategy in resource allocation.* London: The MIT Press.

Vassolo, R. S., Anand, J., & ve Folta, T. B. (2004). Non-additivity in portfolios of exploration activities: A real options-based analysis of equity alliances in biotechnology. *Strategic Management Journal, 25*, 1045–1061.

Werner, S., Brouthers, L. E., & Brouthers, K. D. (1996). International risk and perceived environmental uncertainty: The dimensionality and internal consistency of Miller's measure. *Journal of International Business Studies, 27*(3), 571–587.

THE COEVOLUTION OF ALLIANCES AND INDUSTRIES: HOW INDUSTRY TRANSFORMATION INFLUENCES ALLIANCE FORMATION AND VICE VERSA

Christian Goeke, Martin Gersch and Jörg Freiling

ABSTRACT

The paper investigates the role of alliances in periods of industry transformation. It addresses the research question why firms ally in dynamic environments. This takes place with an interactive qualitative research design and fieldwork in the changing German health care sector between 2004 and 2007, primarily using qualitative longitudinal data from a focus group panel. From the theoretical side, the resource- and competence-based views have proven useful for alliance research. For our theory-driven investigation we applied the perspective of the competence-based theory of the firm and extended this view by insights from the Austrian School in order to cover developments on multiple levels of analysis in an integrated way.

A Focused Issue on Identifying, Building, and Linking Competences
Research in Competence-Based Management, Volume 5, 79–109
ISSN: 1744-2117/doi:10.1108/S1744-2117(2010)0000005007

On an aggregated level we elaborate a taxonomy of three categories reflecting motivations and alliance types against the background of industry transformation:

(1) *closing resource and competence gaps in so-called "gap-closing alliances,"*
(2) *preparing for unexpected developments in so-called "option networks," and*
(3) *intending to proactively exert influence on the relevant business environment in so-called "steering alliances" as an alternative way to enhance fit.*

For each alliance type, propositions are derived and validated. Summarizing the findings from a meta point of view, a twofold role of collaborative arrangements turned out: On the one hand agents are pushed into cooperation with others in order to manage change and uncertainty in transforming business environments. But on the other hand joint forces themselves act as an accelerator of industry transformation and thereby as a jolt to other economic agents.

INTRODUCTION

Dynamic competition and the need for continuous strategic renewal have attracted growing attention among strategic management scholars. It is argued that these phenomena appear increasingly frequent and intense in more and more industry sectors (e.g., D'Aveni, 1994, p. 4; Eisenhardt & Martin, 2000; Porter & Rivkin, 2000; Wiggins & Ruefli, 2005, p. 895). Continuously, but at varying degrees, a crossfire of environmental jolts changes entire industry settings and surprises organizations forcing them to adjust their business models, market offerings, and/or strategies (Meyer, 1982, p. 515). The sources of such uncertainty-causing jolts are numerous: technological innovations, governmental action, changing customer needs, international competition, and/or new competitors, just to mention a few (Porter & Rivkin, 2000; Prahalad, 1995). In extreme cases such changes even transform entire industries (Gersch & Goeke, 2006).

Evidence exists that firms consider collaboration with others as one appropriate means to master the uncertainties and unforeseen events they are facing in turbulent and continuously changing environments despite the numerous threats of opportunistic behavior which might occur (Carson,

Madhok, & Wu, 2006; Dyer, 1997; Gomes-Casseres, 2006; Gulati, Nohria, & Zaheer, 2000b; Nielsen & Rikama, 2004; Silverman & Baum, 2002). At the same time setting up cooperative arrangements itself can mean another change of the relevant business environment to all nonparticipating agents.

The argument is brought forward that continuous change processes on both firm and market/industry level can only be scrutinized with evolutionary research programs (Jacobson, 1992; Nelson & Winter, 1982, p. 164; Rothaermel & Hill, 2005). Against this background we consider it a promising starting point to interpret firms' decisions to cooperate with others as an event in organization–environment coevolution (Baum & Singh, 1994). With regard to collaborative arrangements, many advances have been made to understand the coevolution of the participating organizations (Koza & Lewin, 1998, 1999; Volberda & Lewin, 2003). However, in the field of organization–environment coevolution the role and motivations of interfirm cooperation have not been explored in depth from a theoretical point of view, yet. Questions like "How and why do firms set up alliances to master the adverseness of environmental dynamics?" or "Is there a difference between alliances' and single organizations' actions to influence industry evolution?" seem to remain unanswered, yet. At least, they are either treated only marginally (e.g., from a learning perspective, cf. Lewin, Long, & Carroll, 1999) or for very particular forms of environmental dynamics (e.g., for technological discontinuities, cf. Rothaermel & Hill, 2005).

Our respective understanding of "cooperation" is wide. It covers all those coordinated activities of organizations that intentionally define explicit joint aims and activities in order to better achieve their individual and organizational (sometimes hidden) aims (cf. also Huxham & Vangen, 2004, pp. 192–193). The answer to the research question is therefore directed to an understanding of cooperation as being primarily between organizations (not intra-organizational) and comprising the full range of positively and negatively oriented interorganizational relationships (Huxham & Vangen, 2005, p. 4).

We address the research question why firms ally in dynamic environments embedded into Maxwell's (2005) interactive model of research design. Interested in the role and nature of cooperative arrangements concerning continuous change processes on both firm and market/industry level, we apply a resource- and competence-based view of the firm to analyze organizational-level issues in combination with insights from the Austrian School for the market/industry level, a respective analysis of organization–environment coevolution (Freiling, Gersch, & Goeke, 2008). The study will strongly focus on coevolutionary aspects, i.e., how alliance formation affects industry transformation and vice versa (and thereby mainly cut off unidirectional effects). The theoretical choice and the respective choice of a research design limits availability of methods for empirical work. For our fieldwork conducted in the highly dynamic German healthcare sector, we therefore made use of a set of qualitative methods being detailed further below.

LITERATURE REVIEW

It is argued that orthodox strategy and industrial organization-based analysis of change fail to tackle observable and continuous change processes in the relevant business environment as well as accompanying firm challenges adequately (Lockett & Thompson, 2001). With their seminal "Evolutionary Theory of Economic Change" Nelson and Winter (1982) fostered an evolutionary perspective on strategic management. For reasons further explained below, we will refer to the Austrian School's market process theory as one possible way of applying an evolutionary thinking (Witt, 1992).

In a nutshell, the Austrian School considers entrepreneurship and agents' alertness as driving forces for economic development and changes, founding their school of thoughts on the core basic assumptions of (1) methodological individualism, (2) subjectivism, (3) relevance of time, (4) radical uncertainty, (5) "homo agens/acting man" as the model of man, and a (6) non-consummatory approach combined with moderate voluntarism (Freiling et al., 2008; Vaughn, 1994). The agents' knowledge is incomplete and asymmetrically distributed. Economic agents gain new knowledge through every market process (e.g., transactions). In this sense, even "small events" in the market process might be meaningful. On the basis of new knowledge accessed they build new expectations and revise their plans as well as market offerings, always seeking to enhance competitiveness, creatively destroying old ideas or concepts (Schumpeter, 1934) and using competition as a discovery process (Hayek, 1978).

In their inquiries into firm cooperation after technological discontinuities – as one form of environmental dynamics – Rothaermel and Hill (2005) emphasize the relevance of an interrelated firm and market/industry level scrutiny as well. In this context they also stress the explanatory power of the Austrian School for the market/industry level, but not without pointing out the significance of firm heterogeneity for the analysis. For a long time scholars analyzing the Austrian School have argued that there is a "missing chapter" concerning this issue, namely the configuration adjustment of firms in order to set up competitive offerings to the market (Fagerberg, 2003; Witt, 1999). The idea that resource- and competence-based view have the potential to close this gap has already been introduced by a couple of scholars (e.g., Lockett & Thompson, 2001). Amongst others, this idea has recently been anchored very fundamentally by Foss and Ishikawa (2007) and Freiling et al. (2008). Applying the Lakatos (1978) methodology of scientific research programs, the latter showed that the mainstream of the Austrian School is compatible in terms of philosophy of science, even in its hard-core basic assumptions, with a reconceptualized resource- and competence-based approach being able to provide a "competence-based theory of the firm" (Freiling et al., 2008). Economic activity is then embedded into idiosyncratic development paths as a sequence of irreversible decisions and events on both the firm and market level. This can even allow for path dependencies when developments show momentum and self-enforcing effects due to positive feedbacks and/or increasing returns (Arthur, 2000).

All in all, Austrian School and a competence-based view of the firm seem to have the potential for a consistent theoretical framework to conduct integrated analyses of the coevolution of change processes on the organizational level (competence theory) and market/industry level (Austrian School) and thereby also in order to analyze cooperation decisions in dynamic environments (Freiling et al., 2008).

The resource- and competence-based view have become increasingly popular (Sanchez, Heene, & Thomas, 1996; Teece, Pisano, & Shuen, 1997; Barney & Clark, 2007) when examining the nature and causes of firm competitiveness. They are a somewhat "state-of-the-art" concept in strategic management literature. Firms are understood as distinct bundles of resources and competences that have evolved over time and are embedded in their relevant business environment. Within firms homogeneous assets, which can typically be procured in markets, are subject to a firm-specific upgrading process. This process is primarily made up of (re)bundling and learning. Permanently required and arranged upgrades finally contribute to the actual and future firm competitiveness. Furthermore, competences have the character of a repeatable ability of rendering competitive output with these resources, based on knowledge, usually nonrandomly managed by rules, and channeled by routines (Becker, 2004). They enable goal-oriented processes to arrange future readiness for action and potentials to render concrete input to the market. Competences cater for a conservation of competitiveness and if so they might even represent a substantial precondition to achieve competitive advantages. Such upgrading processes necessarily follow idiosyncratic, firm-specific paths. Thereby they account for firms' heterogeneity in order to explain performance differences not bound to existing market structures.

While recently endeavors have also been made to investigate deeper into the processes underlying the building and leveraging of competences (e.g., Freiling et al., 2008; Sanchez & Heene, 2004), it has formerly often been assumed that firms "somehow" develop them internally (Gulati, Nohria, & Zaheer, 2000a, p. 207) and more or less autonomously. Recent research sheds light on the so-called "firm-addressable" resources and competences (Sanchez et al., 1996). They are external to a firm and can be levered to other firms by various forms of collaborative arrangements (Eisenhardt & Schoonhoven, 1996; Gulati, 1999).

The emphasis drawn in literature on collaboration and cooperation against the background of resource- and competence-based approaches primarily aims at mechanisms of protection or building up new own resources and competences (Prévot, 2006). In this regard, opportunistic behavior in terms of "races-to-learn" or "outlearning" of alliance partners is also addressed (Hamel, 1991; Doz & Hamel, 1998). However, the so-called "relational view" (Duschek, 2004; Dyer & Singh, 1998) follows a different path as to applying a network perspective to resources and competences with a trend of deconstructing the formerly integrated value chains (Bresser, Heuskel, & Nixon, 2000). Thus, the relational view assumes a shift of competition from the firm level to alliances as (at least *de facto*) owners of competences (see also Gomes-Casseres, 1994).

Extant resource- and competence-based work on interfirm cooperation and firms' cooperation decisions accordingly seems to lack an explicit consideration of what Gulati (1998) identifies as a shortfall of research on cooperation in general. He criticizes that a one-sided focus on cooperations/networks/alliances as unit of analysis does not take into account the actions of other firms or the relationships in which they themselves are already embedded, and rather ignores interactive elements of the market through which participants discover market information via their interactions in the market (Gulati, 1998). He argues that it is not only the interaction with the market that most research contributions on collaborative business lack, but also the broader institutional context in which they are placed and embedded (Gulati, 1998, p. 302). This is why we take a strictly coevolutionary point of view as described above when addressing our research question as to why firms ally in dynamic environments. In doing so, the competence-based theory of the firm enables the analysis of developments on the firm level and the Austrian School for the level of aggregates as markets or industries.

RESEARCH DESIGN AND METHODS

Generally, market process theory applied in this paper is associated with particular challenges to empirical research and methodological opportunities. Facing the subjectivist nature and the positioning of market process theory as a part of the interpretative paradigm (Burrell & Morgan, 1979; Freiling et al., 2008), the traditional anchor point of critical rationalism – as formulated by Popper (1945) – is not adequate. There is a limited opportunity to generalize findings when idiosyncrasies apply. Given the above-mentioned basic assumptions of methodological individualism, subjectivism, radical uncertainty, "homo agens," relevance of time, and moderate voluntarism, the appropriateness of formalized quantitative empirical work is doubtful. For this reason we found it appropriate to borrow qualitative methods from social sciences although they do not seem to be too much accepted in the economic scientific community, yet. However, they finally made us able to follow Hayek's (1964) remedy from his seminal "Theory of complex phenomena" and seek to identify patterns within evolutionary development processes. The patterns and propositions to be derived then fill the protective belt around the above-mentioned hard-core elements of this school of thought (Lakatos, 1978).

Doing so, the set of qualitative methods of empirical research we apply is basically embedded into Maxwell's (2005) interactive approach to qualitative research designs. Fig. 1 gives a survey on cornerstones of our research visualized in Maxwell's framework.

As already mentioned in the introduction, the research question of why firms ally in dynamic environments was derived from evidence gained when we sought a general understanding of organization–environment coevolution processes. For a theoretically consistent analysis of this research question, we had market process theory and especially its basic assumptions and mechanisms as outlined above as the conceptual framework in mind when conducting the interactive and iterative fieldwork for this paper. To ensure comprehensive analytical understanding of the units of analysis we followed the recommendation to focus on one industry sector in this study (Charmaz, 2006), namely the German pharmaceutical industry between 2004 and 2007.

Because of the early stage of research we adopted a series of exploratory case studies (Eisenhardt, 1989; Leonard-Barton, 1990; Yin, 2008) and performed data collection and analysis as an interrelated process.

We chose the German health care sector as the context for our fieldwork as it shows defining features of a transforming industry sector, especially in

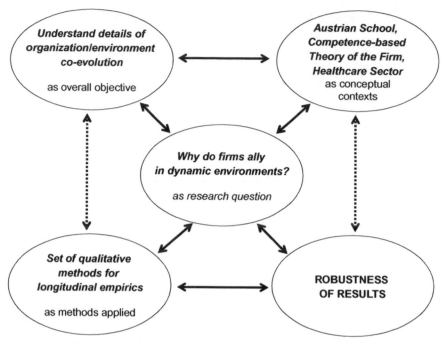

Fig. 1. Research Design (Adapted from Maxwell, 2005).

the pharmacies' market stage, particularly beginning with a comprehensive health care system reform in 2004. Amongst other triggers, this – for the German market radical – reform legalized mail-order drug retail (thereby shifting the scope of competition from a local to the national level through a new distribution channel), the establishment of chains of pharmacies (thereby enabling the formation of larger entities), an abolishment of price-control for nonprescription drugs (thereby causing price competition) and a shift from price-based to a fixed commission for prescription drugs, just to mention some details that were accompanied by observable changes to business models, too. All these changes became effective on January 1, 2004, facilitating the observation of interrelated change processes on industry and firm level, literally speaking, in an incubator.

Our case studies were backed up by using multiple sources of data, comprising focus group workshops, expert interviews, Delphi analysis, questionnaires, written primary and secondary documents (memos, newspaper articles, analyst reports, internal documents), and direct observations. In order to "catch reality in flight" (Pettigrew, Woodman, & Cameron,

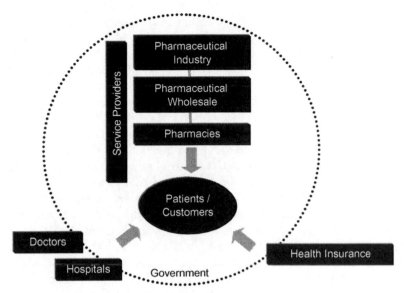

Fig. 2. The German pharmaceutical industry value chain.

2001, p. 698) when addressing the underlying and other research questions on industry transformation and organization–environment coevolution, we set up a panel of 14 upper management executives from all relevant value chain stages in the German health care sector as visualized in Fig. 2 for longitudinal analyses.

In roughly quarterly focus group workshops with the panelists, recent developments in the German health care sector are analyzed, topics of former meetings revisited, and our research results and ideas commented on from the practitioners' side. One ambition of the longitudinal character of the analyses with the executive panel is to identify and analyze mechanisms causing observable change processes and development paths. This long-term relationship with the executive panelists turned out to be valuable insofar as trust could be generated in order to share confidential information, as well, which we consider as an essential input to our qualitative research.

To explore features, entrepreneurial challenges and conceived solutions to master organization–environment coevolution in transforming industries, we conducted a three-round Delphi analysis (Dalkey, 1969; Linstone & Turoff, 1975) on these issues, with special regard to the German health care sector within the executive panel from March to June 2005. In many respects – but still quite unstructured – a special relevance of diverse forms of interfirm collaboration was revealed. After the Delphi analysis we held a concluding interactive focus group workshop (Cowley, 2000; Morgan, 1997) with the panelists in June 2005 reflecting the results of the three questionnaire rounds. Subsequent categorizing of the focus group discussions on interfirm cooperation allowed us to formulate three – not necessarily mutually exclusive – common bases for collaborative advantage purely against the background of environmental dynamics (cf. the "Results" section).

To achieve further validation of these categories (Charmaz, 2006) we applied an embedded single case design (Yin, 2008) for the three categories as a means of what would be called theoretical sampling in grounded theory (Glaser & Strauss, 1967). Based on group discussions in the executive panel and following the logic of formulating "pattern predictions" in the Hayekian sense, we chose cases for in-depth analyses of each category in order to derive our findings and formulate propositions. Again, starting with a questionnaire for the panel in December 2005, a focus group workshop in June 2006 exclusively considering the three categories of cooperation was held and numerous personal and telephone interviews were conducted and available secondary data used for triangulation. As the main intent of theoretical sampling is not to look for a kind of population representativeness, but rather for theory construction (Charmaz, 2006, p. 6), we consider the single case design as viable for this stage of research. To meet the concerns of the evolutionary theory background we gathered data from numerous points in time in order to achieve a longitudinal design of the case studies (Abbott, 2001; Beverland & Lockshin, 2003; Burgelman, 1994, 1996; Leonard-Barton, 1990) to identify and analyze mechanisms that cause change processes and development paths. Consistent to our conceptual framework we model and interpret experiences on the market/ industry level with market process theory and on the firm level with the aforementioned competence-based theory of the firm.

For improving the quality of the research, a number of procedures were adopted throughout the study. To justify the trustworthiness of the results we reviewed numerous sets of criteria (e.g., Flint, Woodruff, & Gardial, 2002; Miles & Huberman, 1994; Yin, 2008). Like other authors in the field of management science (e.g., Beverland & Lockshin, 2003, p. 656), we adopted the result of Flint et al.'s (2002, pp. 104–106) review on relevant criteria for evaluating the trustworthiness of our work (Table 1). We took credibility, transferability, dependability, confirmability, and integrity from interpretive research (Hirschman, 1986; Lincoln & Guba, 1985) as well as the criteria of fit, understanding, generality, and control from grounded theory (e.g., Strauss & Corbin, 1998).

Table 1. Check of Trustworthiness Applying the Criteria of Flint et al. (2002).

Trustworthiness Criteria	Method of Addressing in This Study
Credibility: Extent to which the results appear to be acceptable representations of the data	Conducted interviews and market observation continually for 4 years, with the panel experts for 1.5 years Third persons involved in categorizing Findings and milestones presented for discussion and adjustment of the executive panel (which provided the majority of data) Protocols with interpretations regularly returned to participants Extraction of results through a research team of three with mutual justification of the results Result: Emergent findings and propositions were altered and expanded
Transferability: Extent to which findings from one study in one context will apply to other contexts	Theoretical sampling Weakness, that results were generated exclusively with data from the health care sector was tackled through the abstract development of findings consistent to market process theory basic assumptions. Additional discussions with representatives from the steel, music, and education sector, who basically confirmed the findings for their industry as well Result: Findings were represented by multiple data sources and all panelists
Dependability: Extent to which the findings are unique to time and place; the stability or consistency of explanations	Design as longitudinal analysis (including interviewees focus groups members) Panelists and interviewees reflected on current and recent events and experiences Results not anchored in "fixed real world events" Result: Found consistency in the phenomena for multiple points in time; consistency in the participants' stories
Confirmability: Extent to which interpretations are the result of the participants and the phenomenon as opposed to researcher bias	Milestones of research also presented and discussed with other researchers on conferences and interdisciplinary research workshops at our university Comprehensive industry image through participants from every value chain stage in the German health care sector Result: Findings and propositions were altered and expanded

Table 1. (*Continued*)

Trustworthiness Criteria	Method of Addressing in This Study
Integrity: Extent to which interpretations are influenced by misinformation or evasions by participants	Trust built with longitudinal participants (interviewees, panelists) Nonthreatening nature of interactive elements, motivation to achieve "win-win" situations with the participants Always numerous sources of data Triangulation with comprehensive secondary data When nonconfidential, protocols were returned to all panelists with the request to comment irregularities Eyes open for participants trying to evade the issues being discussed Result: Participants were very open about issues being discussed; no evidence for missing integrity
Fit: Extent to which findings fit with the substantive area under investigation	Through interactive approach always having in mind research goal and research question Through interpretative approach always having in mind the conceptual/theoretical framework Result: Findings were more deeply described, also backed with extant literature on the topics
Understanding: Extent to which participants buy into results as possible representations of their world	Written survey on importance and relevance with the panelists after concluding focus group workshop confirmed relevance of the three motives to ally Ongoing presentation of findings and interpretations with colleagues, participants, and in industry forums Result: Colleagues and practitioners bought into the findings
Generality: Extent to which findings discover multiple aspects of the phenomenon	All interactively generated data (interviews, focus group workshops, questionnaires) gave explicit opportunities for new facets of phenomena Repeated (longitudinal) interviews with numerous key informants Result: Captures multiple aspects of the phenomenon
Control: Extent to which organizations can influence aspects of the theory	Panelists and interviewees would have some degree of control over their organizations' cooperation decisions (strategic intention), not however on detailed outcome Result: Involvement of the participants in the issue exists

RESULTS

Taxonomy of Three Evolutionary Reasons to Team Up

Within the number of particular motivations for single agents to ally with others, on a higher level of abstraction three categories of basically nondyadic motivations for cooperation were figured out in the fieldwork (cf. also Goeke, 2008). Fig. 3 briefly summarizes the basic idea of the categories before each shall be characterized in detail and by first propositions against the aforementioned theory background.

To make them more handy for the subsequent detailed analysis, we transformed the three motivations into resulting alliance types: gap-closing alliances, option networks, and steering alliances. However, this should not imply that aspects of all three motivations cannot show up in combination in a concrete case.

The subsequent paragraphs shall outline the validated findings of our qualitative empirical research. According to the interactive approach we follow (Maxwell, 2005), the findings to be outlined are integrated into and reflected against the context-relevant theory and former work.

Gap-Closing Alliances
Within the research on timing and diffusion of technological innovations the concept of so-called "strategic windows" or "windows of opportunity"

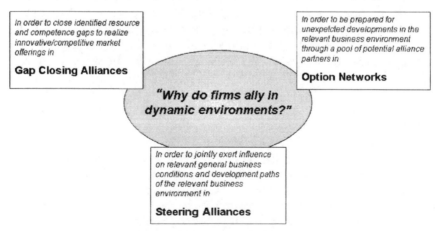

In order to close identified resource and competence gaps to realize innovative/competitive market offerings in

Gap Closing Alliances

In order to be prepared for unexpected developments in the relevant business environment through a pool of potential alliance partners in

Option Networks

"Why do firms ally in dynamic environments?"

In order to jointly exert influence on relevant general business conditions and development paths of the relevant business environment in

Steering Alliances

Fig. 3. Taxonomy of three bases for collaborative advantage in dynamic environments.

(Abell, 1989; Tyre & Orlikowski, 1994) is very popular and describes special phases after discontinuities as playing fields to explore and modify new alternatives. They are either characterized by significant exogenous changes which jeopardize existing firm competitiveness and enforce a reaction (Abell, 1989). Or they are characterized as promising to launch new market offerings based on one's own inventions. Strategic windows or windows of opportunity are made up of interpretations and channeled by the strategic logic (Sanchez et al., 1996) in use. Given the assumptions of radical uncertainty, subjectivism, and firm heterogeneity inherent to the resource- and competence-based view, each firm has its individual perception of what are or could be windows of opportunity and worth making efforts to prepare adequate reactions.

Leveraging this idea to a more general perspective there are windows of opportunity continuously opening up for alert and entrepreneurial firms to create new market offerings or business model innovations. External drivers – as causes for new ideas or effects of change decisions of other agents – can be of technological or regulative nature, action of big agents, effects of globalization, or on a more general level: new relevant knowledge. Accessing new knowledge in a market-process-based (Austrian School) rationale again and again prompts economic agents to rethink their own "entrepreneurial theory" of what current market requirements are (Harper, 1995, p. 136).

This contains a vision of so-called "strategic architectures" (Hamel & Prahalad, 1994). Based on these architectures the required inputs, resources, and competences for competitive output in order to react adequately on a window of opportunity can be identified. Hence, a kind of "window of readiness for action" can be regarded as a necessary counterpart of the "windows of opportunity." A window of readiness for action indicates that a firm is ready and willing to take the chances market processes offer, e.g., by configuring new market offerings.

Typically, preparing new "windows of readiness for action" involves changes of the firm's required resources and competences necessary to render competitive output. At least by implicitly conducting a competence-gap analysis (Klein & Hiscocks, 1994), the firm figures out which resources and competences will be necessary to achieve a fit to the desired market offerings and anticipated market requirements (e.g., Zajac, Kraatz, & Bresser, 2000). Timing strategies for this process have to achieve a fit as soon as/as long as the window of opportunities is open. To manage transactions in the market and thus to be competitive is the firm's target when synchronizing the processes of accumulating required resources and

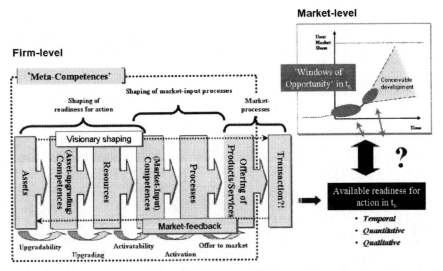

Fig. 4. Synchronization of feasible market-offerings with external windows of opportunity.

competences with the windows of opportunity (Andersson & Mattsson, 2006). Given inevitable market feedback loops of adjustment and conceivable first-mover advantages (Lieberman & Montgomery, 1988, 1998), the period for synchronization of windows of opportunity and windows of readiness for action (Fig. 4) can be extremely short and therefore make resource-/competence-building impossible.

Especially in rapidly changing environments, necessary timing strategies make it impossible for a firm to build up required resources and competences by itself. Agents are often not able to build the required resources and competences autonomously in a way that is fast enough or fits the desired quality. A purchase of generic assets with a subsequent development into resources or competences is therefore considered unrealistic as it is time-consuming, cost-intensive, and still has an uncertain outcome.

Followed by an analysis of existing resource and competence gaps, firms find an appropriate way to attain their desired and necessary readiness for action also through cooperation with other agents who possess the required resources and competences and who are able to lever them into different contexts.

Proposition 1. When strategic windows open in relevant markets/ industries, firms make use of alliances for gap closing in order to overcome critical resource and competence shortcomings and to set up new/changed business models.

Additionally, there is radical uncertainty whether the future will evolve as imagined at all, and the resource and competence accumulation process is successful. With regard to the external uncertainty (will the market adopt the innovation?) and the threat of idiosyncratic migration paths, a gap-closing alliance is an appropriate means to test the conceived strategic architecture without losing the flexibility to reconfigure the business system adequately if required. This reconfiguration can on the one hand be incremental in terms of reaction to the market's feedback loops through every performed (or missed) transaction (concerning requirements on the product level, timing, or quantity). On the other hand a complete strategic change (and annulment of the whole gap-closing alliance) is feasible, too. Especially in early phases of new strategic architectures there is usually a continuous adaptation process as to the required profile of resources and competences. Here we can refer to Leonard-Barton's (1992) findings that given a considerable external pressure for change, existing internal resources and competences can contribute to organizational inertia. Especially those resources and competences with a high specificity regarding usage or organizational embeddedness have the potential to become "core rigidities" (Gersch & Goeke, 2006; Ghemawat, 1991). Then the motto of gap-closing alliances is: "Firms form partners for the dance – but when the music stops, they can change them" (Richardson, 1972, p. 896).

Proposition 2. The higher the (initial) specificity in use of new resources and competences required to introduce product and/or business model innovations, the more likely the firms choose gap-closing alliances in order to attain them instead of building these by themselves.

Returning to a broader evolutionary context, new alternatives on how to serve market requirements typically have an impact on the relevant business environment for other agents too. New knowledge as the basis for their individual plans will be created and will force them to (re)act, sometimes initiating an endless sequence of processes of creative destruction of formerly competitive market offerings. Observations being made in single points of time should always be made against the background that they are milestones on idiosyncratic development paths. These development paths are featured by a sequence of irreversible decisions and events on the market and firm level (Ariño & de la Torre, 1998).

To other market participants the implementation of such a business model innovation itself serves as a trigger of industry transformation. In this manner agents embedded in a gap-closing alliance are driven by one trigger of industry transformation (in the case of German pharmacies a change in legal environment), and through their own action – as coevolutionary process – they themselves trigger the transformation process through enhancing the degree of competition within an industry (Gulati et al., 2000a, p. 206).

The potential for proactive entrepreneurs to bring discontinuities into markets or industries can be enhanced by this. Through coupling internal and external potentials, a network is generated which contributes to "asset mass efficiencies" (Dierickx & Cool, 1989) on the one hand and creates potentials for synergies despite an enhanced systemic complexity.

Proposition 3. When gap-closing alliances accelerate launches of radical product/business model innovations for firms, they serve as an environmental jolt to other organizations in affected industries/markets and thereby themselves accelerate and direct environmental change processes.

Option Networks
While gap-closing alliances are useful to take profit from windows of opportunity when an agent is not able or not willing to set up an adequate readiness for action by herself/himself, option networks serve as an earlier 'line of defense' against unforeseeable and maybe threatening developments. The argument here is similar to the one of the early joint venture literature, where it is argued that a JV serves as an option for acquisition, while the option is often executed in reaction to product market triggers (Kogut, 1991).

Given anticipated probability and velocity of change in the relevant business environment, the funnel of conceivable future market requirements is very wide. This is because there is uncertainty concerning the paths and directions of adaptations as to readiness for action in the future. As future strategic windows or windows of opportunity do not yet exist (O'Neill, 2000; Shackle, 1972), alert agents cannot possess the required knowledge for serious predictions. Therefore, they try to anticipate conceivable triggers-to-come or trajectories within an industry (Dosi, 1982). As soon as their estimate of probability for certain trajectories exceeds a critical level, they will prepare themselves for an adequate reaction. Ideally they seek to create options to (re)act to any presumed change regarding market requirements and environmental conditions.

One facet of doing so is to implement a network of contacts to potential partners, without necessarily working together operationally today. It is thereby a form of "unstructured cooperation" (Spedale, 2003), regularly not linked through institutional arrangements, but at least a pre-stage to it, in order to set one up if necessary. As a kind of "today-for-tomorrow" strategy (Abell, 1999, p. 76) for early phases of competition (Hamel & Prahalad, 1994), option networks do not only build a basis for a later distribution of value chain activities of a not yet exactly defined business model to several agents (Bresser et al., 2000), they also give especially hub firms the possibility to access the resources and competences of their contacts (Portes, 1998, p. 3; Zaheer & Bell, 2005, p. 810). To ensure access to a large pool of resources and competences when necessary is one of the activities to enlarge future trajectories for conceived action. It is goal oriented, concerning alertly anticipated clusters of required resources and competences.

Option networks are estimated to be especially crucial either to secure access to those external resources or competences that are rare or for the case of highly specific internal ones. However, resource and competence specificity is always related to one point in time. By a goal-oriented development and up-valuing of one or more conceivable second-best alternatives, option networks can contribute to a despecification. They can thereby serve as an "emergency exit" when the first-best use is omitted for any reason.

While it is argued in action research literature to avoid collaboration if there is a choice, this piece of advice does not seem to hold true for option networks due to its nonobvious form of collaborative advantage (Huxham & Vangen, 2004, p. 200, 2005, p. 37). Not preparing for future alliances through option networks does not hurt organizations and actual output today, but it might do so in the form of inflexibilities when reactions are required tomorrow.

The implementation of the basic idea of option networks takes place in numerous variants: There are very loose forms to coordinate a conceivable further cooperation, e.g., in standard-setting committees or roundtables for informal discussions on future developments, but also tighter ones with ready-prepared detailed plans about business models, modularity and interfaces, business processes, etc.

Proposition 4. According to the perceived degree of environmental dynamics with a substantial ambiguity as to conceivable future conditions and expected resource and competence gaps, agents span (and continuously revise) networks of potential cooperation partners for anticipated clusters of future conditions.

Proposition 5. Agents seeking to reduce or avoid the risk of inflexibilities manage their individual option network to attain alternatives for originally intended first- or second-best uses of (initially) highly specific resources and competences.

The basic idea also holds true for the case when a current cooperation partner breaks away (e.g., through bankruptcy). Besides reactivity issues, option networks and lose ties as described above can also contribute to a reduction of uncertainty to the participating agents (Gulati, 1998, p. 295; Meyer, Brooks, & Goes, 1990, p. 107; Ahuja, 2000). There is not only access to resources and competences when needed, but expectations and paths of future internal development can also be aligned if necessary. This takes place either with direct partners or – taking advantage from the so-called "small world effect" (Milgram, 1967) – even with competitors. If there is an appropriate "relational quality" (Ariño, de la Torre, & Smith Ring, 2005) in an option network, essential preparations for, e.g., a gap-closing alliance are conducted and therefore for an alert codevelopment of new strategic architectures (Hamel & Prahalad, 1994; Huygens, Baden-Fuller, van den Bosch, & Volberda, 2001; Volberda & Lewin, 2003). This includes "dry practices" through cooperation in noncore activities like R&D on peripheral issues or allying in form of first/preliminary concrete institutional arrangement, which give the opportunities of joint development/experiencing/modification of routines and business processes.

Proposition 6. The more restricted the choice of partners for conceivable future necessities to collaborate, the more the agents are forced to undertake endeavors to ensure access to these potential partners in advance.

Proposition 7. Interacting with option networks makes individual agents feel to better double-check their "theory" on future development paths and mechanisms and thereby also serves as another source of relevant information.

One feature of gap-closing alliances was the ability to set up a required constellation of resources and competences responding to a window of opportunity that opens for business model innovations or new forms of output. Timing was identified as one critical factor for success. But even as the procedure of initiating a gap-closing alliance passes through a couple of phases (decision to ally, find potential alliance partners, negotiate with potential partners, adjust the collaboration to overcome isolating mechanisms, or simply configure process interfaces), such an alliance cannot be set up from one day to another. All in all, option networks also apply to shorten initiation-related learning issues (Hibbert & Huxham, 2005) when collaboration becomes operative. Though windows of opportunity are considered firm specific, those agents or groups who are able to undergo the above-mentioned phases first might have the greatest potential to act as challengers to all other incumbents' competitive positions and thereby are actively able to create migration paths of elements and relations in the market and thus drive the industry transformation.

Proposition 8. When an option network facilitates a superior timing strategy for agents to introduce product/business model innovations, it further levers the effects of gap-closing alliances to push environmental dynamics.

To summarize, spanning of option networks is considered to be an adequate means to master the adverse conditions that agents are facing in turbulent organization–environment coevolution and to "place the beds" on different clusters of development paths (Garud & Rappa, 1994, p. 347). Its main function is to prepare in order to be able to react to a greater variety of conceivable developments of the relevant business environment. So, primarily, setting up an option network is a venture driven by the awareness of continuously changing market requirements. But basically through their expected time and cost advantages, participating agents are able to seize their given opportunities immediately when the scenario for which they have spanned an option network becomes effective. Then they will switch their option network to the required form of institutional arrangement and really accelerate and drive transformation processes with respect to elements and relations within a market. Given the increase of knowledge over time, agents also question the composition of their own option networks again and again and constantly rethink, enlarge, or scale down the network of options, according to estimated future developments.

Steering Alliances
"Forecasting the future or shaping it?" (Simon, 2002) – The basic idea of "steering alliances" is somewhat different to the two preceding ones. They

directly aim at goal-oriented attempts to exert influence and to steer changes in the relevant business environment, basic conditions underlying every market process, or migration paths of industry transformation in a way that is advantageous for participating agents. Acknowledging their discretionary potential to act (moderate voluntarism), agents seek to achieve strategic fit this way (Morgan & Hunt, 2002; Volberda & Lewin, 2003; Zajac et al., 2000).

Proposition 9. When different agents recognize their possibilities of coinfluencing their relevant environment, they actively seize this as a strategy to conserve or enhance their own competitiveness.

Accordingly, instead of being forced to follow disadvantageous paths, agents rather choose to jointly initiate, force, vary, and/or break paths (Arthur, 2000; David, 1994; Garud & Karnøe, 2001) (not necessarily self-reinforcing ones). Thereby, it is their purpose to direct or at least to influence the never-ending sequence of decisions and events determining the relevant business environment.

Starting with the awareness of these mechanisms (i.e., that agents are well able to exert influence on their relevant business environment up to a certain extent) it is assumed that the influence can rather be activated through pooling interests and conducting joint actions in adequate networks. It is observable that agents who have similar interests concerning future developments of their relevant business environment group together. Also in our studies, alliances prove to be more effective compared to autonomous actions for at least the following reasons:

(1) pooling of influence purely for size reasons (market-power and opinion-leading) and for the coordination of the contacts and networks of the participating agents,
(2) synchronizing of influencing action as it can be relatively inefficient if each agent tries to influence developments by herself/himself (maybe even into different directions). Individual endeavors might even hamper,
(3) reducing the probability of opportunistic behavior/unforeseeable action of other agents, and
(4) seizing the advantages of coordinated measures to initiate, steer, break, and correct paths (Ackermann, 2003, p. 232; Dietl, 1993, p. 74) in order to proactively and alertly realize new strategic architectures.

Identifying and acknowledging the joint use of mechanisms is the core idea of steering alliances. This does not necessarily presume that all participating agents have the same objectives in taking joint measures of exerting influence.

Proposition 10. Those agents team up in a steering alliance who consider similar actions or directions of taking influence on their relevant business environment as adequate to foster the achievement of their individual goals.

The activities of such steering alliances can be described in at least two ways: either as an intervention into the evolution of institutional rules (so-called "secondary institutions") or by managing the expectations of other market participants in form of a self-fulfilling (Merton, 1948) or a self-destroying prophecy.

Market processes of agents are always embedded into an institutional context that structures the relations between the agents (North, 1990). Against the explicit background of the convertibility over time and thereby widely extending the property rights theory thinking, Dietl (1993, p. 67) develops a hierarchy of institutions which is highly applicable to characterize the subject matter of steering alliances. The so-called "fundamental institutions" (generally accepted rules and norms, e.g., human rights, constitutions, languages, or money) that are not subject to intentional manipulation form the frame for further levels of derived secondary institutions as regulating systems. Such secondary institutions can (and must) be subject to a goal-oriented creation (Picot, Dietl, & Franck, 2005, p. 13) within the borders of primary institutions. Embedded into evolutionary developments of relevant markets and industries, so-called "points of bifurcation" (Ackermann, 2003; Christensen, Suárez, & Utterback, 1998) for particular secondary institutions can be identified over time. At these points of bifurcation a positioning of future cornerstones of the institutional contexts appears to be promising. This can comprise the setting of technical standards and norms, trade terms, accounting standards, or any further form of industry regulation or (de)regulative governmental action, just to name a few.

Steering alliances aim at the development and manipulation of such institutions. Their creation and manipulation partly takes place centrally and explicitly at the already-mentioned points of bifurcation. Additionally, there is oftentimes even a small number of persons who decide on them (e.g., members of the legislature or of standardization boards). These members make their decisions at specific points in time and subjectively. Due to these preconditions for decisions it is assumed that, e.g., through selective information supply to the decision makers, their decisions can basically be influenced or steered. A well-known example for the successful work of steering alliances is lobbying in connection with new legal initiatives (being particularly popular in the German health care sector that we investigated).

Proposition 11. When multiple agents intentionally provide selective information to decision makers on secondary institutions in a coordinated way, they enhance the likelihood of achieving their desired configuration of these institutions.

Within the system of codified primary and secondary institutions there still remains room to structure bilateral and multilateral relations (concerning institutional arrangements and the execution of market input processes) (Dietl, 1993). Under radical uncertainty the expectations of individual agents form the basis of their decision concerning this leeway. By using their own leeway, agents themselves form a facet of the indefinite, undefined future. The forcing desirable and possible development paths of markets/industries happens in two ways:

(1) by credible signaling concerning own future conduct and/or
(2) through selective distribution of information and one-sided public interpretation of available data.

Through strong commitments (e.g., highly specific investments or alternative lock-ins) agents are able to signal their future conduct toward the market credibly. If such a commitment on a very specific development path by more than one agent takes place in a coordinated manner, the resulting signal to third agents are enhanced. This tends to make other agents underestimate the undetermined character of future developments.

Proposition 12. When multiple agents show strong commitment for a very specific scenario x in the undetermined future, the expected probability of other agents that scenario x will effectively become true increases.

Resources and competences generally show a more or less high specificity concerning partners and/or usages (Gersch & Goeke, 2006; Ghemawat, 1991; Ghemawat & del Sol, 1998). A change in market requirements that is accompanied with a changing first- and/or second-best alternative for use can therefore also be considered as a threat of invalidation of available resources and competences. Seeking competitiveness, agents force those environmental development paths, which allow a continuous first-best usage of their potentials. This can mean a goal-oriented stabilizing of existing environmental conditions as well an intended destabilizing. The latter is especially forced by those with superior reactivity compared to competitors. Again and again they try to surprise other (competing) market participants through forced discontinuities.

Proposition 13. The higher the specificity of resources and competences from agent's point of view, the more measures (s)he will undertake to exert influence on the relevant environmental conditions.

However, at the same time they endeavor to have a set of second-best alternatives (e.g., by option networks) ready. This shows that the three elaborated alliance types are not mutually exclusive.

(Bounded) rationally acting agents adapt the future scenario as signaled by the steering alliances with a high probability. Consequently they will direct their own competence building and leveraging toward that development path and thereby actively ride the self-fulfilling prophecy. In a world of incomplete knowledge, in which agents form their expectations in interpreting their available information (Lachmann, 1984), it seems possible to influence expectations without risky commitments too. Conceivable forms can be selective provision of information and amplifying signals in the market. Betting that these mechanisms work, it can be the joint goal of alert agents in a steering alliance to force a very specific path of development through their conduct and aim at a self-fulfilling prophecy concerning a scenario they desire. This does not need to be restricted only to strategic competence groups (Rese, 2002), who possess similar profiles of resources and competences and are therefore willing to achieve a business environment that matches its existing preconditions (readiness for action, option networks, etc.) best. In almost the same manner, but on a more general level, it can mean the formation of groups of agents from different markets within an industry or from unrelated industries. They would be interested in the same development path of a relevant business environment, namely one which they consider to be most compatible to their existing or potential readiness for action or in which they see the greatest potential for their future competitiveness or even competitive advantages. Precondition for joint actions is the identification of relevant "points of bifurcation," i.e., periods/points in time in which it comes to setting the course for relevant business environment and joint targets at these points of bifurcation.

SUMMARY AND OUTLOOK

Applying Maxwell's (2005) interactive model of research design and the case study method, we performed a theory-driven exploration on the question of why firms ally in dynamic environments.

On the basis of market process theory, our findings comprised a taxonomy of three evolutionary motivations, i.e., alliance types:

1. closing resource and competence gaps in so-called "gap-closing alliances,"
2. preparing for unexpected developments in so-called "option networks," and
3. intending to exert influence on the relevant business environment in so-called "steering alliances" (as another way to enhance fit).

This taxonomy can be regarded as one milestone in addressing details of how and why firms set up alliances to master the adverseness of environmental dynamics. Further, it adresses if there is a difference between alliances' and individual agents' influence on the industry evolution.

With regard to these three categories of cooperation, first propositions were elaborated, which are consistent to an understanding of organization–environment coevolution applying the Austrian School to analyze market and industry level in combination with the competence-based theory of the firm to analyze the firm level. Reflecting the findings from a meta point of view, a twofold role of collaborative arrangements turns out: On the one hand agents are pushed into cooperation with others in order to manage change and uncertainty in transforming business environments. But on the other hand joint forces themselves act as an accelerator of industry transformation and thereby as a jolt to other economic agents.

Though the findings fulfill vital requirements concerning the trustworthiness of qualitative research for this stage, we are aware that the investigations on our research question have by far not come to an end, yet. In fact, the propositions and findings must and should be subject to continuous extension and refinement in further fieldwork (Hayek, 1964), also meeting the particular empirical requirements of evolutionary theories.

Another novelty in approaching the research question refers to the theoretical side. Taking up recent research, which points out the compatibility of the Austrian School and resource- and competence-based research, we try a first application to analyze and understand cooperation decisions as an event in organization–environment coevolution. However, the in-depth interlocking of both research programs to one consistent school of thought is still in its infancy, and seems to have the potential to address further research questions in the industrial dynamics context.

REFERENCES

Abbott, A. (2001). *Time matters: On theory and method*. Chicago, IL: University of Chicago Press.

Abell, D. F. (1989). Strategic windows. *Journal of Marketing, 42*(3), 21–26.

Abell, D. F. (1999). Competing today while preparing for tomorrow. *Sloan Management Review, 40*(3), 73–81.

Ackermann, R. (2003). Die Pfadabhängigkeitstheorie als Erklärungsansatz unternehmerischer Entwicklungsprozesse. In: G. Schreyögg & J. Sydow (Eds), *Strategische Prozesse und Pfade, Band 13 Managementforschung* (pp. 225–255). Wiesbaden: Gabler.

Ahuja, G. (2000). Collaboration networks, structural holes, and innovation: A longitudinal study. *Administrative Science Quarterly, 45*(3), 425–455.

Andersson, P., & Mattsson, L.-G. (2006). Timing and sequencing of strategic actions in internationalization processes involving intermediaries: A network perspective. In: C. A. Solberg (Ed.), *Relationship between exporters and their foreign sales and marketing intermediaries. Advances in international marketing* (Vol. 16, pp. 297–326). Bingley: Emerald.

Ariño, A., & de la Torre, J. (1998). Learning from failure: Towards an evolutionary model of collaborative ventures. *Organization Science, 9*(3), 306–325.

Ariño, A., de la Torre, J., & Smith Ring, P. (2005). Relational quality and inter-personal trust in strategic alliances. *European Management Review, 2*, 15–27.

Arthur, W. B. (2000). *Increasing returns and path dependence in the economy*. Ann Arbor, MI: University of Michigan Press.

Barney, J. B., & Clark, D. N. (2007). *Resource-based theory: creating and sustaining competitive advantage*. Oxford: Oxford University Press.

Baum, J. A. C., & Singh, J. V. (1994). Organization–environment coevolution. In: J. A. C. Baum & J. V. Singh (Eds), *Evolutionary dynamics of organizations* (pp. 379–401). Oxford: Oxford University Press.

Becker, M. C. (2004). Organizational routines: A review of the literature. *Industrial and Corporate Change, 13*(4), 643–677.

Beverland, M., & Lockshin, L. (2003). A longitudinal study of customers' desired value change in business-to-business markets. *Industrial Marketing Management, 32*(8), 653–666.

Bresser, R. K. F., Heuskel, D., & Nixon, R. D. (2000). The deconstruction of integrated value chains. In: R. K. F. Bresser, M. A. Hitt & R. D. Nixon (Eds), *Winning strategies in a deconstructing world* (pp. 1–21). Chichester: Wiley.

Burgelman, R. A. (1994). Fading memories: A process theory of strategic business exit in dynamic environments. *Administrative Science Quarterly, 39*(1), 24–56.

Burgelman, R. A. (1996). A process model of strategic business exit: Implications for an evolutionary perspective on strategy. *Strategic Management Journal, 17*, 193–214.

Burrell, G., & Morgan, G. (1979). *Sociological paradigms and organisational analysis: Elements of the sociology of corporate life*. London: Heinemann.

Carson, S. J., Madhok, A., & Wu, T. (2006). Uncertainty, opportunism, and governance: The effects of volatility and ambiguity on formal and relational contracting. *Academy of Management Journal, 49*(5), 1058–1077.

Charmaz, C. (2006). *Grounded theory. A practical guide through qualitative analysis*. Thousand Oaks, CA: Sage.

Christensen, C. M., Suárez, F. F., & Utterback, J. M. (1998). Strategies for survival in fast-changing industries. *Management Science, 44*(12), S207–S220.

Cowley, J. C. P. (2000). Strategic qualitative focus group research – Define and articulate our skills or we will be replaced by others. *Journal of the Market Research Society, 42*(1), 17–38.

Dalkey, N. C. (1969). The Delphi Study of Group Opinions, Rand Corp., RM 5888 PR.

D'Aveni, R. A. (1994). *Hypercompetition: Managing the dynamics of strategic maneuvering.* New York: Free Press.

David, P. A. (1994). Why are institutions the carrier of history? Path dependence and the evolution of conventions, organizations and institutions. *Structural Change and Economic Dynamics, 5,* 205–220.

Dierickx, I., & Cool, K. (1989). Asset stock accumulation and sustainability of competitive advantage. *Management Science, 35*(12), 1504–1511.

Dietl, H. (1993). *Institutionen und Zeit.* Tübingen: Mohr.

Dosi, G. (1982). Technological paradigms and technological trajectories. *Research Policy, 11*(3), 147–162.

Doz, Y. L., & Hamel, G. (1998). *Alliance advantage: The art of creating value through partnering.* Boston: Harvard Business School Press.

Duschek, S. (2004). Inter-firm resources and sustained competitive advantage. *Management Revue, 15*(1), 53–63.

Dyer, J. H. (1997). Effective interfirm collaboration: How firms minimize transaction costs and maximize transaction value. *Strategic Management Journal, 18*(7), 535–556.

Dyer, J. H., & Singh, H. (1998). The relational view. Cooperative strategy and sources of inter-organizational competitive advantage. *Academy of Management Review, 23*(4), 660–679.

Eisenhardt, K. M. (1989). Building theories from case study research. *Academy of Management Review, 14*(4), 532–550.

Eisenhardt, K. M., & Martin, J. A. (2000). Dynamic capabilities: What are they? *Strategic Management Journal, 21*(10/11), 1105–1121.

Eisenhardt, K. M., & Schoonhoven, C. B. (1996). Resource-based view of strategic alliance formation: Strategic and social effects in entrepreneurial firms. *Organization Science, 7*(2), 136–150.

Fagerberg, J. (2003). Schumpeter and the revival of evolutionary economics. *Journal of Evolutionary Economics, 13,* 125–159.

Flint, D. J., Woodruff, R. B., & Gardial, S. F. (2002). Exploring the phenomenon of customers' desired value change in a business-to-business context. *Journal of Marketing, 66*(4), 102–117.

Foss, N. J., & Ishikawa, I. (2007). Towards a dynamic resource-based view: Insights from Austrian capital and entrepreneurship theory. *Organization Studies, 28*(5), 749–772.

Freiling, J., Gersch, M., & Goeke, C. (2008). On the path towards a competence-based theory of the firm. *Organization Studies, 29*(8–9), 1143–1164.

Garud, R., & Karnøe, P. (2001). Path creation as a process of mindful deviation. In: R. Garud & P. Karnøe (Eds), *Path Dependence and Creation* (pp. 1–38). London: Lawrence Erlbaum Associates.

Garud, R., & Rappa, M. A. (1994). A socio-cognitive model of technology evolution: The case of cochlear implants. *Organization Science, 5*(3), 344–362.

Gersch, M., & Goeke, C. (2006). Industry transformation. Conceptual considerations from an evolutionary perspective. *International Journal of Business Market Management, 1*(2), 151–181.

Ghemawat, P. (1991). *Commitment: The dynamic of strategy.* New York: Free Press.

Ghemawat, P., & del Sol, P. (1998). Commitment vs. flexibility. *California Management Review*, *40*(4), 26–42.

Glaser, B. G., & Strauss, A. L. (1967). *The discovery of grounded theory: Strategies for qualitative research*. New York: de Gruyter.

Goeke, C. (2008). *Unternehmenskooperation und Branchentransformation*. Wiesbaden: Gabler.

Gomes-Casseres, B. (1994). Group versus group: How alliance networks compete. *Harvard Business Review*, *72*(4), 62–74.

Gomes-Casseres, B. (2006). How alliances reshape competition. In: O. Shenkar & J. J. Reuer (Eds), *Handbook of strategic alliances* (pp. 39–53). Thousand Oaks, CA: Sage.

Gulati, R. (1998). Alliances and networks. *Strategic Management Journal*, *19*, 293–317.

Gulati, R. (1999). Network location and learning: The influence of network resources and firm capabilities on alliances formation. *Strategic Management Journal*, *20*, 397–420.

Gulati, R., Nohria, N., & Zaheer, A. (2000a). Strategic networks. *Strategic Management Journal*, *21*, 203–215.

Gulati, R., Nohria, N., & Zaheer, A. (2000b). Guest editors' introduction to the special issue: Strategic networks. *Strategic Management Journal*, *21*, 199–201.

Hamel, G. (1991). Competition for competence and inter-partner learning within international strategic alliances. *Strategic Management Journal*, *12*, 83–103.

Hamel, G., & Prahalad, C. K. (1994). *Competing for the future*. Boston, MA: Harvard Business School Press.

Harper, D. A. (1995). *Entrepreneurship and the market process*. London: Routledge.

Hayek, F. A. V. (1964). The theory of complex phenomena. In: M. Bunge (Ed.), *The critical approach to science and philosophy. Essays in honor of K. R. Popper* (pp. 332–349). New York: The Free Press.

Hayek, F. A. V. (1978). Competition as a discovery problem. In: *New studies in philosophy, politics, economics, and the history of ideas*. London: Routledge.

Hibbert, P., & Huxham, C. (2005). A little about the mystery: Process learning as collaboration evolves. *European Management Review*, *2*(1), 59–69.

Hirschman, E. C. (1986). Humanistic inquiry in marketing research: Philosophy, method, and criteria. *Journal of Marketing Research*, *23*(August), 237–249.

Huxham, C., & Vangen, S. (2004). Doing things collaboratively: Realizing the advantage or succumbing to inertia? *Organizational Dynamics*, *33*(2), 190–201.

Huxham, C., & Vangen, S. (2005). *Managing to collaborate*. London: Routledge.

Huygens, M., Baden-Fuller, C., van den Bosch, F. A. J., & Volberda, H. W. (2001). Co-evolution of firm capabilities and industry competition: Investigating the music industry, 1877–1997. *Organization Studies*, *22*(6), 971–1010.

Jacobson, R. (1992). The "Austrian" School of Strategy. *Academy of Management Review*, *17*(4), 782–807.

Klein, J. A., & Hiscocks, P. G. (1994). Competence-based competition: A practical toolkit. In: G. Hamel & A. Heene (Eds), *Competence-based competition* (pp. 183–212). Chichester: Wiley.

Kogut, B. (1991). Joint ventures and the option to expand and acquire. *Management Science*, *37*(1), 19–33.

Koza, M. P., & Lewin, A. Y. (1998). The co-evolution of strategic alliances. *Organization Science*, *9*(3), 255–264.

Koza, M. P., & Lewin, A. Y. (1999). The coevolution of network alliances. *Organization Science*, *10*(5), 638–653.

Lachmann, L. M. (1984). Die Wissenschaft vom menschlichen Handeln. In: L. M. Lachmann (Ed.), *Marktprozess und Erwartungen* (pp. 97–112). München, Wien: Philosophia.

Lakatos, I. (1978). *The methodology of scientific research programmes, philosophical papers Vol. 1* (Worrall, J., & Currie, G. Eds). Cambridge: Cambridge University Press.

Leonard-Barton, D. (1990). A dual methodology for case studies: Synergistic use of a longitudinal single site with replicated multiple sites. *Organization Science, 1*(3), 248–266.

Leonard-Barton, D. (1992). Core-capabilities and core-rigidities: A paradox in managing new product development. *Strategic Management Journal, 13*(Summer), 111–126.

Lewin, A. Y., Long, C. P., & Carroll, T. N. (1999). The coevolution of new organizational forms. *Organization Science, 10*(5), 535–550.

Lieberman, M. B., & Montgomery, D. B. (1988). First-mover advantage. *Strategic Management Journal, 9*(5), 41–48.

Lieberman, M. B., & Montgomery, D. B. (1998). First-mover-(dis)advantages: Retrospective and link with the resource-based view. *Strategic Management Journal, 19*, 1111–1125.

Lincoln, Y., & Guba, E. G. (1985). *Naturalistic inquiry*. Beverly Hills: Sage.

Linstone, H. A., & Turoff, M. (1975). Introduction. In: H. A. Linstone & M. Turoff (Eds), *The Delphi method. Techniques and applications* (pp. 3–12). London: Addison-Wesley.

Lockett, A., & Thompson, S. (2001). The resource-based view and economics. *Journal of Management, 27*, 723–754.

Maxwell, J. A. (2005). *Qualitative research design: An interactive approach*. Thousand Oaks, CA: Sage.

Merton, R. K. (1948). The self-fulfilling prophecy. *Antioch Review, 8*, 193–210.

Meyer, A. D. (1982). Adapting to environmental jolts. *Administrative Science Quarterly, 27*, 515–537.

Meyer, A. D., Brooks, G. R., & Goes, J. B. (1990). Environmental jolts and industry revolutions: Organizational responses to discontinuous change. *Strategic Management Journal, 11*(4), 93–110.

Miles, M. B., & Huberman, M. (1994). *Qualitative data analysis. An expanded sourcebook* (2nd ed.). Thousand Oaks, CA: Sage.

Milgram, S. (1967). The small world problem. *Psychology Today, 1*, 62–67.

Morgan, D. L. (1997). *Focus groups as qualitative research* (2nd ed.). Thousand Oaks, CA: Sage.

Morgan, R. M., & Hunt, S. D. (2002). Determining marketing strategy: A cybernetic systems approach to scenario planning. *European Journal of Marketing, 36*, 450–478.

Nelson, R. R., & Winter, S. G. (1982). *An evolutionary theory of economic change*. Cambridge, MA: Belknap.

Nielsen, P. B., & Rikama, S. (2004). Inter-enterprise relations – First results from the EUROSTAT ad hoc survey. Paper presented at the OECD Workshop on Services, 15–16 November 2004, Paris.

North, D. C. (1990). *Institutions, institutional change and economic performance*. Cambridge: Cambridge University Press.

O'Neill, J. (2000). "Radical subjectivism": Not radical, not subjectivist. *The Quarterly Journal of Austrian Economics, 3*(2), 21–30.

Pettigrew, A. M., Woodman, R. W., & Cameron, K. S. (2001). Studying organizational change and development: Challenges for future research. *Academy of Management Journal, 44*(4), 697–713.

Picot, A., Dietl, H., & Franck, E. (2005). *Organisation. Eine ökonomische perspektive* (4th ed.). Stuttgart: Schäffer-Poeschel.

Popper, K. R. (1945). *The open society and its enemies volume 2: The high tide of prophecy: Hegel, Marx and the aftermath*. London: Routledge.

Porter, M. E., & Rivkin, J. W. (2000). Industry transformation, Note 9-701-008, Harvard Business School.

Portes, A. (1998). Social capital: Its origins and applications in modern sociology. *Annual Review of Sociology, 24*, 1–24.

Prahalad, C. K. (1995). Weak signals versus strong paradigms. *Journal of Marketing Research, 32*(3), iii–viii.

Prévot, F. (2006). The management of competences in the context of inter-organizational relations. Paper presented at the International Symposium on the Competence Perspective in Management Education, Practice and Consulting, University of Stellenbosch Business School, Bellville/Cape Town (South Africa).

Rese, M. (2002). Zur Existenz strategischer Kompetenzgruppen-Eine ökonomische Betrachtung. In: K. Bellmann, J. Freiling, P. Hammann & U. Mildenberger (Eds), *Aktionsfelder des Kompetenz-Managements* (pp. 257–274). Wiesbaden: Gabler Edition Wissenschaft.

Richardson, G. B. (1972). The organisation of industry. *Economic Journal, 82*(327), 883–896.

Rothaermel, F. T., & Hill, C. W. L. (2005). Technological discontinuities and complementary assets: A longitudinal study of industry and firm performance. *Organization Science, 16*(1), 17–52.

Sanchez, R., & Heene, A. (2004). *The new strategic management*. New York.

Sanchez, R., Heene, A., & Thomas, H. (1996). Introduction: Towards the theory and practice of competence based competition. In: R. Sanchez, A. Heene & H. Thomas (Eds), *Dynamics of competence-based competition: Theory and practice in the new strategic management* (pp. 1–35). Oxford: Pergamon.

Schumpeter, J. A. (1934). *The theory of economic development*. Cambridge, MA: Harvard University Press.

Shackle, G. L. S. (1972). *Epistemics and economics*. Cambridge: Cambridge University Press.

Silverman, B. S., & Baum, J. A. C. (2002). Alliance-based competitive dynamics. *Academy of Management Journal, 45*(4), 791–806.

Simon, H. A. (2002). Forecasting the future or shaping it? *Industrial and Corporate Change, 11*(3), 601–605.

Spedale, S. (2003). Technological discontinuities: Is co-operation an option? *Long Range Planning, 36*(3), 253–268.

Strauss, A., & Corbin, J. (1998). *Basics of qualitative research: Techniques and procedures for developing grounded theory* (2nd ed.). Thousand Oaks, CA: Sage.

Teece, D. J., Pisano, G., & Shuen, A. (1997). Dynamic capabilities and strategic management. *Strategic Management Journal, 18*(7), 509–533.

Tyre, M. J., & Orlikowski, W. J. (1994). Windows of opportunity: Temporal patterns of technological adaptation in organizations. *Organization Science, 5*(1), 98–108.

Vaughn, K. I. (1994). *Austrian economics in America. The migration of a tradition*. Cambridge: University Press.

Volberda, H. W., & Lewin, A. Y. (2003). Guest editors' introduction: Co-evolutionary dynamics within and between firms: From evolution to co-evolution. *Journal of Management Studies, 40*(8), 2111–2136.

Wiggins, R. R., & Ruefli, T. W. (2005). Schumpeter's ghost: Is hypercompetition making the best of times shorter? *Strategic Management Journal, 26*, 887–911.

Witt, U. (1992). Turning Austrian economics into an evolutionary theory. In: B. Caldwell & S. Boehm (Eds), *Austrian economics: Tensions and new directions* (pp. 215–236). Boston, MA: Kluwer.

Witt, U. (1999). Do entrepreneurs need firms? A contribution to a missing chapter in Austrian economics. *Review of Austrian Economics, 11*, 99–110.

Yin, R. K. (2008). *Case study research: Design and methods* (4th ed.). Thousand Oaks, CA: Sage.

Zaheer, A., & Bell, G. G. (2005). Benefiting from network position: Firm capabilities, structural holes, and performance. *Strategic Management Journal, 26*, 809–825.

Zajac, E. J., Kraatz, M. S., & Bresser, R. K. F. (2000). Modeling the dynamics of strategic fit: A normative approach to strategic change. *Strategic Management Journal, 21*, 429–453.

THE ROLE OF DISTRIBUTED COMPETENCES FOR STANDARD-SETTING COMMUNITIES: THE CASE OF INDUSTRIAL AUTOMATION

Alexander Gerybadze and André Slowak

ABSTRACT

The competence-based management approach has shed light on how firms represent open systems that link assets, strategic logic, and capabilities in order to create new competences. Nonetheless, we find that there are too few empirical studies that illustrate how competences are distributed within an industry. The following case study is based on an in-depth analysis of innovation and standards-formation in industrial automation. Two examples, the standard-setting community PROFIBUS and the field bus-related sensor consortium IO-Link are used to analyze partnership arrangements and competence-distribution patterns.

This study is based on qualitative interviews and it uses patent data to judge competences of a standard-setting community's partner firms. Referring to the empirical case of IO-Link, we show how the integrator firms' competence-leveraging can be significantly affected by new technology approaches that reason a novel deployment of capabilities.

A Focused Issue on Identifying, Building, and Linking Competences
Research in Competence-Based Management, Volume 5, 111–142
ISSN: 1744-2117/doi:10.1108/S1744-2117(2010)0000005008

It seems that the deployment of resources depends not only on industry segmentation, but also on the firms' coordinated agenda concerning innovative, new functionality of a given standard. Our patent analysis also mirrors the variety of knowledge within a standard-setting community. Furthermore, we develop a concept of layered business systems, that is, a terminology of knowledge, organizational, and technology domains. Standard-setting communities bundle complementarity assets, they make their member firms create both proprietary and open technology, and they integrate knowledge across industry boundaries.

1. INTRODUCTION

Field buses are a technology to connect machines, robots, and components in a factory or process plant. They are, however, also used in other industries such as white goods (e.g., field bus *CAN*) or automotive backbone and control systems (particularly *CAN/LIN* and *FlexRay*). The economic history of industrial automation goes back to the idea to reduce cabling and to replace mechanical controls by electronic controls. Industrial automation generally has three separate market segments: factory, process, and building. Factory automation is characterized by ambitious real-time requirements and robotic and motion components. Process automation provides technology for safe and efficient industrial processing, for example, processing chemicals on large scale. (This also includes the monitoring of processes.) Building automation concerns low-tech automation, but also IT-infrastructure in industrial buildings. Note that this paper only deals with factory automation. Recently, the field bus market has been dominated by the standards *DeviceNet*, *EtherNet/IP* and *CompoNet*,[1] *CC-Link*,[2] and *PROFIBUS & PROFINET*.[3] An example of factory automation is Siemens' SIMATIC S7 field bus network for automated door stores in car assembly (cf. Siemens, 2008). The network consists not only of machines, robots and logistics, controls interfaces/displays, controls hardware such as terminals/ industrial PCs, interface displays, components and sensors, but also software specialized for the business case (e.g., inventory management). Doors are removed so that workers can fit interior car components more easily; then, they are carried to storage and delivered back to assembly just in time. A process plant network differs from this case example in two ways. First, specialized terminals and displays for batch processes are added. Second, there are so-called ex-zones where devices and sensors need to be intrinsically safe. Process plants implement both factory and process automation networks. Process automation helps the key processes such as chemical reactions or treatment of chemicals with different liquids.[4] Automation hardware consists of mechanical parts, (micro)electronics, input/output interfaces, and the ability to send as well as to read data in conformity with the overall network. Technically, automation software includes tools for programming automation hardware (parameterization), simulation tools, and visualization for human–machine interfaces. Note that besides hardware-based control devices, automation control devices can also be virtually integrated into a standard PC (so-called "soft-PLCs").

Standard-setting studies merely analyze the process of standard specification (e.g., Farrell & Simcoe, 2009), diffusion patterns (Rogers, 2003; Geroski, 2000), firm roles and governance in standard-setting communities (e.g., Gerybadze, 2008; Schweikle, 2009), intellectual property and standards,[5] and methods of standard-setting (Funk, 2009). The economics of standards rather deals with macroeconomic considerations (cf. Blind, 2004) and competing standards, particularly standard wars and network effects (cf. Shapiro & Varian, 1999a, 1999b; Farrell & Klemperer, 2007). Besides the empirical investigation of competences in standard-setting communities from non-HT industries, there is a research gap in how competence profiles of partners affect the design of a standard.

Besides a variety of definitions, we follow the definition by Sanchez:

> Competence is the ability to sustain the coordinated deployment of assets in ways that help a firm achieve its goals. … First, competence must include the ability to respond to the dynamic nature of an organization's external environment and of its own internal processes. The requirement of sustainability in the above definition of competence encompasses both forms of dynamics. … Second, competence must include an ability to manage the systemic nature of organizations and of their interactions with other organizations. … Third, competence must include an ability to manage the cognitive processes of an organization. … Fourth, competence must include the ability to manage the holistic nature of an organization as an open system (2004, p. 521).

This paper only accounts for a fraction of that competence construct, namely, competence as the ability to sustain the coordinated deployment of the firm's STI-base in standard-setting processes. Complementarily, we argue that (strategic) competences of the firm pursue competitive advantage, they configure resources, they take time to acquire and they are difficult and time-consuming to imitate (cf. Hall, 2000). Patents can be taken as an indicator of competence in various ways. For instance the number of new patents per R&D spending inter alia expresses R&D productivity (Carayannis & Alexander, 2002). Patents also express that technology of a firm is of potential economic benefit, they particularly measure explicit codified elements of competence (Knudsen, 2005), or they may be used to measure the divergence of partners' technological specialization and their technological proximity (Colombo, 2003). In this paper, they are just used to describe each standard-setting partner's STI-base. A quite extensive measurement approach of competence is provided by Ritter and Gemünden (2004) on the basis of a survey. For more information on patents portfolios as a measure of diversification and market positioning of a firm, see Patel (1999) and Patel and Pavitt (1997).

Standard-setting communities in this paper are populations of firms that collaborate with the purpose to advance and to diffuse a consistent and integrated set of technical standards. System integrators are defined as follows, "Loosely coupled organizations are led by system integrators. System integrators are more than the assemblers that operate within core networks. System integration includes the technological and organizational capabilities to integrate changes and improvements in internally and externally designed and produced inputs within an existing product architecture" (Brusoni, Prencipe, & Pavitt, 2001, p. 614). Research from several innovation surveys shows that firms use *lead time*, *patents*, and *secrecy* to appropriate their product innovations. Furthermore, patents also serve other strategic goals such as blocking other firms or providing bargaining power in cross-licensing negotiations (cf. Hall, 2009). Machinery and electrical equipment represent complex technologies where products are systems formed of components and several technologies. Patent strategy thus pursues portfolio maximization; patents are particularly used in negotiations and to prevent litigation (von Graevenitz et al., 2007, p. 10ff; Hall, 2009, Table 3 on p. 10). Our paper sheds light on how the patent portfolios of standard-setting partners differ in size and technology fields that the patents cover. We take patents as an indicator of technological competence.[6] Each firm can be described by a patents/IPC count-profile for selected technology fields (for methodology see Schmoch, 1995; Knudsen, 2005).[7]

Fig. 1 illustrates the flow of arguments and structure of this paper. Within the next section we characterize the industry's knowledge landscape as one of a low and medium industry with a strong foundation in mechanical engineering. Section 3 provides a case study on both *PROFIBUS* and *IO-Link*. *PROFIBUS* is a standard-setting community, whereas *IO-Link* originally represented a project consortium of that community but meanwhile created a sensor-bus standard that is applied to several field bus standards, not only *PROFIBUS*. This section also refers to different types of essential patents. Then, a patent count is conducted in

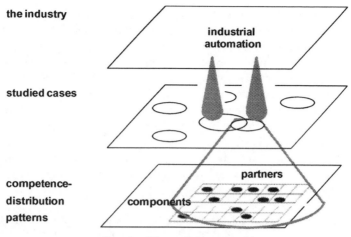

Fig. 1. Flow of Arguments.

order to draw technology profiles of the different *PROFIBUS* core members. Section 4 discusses our concept of competence-distribution patterns. We formulate the idea of a business system that spans knowledge, organization, and technology. Finally, Section 5 concludes our paper. Our study focuses on competence-distribution and patents as R&D output from competence. Note that we do not analyze the structure of an industry (industry architectures, cf. Jacobides, Knudsen, & Augier, 2006; or firm boundaries, cf. Jacobides & Billinger, 2006), but the structure of a standard-setting community.

2. THE INDUSTRY'S KNOWLEDGE LANDSCAPE

Essential characteristics of the standard-setting and innovation process dynamics in industrial automation are as follows. The science and knowledge base spans a *diverse array of capabilities*; it covers various industries such as information and telecommunications, engineering – mechanical engineering, electronics, electro-mechanics – and others. Furthermore, business cases in factory, process, and specific niche segments may overlap and thus interfere. The more systems of technical standards become integrated, the more high investment costs and increased time to operation makes industrial users call for standards that endure over the plant and factory life cycle. In a *market with network effects* from an installed-base such as in industrial automation, users are not willing to implement standards that do not have a global community of supporters. Also note that Industrial Ethernet field buses or wireless technology from consumer markets provoke a new standard-setting race where new entrants try to set standards against incumbents.[8] Asian vendors, for instance, now influence *International Electrotechnical Commission's* Ethernet real-time specification processes. More precisely, the industry of industrial automation is characterized by an ambiguous relationship between low and high technology. Not only the advancement of own technological knowledge, but also the integration of other industries' technology base drives innovation in non-HT:

> Innovation in low- and medium-tech industries is critically dependent on the absorption of new products and technological spillovers from other industries. Absorptive capabilities need to be combined with other related forms of downstream innovation (design, customer integration, complementary services, changing business models) (Gerybadze & Slowak, 2008, p. 47).

Therefore, standard-setting communities often face the challenge of providing technology superior to that of firms from other sectors operating at the high-technology frontier. In this paper, we argue that leading firms in industrial automation agree on how to distribute competences so that an integrated system of technical standards is created and maintained. The systemic character then creates higher business value than could be extracted from components business. In such a way, industrial automation establishes market imperfections against lower priced consumer technology; and high-technology components are seamlessly integrated into the systems offered to users. Furthermore, global users of field bus technology demand a global certification, global support, and user community-specific advancement of technical standards used in operation. High-norm activities take place particularly in the *International Electrotechnical Commission*, Ethernet and consumer technologies are often specified by the *Institute of Electrical and Electronics Engineers* or sometimes by the World Wide Web Consortium. If relying on proprietary strategies, single firms cannot have the necessary influence on the *International Electrotechnical Commission* as a field bus association. De jure bodies are involved in the standard-setting process also for de facto standards as communities try to standardize the technical environment and influence regulation in favor of their collaborative standards. Multinational firms rely on *high-norm* activities (at de jure bodies) as complementary to other standard-setting capabilities (particularly at the standard-setting communities/de facto). "[High-norm activities] include: the development of standard-setting institutions and regulatory bodies; technical societies, engineering communities and industry associations; and innovation marketing and opinion-building through trade fairs, international exhibitions and conferences" (Gerybadze & Slowak, 2008, p. 49).

Fig. 2 gives an overview of the automation value chain behind factories or process plants (i.e., automotive manufacturing or chemical plants). The more a standard is capable of spanning several value steps of the production value chain, the more it becomes a key asset to industry solutions and thus valuable for integrator firms. Such integrators are big multinational firms with strong automation business segments such as Siemens or technical service firms specialized in factory and plant construction or setup.

Automation solutions rely on knowledge and standards from various domains such as production technologies (particularly manufacturing vs. processing), machinery, or chemistry. These knowledge stocks have to be aligned with and updated by business cases. Thus a patent analysis needs to cover different segments across IPC classes, particularly: mechanical engineering (IPC G: *physics*, IPC F: *mechanical engineering*), controls software tools (several or not patentable) and electronics (IPC H: *electricity*). Note that our patent analysis by nature neglects services, for instance, planning, modernization, advanced visualization of manufacturing process, or simulation of production.

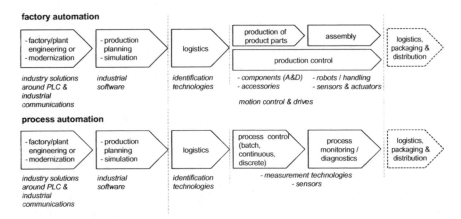

Fig. 2. Industrial Automation Along the Production Technologies Value Chain.

3. THE CASES OF PROFIBUS AND IO-LINK

[PROFIBUS] emerged from a joint industry project in 1987–90 supported by the German Federal Ministry of Research and Technology. The project was accomplished by German firms and universities with strong engineering and IT capabilities, in particular Siemens, Bosch, Klöckner and Moeller, the RWTH Aachen and the Karlsruhe Research Center for Information Technologies (FZI). ... In 1989 the PROFIBUS user Organization (PNO) was founded in order to augment and to maintain the technology designed in the above research project. PROFIBUS International (PI) was set up in 1995. ... Today, PROFIBUS/PROFINET is represented by PROFIBUS and PROFINET International (PI, responsible for user support and technology-marketing), and the PROFIBUS User Organization (PNO, responsible for enhancing technology and influencing coherent international standards) (Gerybadze & Slowak, 2008, p. 52).

The ecology of firms behind the standard-setting community *PROFIBUS* shows how a variety of competences are represented, inter alia by solution providers and integrator firms such as Siemens, ABB, or Endress+Hauser; strong industry users like BASF or Shell and DEA Oil; field bus competitors (Mitsubishi Electric, OMRON, Phoenix Contact, Schneider Electric); prestigious German applied-research institutions from the field of engineering and IT as well as university research in industrial automation; technical specialists and component manufacturers; or technical services firms.[9]

IO-Link was founded as a *PROFIBUS* working group/project consortium in 2003. The project internally announced its first specification draft in 2006. It developed its own protocol that links sensors actively to the field bus networks *PROFIBUS & PROFINET*. Meanwhile the consortium issued interface specifications to several global leading field bus protocols, and thus it is becoming more and more independent from the *PROFIBUS* community. The *IO-Link* protocol allows for active sensor functions such as self-configuration or active status report, for a fast substitution of an outdated sensor unit or the replacement of a broken sensor unit, and for programming with contemporary software tools. One of the project's initiators was one of the leading sensor manufacturers, SICK. Earlier Siemens tried to enforce the working group to build *IO-Link* on its proprietary technology (*IQ-sense*), but the firm could not prevail that approach.

PROFIBUS members organize themselves in regional or country-specific chapters or in application-specific user communities (e.g., *PROFIBUS* competence centers specialized on particular *PROFIBUS*-technology modules; or business activities emerging from use-case specific community projects such as field bus profiles for train automation). Standardization projects within the *PROFIBUS User Organization's* working groups specify components and data formats based on an underlying core standard, *PROFIBUS DP* (conventional technology) and *PROFINET CBA/IO* (*PROFIBUS'* Ethernet technology). Routines linked to de jure standardization are often run by Siemens. The firm is the liaison partner in international bodies. Working groups may also use *Public Available Specifications* that represent a published pre-consensus on the community's project level before standardization at the *International Electrotechnical Commission* takes place. *PROFIBUS* working groups may establish project consortia to formally agree on intellectual property, trademarks, the distribution of work shares, and a preliminary time schedule/milestones for the de jure standardization process (see PNO Guidelines; PNO bylaws; and PNO IPR Policy).

As follows, we will use patents as a proxy for technological competence in standard-setting processes. Brusoni et al. (2001) provide an interesting patent terminology that we use to demonstrate how different levels of technological competence are expressed by the quality of patents.[10] They differentiate between architecture, sub-architecture, functional, and physical patents:

> Architecture patents are those whose abstract describes how components are arranged in a system. Sub-architecture patents are those whose abstract describes how components are arranged in a subsystem. If the main content of the patent abstract describes functional behavior of a system ... we label patents as functional. Physical patents are those whose abstract concerns the physical description of an item or subsystem, i.e., what the system looks like (Brusoni et al., 2001, p. 606).

Architectural patents in the *PROFIBUS* case concern interfaces, basic digital data formats, and network design. *PROFINET CBA* ("component-based automation," see Table 1) describes all components as objects with

Table 1. US Patent 7418305,[a] Method of Generating a Component of a Component-Based Automation System.

Abstract	A computer-implemented method for generating a description of a component of an automation system comprises describing the component as a plurality of inputs and outputs, generating a vendor-independent component description file based on a description of the component as the plurality of inputs and outputs, updating the vendor-independent component description file to include vendor-specific hardware information and hardware control logic, and creating the component based on an updated vendor-specific component description.
IPC	G06F, G06G
Assignee	Siemens Corporate Research, Inc., Princeton, USA

[a] Also see European Patent Application EP1691245A1.

inputs/outputs in a kind of a vendor-independent library. It provides a modular representation of the factory's/plant's arrangement of functional objects, labeled "components of a field bus network." Thus above patent can be considered an architectural element of the *PROFINET* business system. Furthermore, the above patent specifies a method to show not only how a file for the component description is created and updated, but also how it is accessed/functions with hardware. In this sense it is functional. The *IO-Link* case is rather characterized by functional patents, for instance:

> The background of the invention is the networking of sensors, for example of one-dimensional or two-dimensional optical code readers or of laser measuring systems, via a digital fieldbus, for example of the type Profibus or DeviceNet. It is known for this purpose to provide the sensors with their own fieldbus interface which permits a connection of the sensor to the fieldbus and communication between the sensor and the fieldbus. A fieldbus interface integrated in the sensor, however, makes the actual sensor module undesirably expensive and undesirably voluminous for some applications. The relevant sensor is moreover admittedly adapted to a specific fieldbus; but the sensor can no longer easily be used for other fieldbus types (US Patent 7299310, Connection module for the connection of a sensor to a fieldbus).

IO-Link products are available on the market since 2008; leading sensor firms like SICK presented their first products at *Hannover Messe 2007*. In order to become mature, the technology had to be negotiated successfully over several years, and IEC standardization activities (namely IEC 60947-5-2, 3rd ed.) had to be completed in 2007. *IO-Link* trademarks are owned by the firms Balluff (figurative elements) and ifm electronic (name), see WIPO Trademarks 876152 and 913389 (http://www.wipo.int/ipdl/en/madrid/key. jsp?KEY=876152 and http://www.wipo.int/ipdl/en/madrid/key.jsp?KEY= 876152) (Table 2).

Appendix A documents the data on whichthe patent analysis of our paper is based on, and how keywords and patent classification were matched with industrial automation standards technology. Note that we did not use the key words suggested in the appendix, but selected them from patents by IPC-industries-concordance. Appendix B provides a count of covered IPC classes for each applicant.

Fig. 3 shows that Siemens has the most diversified and deepest technology competence profile. The company is particularly strong in IPCs G01, G05, G06, G11, H01, and H04. Siemens' web of competences enfolds the other firms' webs of competence. Siemens is richer than other PROFIBUS' members, with respect to their depth and the variety of patents that are potentially relevant to field bus standards. Fig. 4 shows that the competence profile of other multinational firms – not representing incumbents' driving

Table 2. Triadic Patent Count for the PROFIBUS Community and Integrator Firms in Industrial Automation.

	No. of Patent Families	Share on Sample (%)	Variety in Technology (No. of IPC Covered)
ABB	201	9.5	17
Balluff	2	0.1	2
Beckhoff	0		
Endress+Hauser	139	6.6	15
Festo	39	1.8	8
Gemü	0		
ifm Electronic	0		
Leuze	7	0.3	4
Mesco	0		
Mitsubishi Electric	72	3.4	9
Omron	119	5.6	19
Pepperl+Fuchs	1	0.0	2
Phoenix Contact	2	0.1	2
Rockwell	48	2.3	14
Schneider Electric	80	3.8	13
Sensopart	0		
SICK	27	1.3	9
Siemens	1,372	65.1	25
Softing	0		
Technische Universität München	0		
Turck	0		
Wago Kontakttechnik	0		

Note: N: 2,109 triadic patent families as selected by EPO IPC classification; *N*: 1,862 triadic patent families as selected by USPTO IPC classification.

forces behind the leading standard-setting communities – is more narrowed. Festo has a high number of triadic patents in IPC F15 whereas Endress+Hauser is strong in IPCs G01and G08 particularly. Fig. 5 shows that sensor firms have a weak patent portfolio in comparison to Siemens or Omron. SICK, however, is much stronger than Balluff or Pepperl+Fuchs. Similarly to Fig. 4, the IPC classes F15 and G01 are particularly relevant.

4. THE EMERGENCE AND CONTROL OF COMPETENCE-DISTRIBUTION PATTERNS

Standard-setting in industrial automation takes part in communities and thus in collaboration among firms. Standard-setting communities can be taken for open systems in terms of Sanchez (2004), that is, capabilities are

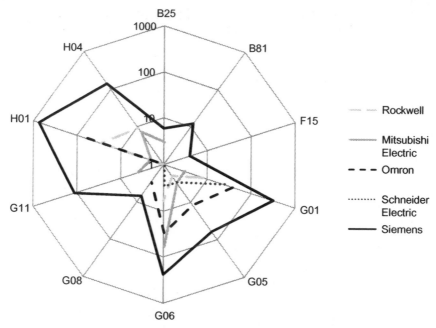

Fig. 3. Integrators' Technology Profile (Incumbents of the Different Standard-Setting Communities). *Note:* Figs. 3 and 4 are presented in logarithmic scale. Fig. 5 plots the number of patents as they are only few.

taken for "repeatable patterns of action in the use of all other assets" (p. 519). There are primarily three reasons why collaboration generates business value for each partner firm. These are

- first, standard-setting communities allow member firms to exploit own knowledge beyond production boundaries, creating as much value for an industry as possible with respect to all accessible assets (both own and disclosed assets by partners);
- second, standard-setting communities provide a precompetitive infrastructure upon which firms base their proprietary activities at product and service markets; and finally
- third, standard-setting communities allow member firms to use modular business systems.

First, firms can use collaborations to advance their knowledge-base. In their paper on selected multitechnology product firms in the market for aircraft engine control systems, Brusoni et al. (2001) present an empirically

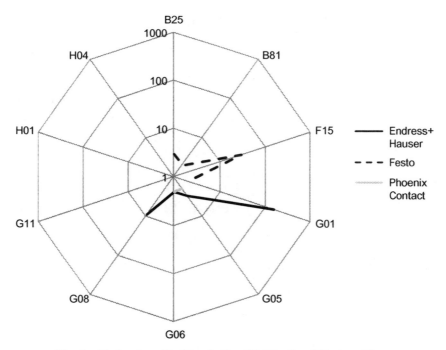

Fig. 4. Technology Profile of other Multinational Partner Firms.

based typology of organizational coupling. They show how product interdependencies and rates of change in component technologies affect the boundaries of the firm and how the producers' supplier network affects knowledge boundaries. As per their definition, multitechnology products "are artifacts made up of components and embody a number of technologies" (Brusoni et al., 2001, p. 597). Their study points out that firms may know "more than they do":

> In a number of sectors, technologies and products have been shown to follow interconnected, yet different, dynamics. More precisely, the knowledge boundaries of firms stretch beyond their production boundaries, and the evolution of their knowledge and product domains unfolds according to different principles. ... Firms invest into broadening their knowledge bases while narrowing down their manufacturing bases (Brusoni et al., 2001, p. 598f).

In industrial automation, there are two observable radical shifts in underlying technology. First, in the last decades, industrial automation controls emerged from mechanical controls systems. Electro mechanics

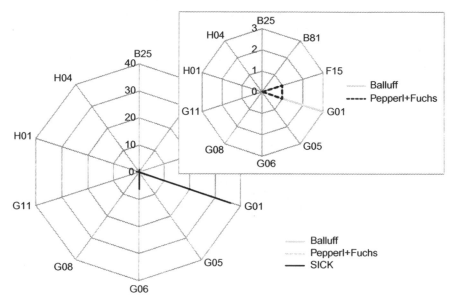

Fig. 5. Sensor Manufacturers' Technology Profile.

became a more and more important basic technology. Second, recently the market has shifted from conventional field buses to Ethernet field buses. Furthermore, *PLC*/industrial controls programming tools, data management, and software to visualize functions and interfaces between subnetworks have gained importance. This is one of Siemens' appropriated strengths: extra functionality to open standards is included in the *SIMATIC* product lines. Apart from analogy in industry and technology dynamics, Brusoni et al. (2001) also evidenced their typology by the use of patent data, namely patent shares of control-system-related patents on the observed interdependent technology fields ("control-system-related technologies"). They describe that one company from their sample labeled as "company C" outsourced production, but maintained technological capabilities via "collaborative agreements with external sources of components and technologies of control systems (suppliers and universities)" (Brusoni et al., 2001, p. 608, p. 611f). That company moved from a loosely coupling to a decoupled network structure. The decoupled network structure is characterized by predictable systemic interdependencies and even rate of change in component technologies. The study concludes that companies moved to predictable system interdependencies/even rate of change, when technology matured. In terms of collaborative standard-setting, we argue that integrators in standard-setting communities should anticipate systemic interdependencies and harmonize rate of change in component standards in order to build and maintain knowledge beyond their own technology portfolio. For instance, PROFIBUS is a matured, non-HT standard with slow rates of technological change. Other standards – consumer technologies, or disruptive component innovations such as IO-Link – show asynchronous, faster rates of change than usual in non-HT.

Second, firms collaborate on standards in order to create a strong infrastructure for their proprietary products.

> [Standards] help create a strong, open, and well-organised technological infrastructure that will serve as a foundation for innovation-led growth. It is often asked whether, on balance, standardization acts more to constrain innovation or to enable innovation. From our perspective these two activities are inextricably linked. Standardization does constrain activities but in doing so creates an infrastructure for subsequent innovation. Well-designed standards should be able to reduce undesirable outcomes. Moreover, standardization is not just about producing norms for given technologies in given markets. Standardization helps to credibility, focus and critical mass in markets for new technologies (Swann, 2000).

In the case provided in this paper, field buses are indeed the "strong, open, and well-organised technological infrastructure" that not only underpin the proprietary products for automation firms, but also allow for specialized technical services. The collaboration on standards within global standard-setting communities also assures that the users of field bus technology can expect positive network effects due to the number of members. "Consumers fear making investments in a network and then becoming 'stranded' because there is insufficient consumer acceptance. Standards may alleviate those concerns, by assuring consumers that the network technology will be adopted" (Balto, 2000). Although standard-setting competition in medium-technology markets such as industrial automation does not follow the winner-takes-it-all patterns of consumer cases such as *VHS/Betamax*, long technology life cycles in production technology to some extent substitute for such effect. Users may rely on those standards that are backed by leading multinational firms and those standard-setting communities which dominate global application domains, because users assume that those standards endure. Users of field bus technology may accept several co-existing standards, but they demand long-term availability of components and continuous, nondisruptive innovation in standards. *Global standards* are thus driven by big firms such as Siemens, Rockwell, or Mitsubishi Electric.

As a third argument, we add that standard-setting communities allow for modular business systems that consist of services, an in-depth and diversified set of component standards, and a common infrastructure. The latter assures for well-defined interfaces. A business system shall be defined as an implicit, underlying agreement between all partners on how knowledge as input; technical standards as intermediate products; and intellectual property, trademarks, and affiliation (status and exclusion rules) are relevant to the business carried out in product and service markets. That is, field bus standards can be conceptualized in terms of modular product architectures where standards deliver stability, but incremental innovations at the component level facilitate technological progress and create innovation-driven market dynamics in a non-HT environment.

> In creating modular architectures, firms may pursue either closed-system or open-system strategies. In a closed-system strategy, a firm creates a proprietary modular architecture intended to accommodate only component variations supplied by the firm. In an open-system strategy, a firm may disclose its interface specifications so that other firms can develop components for its product architecture. Alternatively, a firm may collaborate with other firms in establishing industry standards that define the types of functional components they will use and the interface specifications that will apply to each type of component (Sanchez & Collins, 2001, p. 648).

In the GE-Fanuc case provided by Sanchez and Collins (2001), products are decomposed into key functional components/technology building blocks and fully specified component interfaces. Interface specifications for these key functional components are *frozen* at the beginning of the component development process. Although modular architectures may also serve focused strategic learning and capability development (e.g., Sanchez & Collins, 2001, p. 656), we suggest that in non-HT industries modularization inter alia serves the well-defined distribution of competences for a collaborative, incremental advancement and the coordinated proprietary exploitation of a common STI-base. Note that integrator firms in our case chose a hybrid strategy between proprietary modules and modules that implement open standards technology. System leadership is then not only about how to own technology and crucial components of a standard, but also about how to arrange a fit between proprietary modules and open modules with respect to the rates of technological change. In Sanchez and Collins (2001, p. 648) words, industrial automation firms "collaborate with other firms in establishing industry standards that define the types of functional components they will use and the interface specifications that will apply to each type of component"; at the same time, firms integrate other markets open standards and create some additional proprietary specification

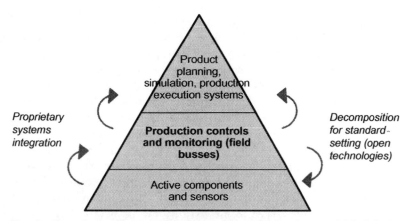

Fig. 6. Proprietary Systems Integration, Open Technology and Modularity.

not disclosed to the standard-setting community (e.g., Siemens *SIMATIC* or proprietary field buses at the component level).

Fig. 6 demonstrates how modular standards architectures allow for proprietary systems integration while creating open technology through technical standards. The modular approach furthermore allows for differentiated *semi-open standards architecture.* Although particular standards are influenced and particular intellectual property is accessed by many members of the standard-setting community, other elements of a standards development are shaped by an exclusive project consortium within the user organization such as *IO-Link* project within *PROFIBUS.* Furthermore, firms add proprietary technologies to open standards. This set of open and closed technology specifications creates the technical standards infrastructure of a business system. The creation of open technology can be thought as system decomposition of the system from field bus level to other levels of automation and production technologies. Note that modularization and thus processes of decomposition need to be enforced by management through technical interface specification. Systems integration describes the re-integration of open, modular innovations (new standard components) into the firm's product offers (proprietary systems of the firm).

> When fully specified and standardized, the interface specifications for a new modular product architecture provide an information structure that implicitly co-ordinates each component development group's activities ... Throughout the modular development process, both top and middle levels of management have a critical role to play in ensuring that all component development groups agree to a set of standardized component interfaces for a modular architecture – and then strictly conform to those interfaces in creating their component designs (Sanchez & Collins, 2001, p. 658).

While standardization leads to unification and does not address individual needs of particular implementations, modularity of standards allows for variety, it promotes compatibility with complementary technologies and increases interoperability between competing component manufacturers through *frozen, but open interfaces*. Sanchez and Collins (2001, p. 648f) point out various strategies of configuring components for delivering new products to the market. Modularity can be used to create most desired models, discovered by "real-time" market research, to customize products for different world regions, to allow for new components increasing product life time (backward compatibility and well-defined interfaces), and to allow for an effective use of common components across product line/within technology platforms. In industrial automation, it seems that frozen interface standards and common basic technology allow for new components that extend the product's life time (particularly, process plant or factory modernization, new functionalities at the machine cell). Fig. 7 suggests a new approach on how to separate an analysis of competence into several layers, namely how firms utilize their knowledge, how they organize the standard-setting process/best dominate standard-setting communities, and how they transform both elements into standard and proprietary product technology.

A proprietary business strategy in the context of distributed standard-setting competences means that each agent or each member firm of a standard-setting community fails decisions about which know-how, IPR,

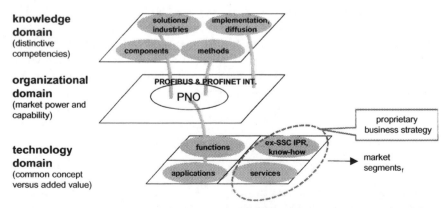

Fig. 7. Design of the PROFIBUS Business System Terminology "Knowledge/ Organizational/Technology Domain" (Based on Brusoni & Prencipe, 2006, p. 185, Figs. 1 and 2).

and other assets to commit to the standard versus which assets to exclusively commit to own products and services delivered at the market.

Our patent analysis has demonstrated that few big multinational firms significantly differ from all other standard-setting community members by the high number of patents and high IPC-class diversification. Thus, leading firms are able to claim superior technology competence in standard-setting negotiations. However, Siemens' control over knowledge architectures did not succeed in the case of *IO-Link*. We find that sensor firms leverage highly firm-specific assets in a niche market: namely, knowing the user, economies of scale from division of labor respective from specialization, and niche product experience. Sensor firms thus allied and claimed that a new standard must be open and in the best case, applicable to conventional sensors physics. Finally, they could turn *IQ-sense* into a bad user choice:

- First, *IQ-sense* was not open technology. It had been introduced into the market by Siemens as a proprietary sensor feature made for and thus primarily compatible to proprietary Siemens control technology (*SIMATIC*). Nonetheless, Siemens would have agreed to add new specifications to the protocol in order to make it open, but was interested in backward compatibility for their installed base of *IQ-sense* sensor users.
- Second, change in physics or interface characteristics of sensors would have implied hardware switching costs for sensor manufacturers as well as for users modernizing their factory/plant (incompatibility of the installed base with the new protocol).
- Third, sensor manufacturers were interested in a field bus-independent intelligent sensor protocol. *IQ-sense* was explicitly made to allow for intelligent sensors in a *PROFIBUS/PROFINET* network whereas the *IO-Link* project consortium rather became loosely coupled to *PROFIBUS* only.

We find that Siemens could not negotiate the design of the intelligent sensor standard to its own advantage, although their patent profile is much richer than those of other sensor firms. The strong patent portfolio of Siemens indicates that it pools distributed competences, whereas SICK is rather a specialized firm. Given their experience from many standard-setting communities, and also their global business presence, Siemens is capable of designing a global standard-setting community in co-operation with other multinational business partners. Both firms – Siemens and SICK – have been explicit on not only what functionality is required for future sensor technology, if it should be open, but also how the sensor bus shall interact with other field buses. However, SICK and other leading sensor

Table 3. Sensor Manufacturers Position in IO-Link.

Capability (Ability to) in the Case of IO-Link	Leading PROFIBUS Firms (e.g., Siemens)	Sensor Firms
Pool distributed competences and apply rich patent portfolio	+	–
Design a global standard-setting community	++	n/a
Formulate a sound strategy: functionality, openness, interplay with other standards	+ (Siemens)	+ (SICK)
Know users and their needs	–	++

Note: –, no ability; –, weak ability; +, strong ability; ++, very strong ability; n/a, no evidence from case.

manufacturers better know the needs of the sensor segment customers than Siemens does. They have the larger installed-base and thus can enforce the claim of backward compatibility. Table 3 summarizes the arguments. We conclude that firms need to address their competitive assets when negotiating standard-setting agendas and technology shape/design of the standard.

5. CONCLUSIONS

Field bus standards are the common technological basis among standard-setting partners in industrial automation, upon which they agree on intellectual property terms, co-ordinate their proprietary market strategies and they can lock in users (the installed base) into long-term investments through industry solutions. We find that competences are different between member firms, they are distributed, but particular members dominate standardization projects. Standard-setting activities require a positioning of the firm with respect to its strengths (assets-based, capabilities) and the standard-setting community's project agendas. Furthermore, we distinguish two strategies of influence: First, integrators may deploy their rich science, technology, and innovation-base in order to ensure their technology becomes essential to a standard. Second, particularly component manu-facturers and niche market specialists may try to bundle a set of strong economic or political arguments against integrators' technology (e.g., switching costs of users, arguing against closed standards/user dependence). We have conducted a patent count analysis to demonstrate how patent portfolios affect the outcome of standards development. Firms should try to achieve best fit between their competitive assets and the standard-setting agenda. They should also try to influence processes at all levels of the business system: relevant knowledge to standards, organization of the standard-setting community and technology shape/design of the standard.

Collaboration on standards allows integrator firms not only to embed high technology by the means of modular systems, but also to focus on high-value activities such as automation systems integration in factories or process plants, energy efficiency or product data management, and advanced simulation. System leadership can be achieved if a group of big multinational firms is able to take a dominant position at all three layers of the business system, that is, the knowledge domain, the organizational domain, and the technology domain. Note that such firms should complement each other in assets and competences. Finally, it seems to be crucial to define what shall be open versus closed in technology. Integrators disclose some variety of competence to standard-setting communities in order to attract members. For instance, Siemens was a major developer of *PROFIBUS* original DP technology and it disclosed architectural patents to *PROFIBUS* (e.g., *PROFINET CBA*). Further research should thus particularly shed light on the firms' motivation to close or to open up technology in the context of standard-setting processes.

NOTES

1. Particularly influenced by Rockwell, OMRON, and Schneider Electric; user organization: ODVA.

2. Particularly influenced by Mitsubishi Electric; user organization: CLPA.

3. Particularly influenced by Siemens; user organization: PROFIBUS & PROFINET International.

4. A nice overview on Siemens process industry automation technology can be found in ARC (2005). On the performance of industry solutions related to adaptiveness also see ARC (2008).

5. For instance, essential intellectual property rights, fraud, and unreasonable/unfair use of intellectual property rights between standard-setting partners and in de jure bodies or research on intellectual property regimes. Cf. Bekkers and West, 2009; Lemley and Shapiro, 2007; Shapiro, 2003; Mueller, 2002; DIME, Sector studies on Open and Proprietary Innovation Regimes, http://www.dime-eu.org/wp14; IPRsTrust: Patents and Antitrust in Standards, Berkman Center at Harvard University, Center of Industrial Economics at Mines ParisTech, Helsinki Law and Technology Center at University of Helsinki and Institute of Economic Research at Hitotsubashi University, http://www.iprstrust.org/academics.

6. Note that patents as indicator of competence only account for a fraction of a firm's science and technology base. A firm may own knowledge which is either kept secret for strategic reasons or which is too implicit to be filed. However, as field bus

standards are developed in inter-firm co-operation/in collaboration, only such knowledge which is disclosed and shared can contribute to a standard. Also note that patent portfolios do not provide any information on the firms' experience and history with regard to standard-setting processes.

7. However, we do not address evolution of patent portfolios, cumulativeness of patents, patenting behavior/strategy in different industry, or specialization measures such as index on revealed technological advantage.

8. Standard-setting, but also competition at the global product market can be taken for a game between leading firms (incumbents) and new entrants or firms from originally non-related markets (challengers), cf. Gerybadze and Slowak (2008) and Fligstein (2001).

9. This paragraph takes from Gerybadze and Slowak (2008, p. 53).

10. Given the state of research (for instance cf. EC, 2005; Hall, Jaffe, & Trajtenberg, 2005; Nakanishi & Yamada, 2007), this is a rather simplistic approach. Nonetheless, Brusoni et al. (2001) best characterizes quality in terms of relevance for product *systems*.

REFERENCES

ARC. (2005). Siemens process industry strategies. ARC White paper, Dedham, MA.

ARC. (2008). Adaptation: The key to business performance from manufacturing IT. ARC White Paper, Dedham, MA.

Balto, D. A. (2000). *Standard setting in a network economy* [speech]. Cutting Edge Antitrust, Law Seminars International. February 17, 2000. US Bureau of Competition, Federal Trade Commission, New York (http://www.ftc.gov/speeches/other/standardsetting.shtm).

Bekkers, R., & West, J. (2009). The limits to IPR standardization policies as evidenced by strategic patenting in UMTS. *Telecommunications Policy, 33*(1–2), 80–97.

Blind, K. (2004). *The economics of standards: Theory, evidence, policy*. Cheltenham: Edward Elgar.

Brusoni, S., & Prencipe, A. (2006). Making design rules: A multidomain perspective. *Organization Science, 17*(2), 179–189.

Brusoni, S., Prencipe, A., & Pavitt, K. (2001). Knowledge specialization, organizational coupling, and the boundaries of the firm: Why do firms know more than they make? *Administrative Science Quarterly, 46*(4), 597–621.

Carayannis, E. G., & Alexander, J. (2002). Is technological learning a firm core competence, when, how and why? A longitudinal, multi-industry study of firm technological learning and market performance. *Technovation, 22*(10), 625–643.

Colombo, M. G. (2003). Alliance form: A test of the contractual and competence perspectives. *Strategic Management Journal, 24*(12), 1209–1229.

EC. (2005). *The value of European patents: Evidence from a survey of European inventors*. Final Report of the PatVal EU Project, HPV2-CT-2001-00013 (http://www.alfonsogambardella.it/PATVALFinalReport.pdf).

Farrell, J., & Klemperer, P. (2007). Coordination and lock-in: Competition with switching costs and network effects. In: M. Armstrong & R. H. Porter (Eds), *Handbook of industrial organization* (Vol. 3, pp. 1967–2072). Amsterdam: North-Holland.

Farrell, J., & Simcoe, T. S. (2009). *Choosing the rules for consensus standardization.* Working Paper, April 28, 2009 (http://ssrn.com/abstract=1396330).

Fligstein, N. (2001). *The architecture of markets. An economic sociology of twenty-first century capitalist societies.* Princeton, NJ: Princeton University Press.

Funk, J. L. (2009). The co-evolution of technology and methods of standard setting: The case of the mobile phone industry. *Journal of Evolutionary Economics, 19*(1), 73–93.

Geroski, P. A. (2000). Models of technology diffusion. *Research Policy, 29*(4–5), 603–625.

Gerybadze, A. (2008). Innovationspartnerschaften, Patentpools und Standardsetzungsgemeinschaften: Verteilung und Zuteilung der Rechte und Neue Organisationsformen. In: M. Eifert & W. Hoffmann-Riem (Eds), *Geistiges Eigentum und Innovation: Innovation und Recht I* (pp. 165–181). Berlin: Duncker & Humblot.

Gerybadze, A., & Slowak, A. (2008). Standard-setting competition and open innovation in non-HT industries: Mechanical engineering and machinery. In: H. Hirsch-Kreinsen & D. Jacobsen (Eds), *Innovation in low-tech firms and industries* (pp. 43–63). Cheltenham: Edward Elgar.

Hall, B. H. (2009). The use and value of patent rights, *UK IP Ministerial Forum on the Economic Value of Intellectual Property*, June 10, 2009, Strategic Advisory Board for Intellectual Property Policy (http://www.sabip.org.uk/forum-hall.pdf).

Hall, B. H., Jaffe, A., & Trajtenberg, M. (2005). Market value and patent citations. *RAND Journal of Economics, 36*(1), 16–38.

Hall, R. (2000). What are strategic competencies? In: Tidd, J. (Ed.), *From knowledge management to strategic competence: Measuring technological, market and organisational innovation* (pp. 26–49). Series in Technology Management, Vol. 3. London: Imperial College Press.

Jacobides, M. G., & Billinger, S. (2006). Designing the boundaries of the firm: From "make, buy, or ally" to the dynamic benefits of vertical architecture. *Organization Science, 17*(2), 249–261.

Jacobides, M. G., Knudsen, T., & Augier, M. (2006). Benefiting from innovation: Value creation, value appropriation and the role of industry architectures. *Research Policy, 35*(8), 1200–1221.

Knudsen, M. P. (2005). Patterns of technological competence accumulation: A proposition for empirical measurement. *Industrial and Corporate Change, 14*(6), 1075–1108.

Lemley, M. A., & Shapiro, C. (2007). Patent hold-up and royalty stacking, CPC07-065, *Competition Policy Center* (http://repositories.cdlib.org/iber/cpc/CPC07-065).

Mueller, J. M. (2002). Patent misuse through the capture of industry standards. *Berkeley Technology Law Journal, 17*(2) (http://www.law.berkeley.edu/journals/btlj/articles/vol17/mueller.pdf).

Nakanishi, Y., & Yamada, S. (2007). *Market value and patent quality in Japanese manufacturing firms.* MPRA Paper No. 10790, Senshu University (http://mpra.ub.uni-muenchen.de/10790/1/MPRA_paper_10790.pdf).

Patel, P. (1999). *Measurement and analysis of technological competencies of large firms.* Draft Report for Dynamic Capabilities, Growth and Large Firms (DYANCOM) project funded by EC Targeted Socio-Economic Research Programme, SOE1-CT97-1078 (http://www.lem.sssup.it/Dynacom/files/D07_0.pdf).

Patel, P., & Pavitt, K. (1997). The technological competencies of the world's largest firms: Complex and path-dependent, but not much variety. *Research Policy, 26*(2), 141–156.

PNO bylaws [Satzung der PROFIBUS Nutzerorganisation e.V.]. (1996). http://www.profibus. com/celummdb/doc/RPA/GERMANY/Satzung_PNO.pdf

PNO Guidelines [Guidelines for the Technical Committees and Working Groups of the PROFIBUS Nutzerorganisation e.V.], Version 3.2, April 16, 2007 (http://www.profibus. com/celummdb/doc/RPA_GERMANY/2007-04-16_pno_tc_wg_guidelines_stand_3_2_ en_released.pdf).

PNO IPR Policy [Intellectual Property Rights Policy of the PROFIBUS Nutzerorganisation e.V.], Version 1.1, April 16, 2007 (http://www.profibus.com/celummdb/doc/RPA_GER-MANY/2007-04-16_pno_ipr_stand_1_1_en_released.pdf).

Ritter, T., & Gemünden, H. G. (2004). The impact of a company's business strategy on its technological competence, network competence and innovation success. *Journal of Business Research, 57*(5), 548–556.

Rogers, E. M. (2003). *Diffusion of innovations* (5th ed.). New York: Simon & Schuster International.

Sanchez, R. (2004). Understanding competence-based management: Identifying and managing five modes of competence. *Journal of Business Research, 57*(5), 518–532.

Sanchez, R., & Collins, R. P. (2001). Competing – and learning – in modular markets. *Long Range Planning, 34*(6), 645–667.

Schmoch, U. (1995). Evaluation of technological strategies of companies by means of MDS-maps. *International Journal of Technology Management, 10*(4/5/6), 426–440.

Schmoch, U., Laville, F., Patel, P., & Frietsch, R. (2003). *Linking technology areas to industrial sectors*. Final Report to the European Commission, DG Research. Karlsruhe/Paris/ Brighton (TecInd/Field_ definitions_by_IPC.txt, Compute Time Series Field Definitions by IPC).

Schweikle, R. (2009). *Innovationsstrategien Und Determinanten Des Wettbewerbserfolges: Eine Vergleichende Analyse Japanischer Und Deutscher Unternehmen*. Wiesbaden: Gabler.

Shapiro, C. (2003). Navigating the patent thicket: Cross licenses, patent pools, and standard-setting. *Law and Economics, EconWPA*, 0303005 (http://ideas.repec.org/p/wpa/wuwple/ 0303005.html).

Siemens. (2008). BMW, Dingolfing: Just-in-time doors. Siemens move up, 2-2008: 13-15 (http:// www.automation.siemens.com/magazines/moveup/ftp/MoveUp_2_2008_en.pdf).

Swann, P. (2000). *The economics of standardization*. Final Report for Standards and Technical Regulation Directorate Department of Trade and Industry. Manchester Business School (http://www.berr.gov.uk/files/file11312.pdf).

Shapiro, C., & Varian, H. R. (1999a). *Information rules: A strategic guide to the network economy*. Boston, MA: Harvard Business School Press.

Shapiro, C., & Varian, H. R. (1999b). The art of standards wars. *California Management Review, 41*(2), 8–32.

von Graevenitz, G., Wagner, S., Hoisl, K., Hall, B. H., Harhoff, D., Giuri, P., & Gambardella, A. (2007). *The strategic use of patents and its implications for enterprise and competition policies*. Report for the European Commission (http://ec.europa.eu/enterprise/ newsroom/cf/document.cfm?action=display&doc_id=2475).

APPENDIX A. PATENT SAMPLE (YEARS 1995–2005)

Technology fields related to competence in industrial automation	IPC and/or industrial sector (IPC)[*]
Industry solutions around PLC and industrial communications	39-Industrial process control equip. (G01K, G01L, G05B, G08C), G01R, G06F, H01H
Industrial software	[**]
Identification technologies	[**]
Components (A&D), motion control and drives, wireless networks	34-Electronic components (B81B, B81C, G11C, H01C, H01F, H01G, H01J, H01L), 35-Signal transmission, telecoms (H04Q), F01B, F15B
Robots/handling	B25J
Measurement technologies	G01B, G01F, G01G
Sensors	G01N, G01R, G01S, G01V, G06F, G06K

Notes: The analysis conducted in this paper uses the OECD database on triadic patent families (raw data in text files), updated October 2008. Based on PATSTAT, September 2008. Furthermore, our study is limited to OECD triadic dataset tables for the years 1995–2005.

[*]In Appendix C, we suggest keywords for a semantic analysis. However, this paper does not use keywords in any way. We selected our patent sample with respect to IPC-industry concordance. Also note that our analysis from case to case either only covers a fraction of relevant technologies or may include too many patents. For instance, G06F as a proxy for sensor technology is quite broad.

[**]Our patent selection does not include these technology fields.

The concordance between industrial sectors and IPC subclasses is based on Schmoch, Laville, Patel, and Frietsch (2003). G01K, L also describe a variety of measurement technologies, but they are relevant to industrial communications controls in process industries and thus taken into account.

A patent family is defined as a set of patents taken in various countries for protecting a same invention, i.e. related patents are regrouped into a single record to derive a unique patent family. The OECD's "triadic" patent families are defined as a set of patents filed for at the European Patent Office (EPO), the Japanese Patent Office (JPO) and granted by the United States Patent and Trademark Office (USPTO) that share one or more priority applications (OECD database on triadic patent families).

Applicants included in our patent selection/sample are:

• integrator firms (ex Cisco): Siemens, Rockwell, Omron, Schneider Electric, Mitsubishi Electric;

- all PROFIBUS User Organization "core" members: SIEMENS, Endress+Hauser, TU Munich, WAGO Kontakttechnik, Mitsubishi Electric, Pepperl+Fuchs, SICK, Phoenix Contact, FESTO, Softing, ABB; and
- all *IO-Link* members: Balluff, Beckhoff, Gemü, Festo, ifm electronic, Leuze electronic, Mesco, Pepperl+Fuchs, Phoenix Contact, Schneider electric, Sensopart, SICK, Siemens und Turck.

Queries used to extract data from the database ("MySQL" applied to an "Infobright" database/data warehousing) can be provided on request.

Note that we conducted two separate IPC-analyses for above firm and IPC set. Table B1 illustrates the results if triadic patent families are classified by IPC as stated in the included EPO-patents, Table B2 outlines the results if triadic patent families are classified by IPC as stated in the included USPTO-patents (for tables see Appendix B). We do not take account of any IPC-statement from JPO-patents as JPO-patents included in the OECD dataset come without IPC-classification. PCT filings are not explicitly addressed as well.

APPENDIX B. IPC ANALYSIS FOR PROFIBUS AND IO-LINK; DATA TABLES

Tables B.1 and B.2 provide the detailed descriptive statistics for relevant firms in relevant patent classes. The paper only refers to the EPO patent count. Table B2 (USPTO count) is included to show that results are similar for EPO and USPTO patent analysis. We use the analysis of Table B1 (see Table B2 in the paper).

Table B1. Patent Analysis According to IPC-Classes Stated by the EPO.

Applicant	No. of Patent Families	Share on Sample (%)	Variety in Technology (No. of IPC Covered)	B25J	B81B	B81C	F01B	F15B	G01B	G01F	G01G	G01K	G01L	G01N	G01R
ABB	201	10.5	17	25	0	0	0	1	6	5	0	0	7	11	17
Balluff	2	0.1	2	0	0	0	0	0	2	0	0	0	0	1	0
Beckhoff	0	0.0													
Endress+Hauser	139	7.3	15	0	1	0	0	0	1	101	0	0	22	16	2
Festo	39	2.0	8	3	2	0	0	30	0	1	0	0	1	0	0
Gemü	0	0.0													
ifm Electronic	0	0.0													
Leuze	7	0.4	4	0	0	0	0	0	0	0	0	0	0	0	0
Mesco	0	0.0													
Mitsubishi Electric	72	3.8	9	3	0	0	0	0	1	0	0	0	0	0	0
Omron	119	6.2	19	0	1	0	0	0	5	2	1	12	4	5	1
Pepperl+Fuchs	1	0.1	2	0	0	0	0	1	1	0	0	0	0	0	0
Phoenix Contact	2	0.1	2	0	0	0	0	0	0	0	0	0	0	0	0
Rockwell	48	2.5	14	0	2	1	0	0	0	0	0	0	1	3	3
Schneider Electric	80	4.2	13	0	1	0	0	0	3	0	0	2	0	1	6
Sensopart	0	0.0													
SICK	27	1.4	9	1	0	0	0	0	10	1	0	0	0	2	0
Siemens	1372	71.9	25	6	8	4	0	4	44	14	9	9	32	80	92
Softing	0	0.0													
Technische Universität München	0	0.0													
Turck	0	0.0													
Wago Kontakttechnik	0	0.0		38	15	5	0	36	73	124	10	23	67	119	121

Table B1. (*Continued*).

Applicant	G01S	G01V	G05B	G06F	G06K	G08C	G11C	H01C	H01F	H01G	H01H	H01J	H01L	H04Q
ABB	1	2	9	2	0	3	0	5	20	7	39	0	59	0
Balluff	0	0	0	0	0	0	0	0	0	0	0	0	0	0
Beckhoff														
Endress+Hauser	10	1	3	2	0	9	0	0	2	0	1	1	3	0
Festo	0	0	0	0	0	2	0	0	1	0	0	0	4	0
Gemü														
ifm Electronic														
Leuze	1	1	1	0	5	0	0	0	0	0	0	0	0	0
Mesco														
Mitsubishi Electric	2	0	3	43	16	0	4	0	0	0	0	0	2	7
Omron	2	5	12	11	19	3	0	0	3	2	43	0	10	1
Pepperl+Fuchs	0	0	0	0	0	0	0	0	0	0	0	0	0	0
Phoenix Contact	0	0	2	2	0	0	0	0	0	0	0	0	0	0
Rockwell	1	0	2	6	0	0	1	0	1	0	3	2	22	9
Schneider Electric	3	10	3	3	0	1	0	0	6	0	57	0	7	0
Sensopart														
SICK	13	10	0	1	5	0	0	0	0	0	0	0	1	0
Siemens	38	6	60	175	65	7	110	6	59	10	118	15	531	137
Softing														
Technische Universität München														
Turck														
Wago Kontakttechnik	71	35	95	245	110	25	115	11	92	19	261	18	639	154

Table B2. Patent Analysis According to IPC-Classes Stated by the USPTO.

	No. of Patent Families	Share on Sample (%)	Variety in Technology (No. of IPC Covered)	B25J	B81B	B81C	F01B	F15B	G01B	G01F	G01G	G01K	G01L	G01N	G01R
ABB	183	10.9	15	25	0	0	0	2	5	5	0	0	6	10	14
Balluff	2	0.1	2	0	0	0	0	0	2	0	0	0	0	1	0
Beckhoff	0	0.0													
Endress+Hauser	135	8.0	11	0	0	0	0	0	0	100	0	0	18	14	2
Festo	34	2.0	7	3	0	0	0	26	0	1	0	0	1	0	0
Gemü	0	0.0													
ifm Electronic	0	0.0													
Leuze	7	0.4	3	0	0	0	0	0	0	0	0	0	0	0	0
Mesco	0	0.0													
Mitsubishi Electric	54	3.2	8	1	0	0	0	0	0	0	0	0	0	0	0
Omron	109	6.5	15	0	0	0	0	0	2	2	1	11	4	4	1
Pepperl+Fuchs	1	0.1	2	0	0	0	0	1	1	0	0	0	0	0	0
Phoenix Contact	2	0.1	2	0	0	0	0	0	0	0	0	0	0	2	0
Rockwell	33	2.0	13	0	3	0	0	0	0	0	0	0	1	2	2
Schneider Electric	69	4.1	10	0	1	0	0	0	0	0	2	2	0	1	4
Sensopart	0	0.0													
SICK	24	1.4	7	0	0	0	0	0	1	1	0	0	0	1	0
Siemens	1,209	72.0	23	2	7	0	0	2	15	12	7	7	26	59	71
Softing	0	0.0													
Technische Universität München	0	0.0													
Turck	0	0.0													
Wago Kontakttechnik	0	0.0													
				31	11	0	0	31	26	121	8	20	56	92	94

Table B2. (*Continued*).

	G01S	G01V	G05B	G06F	G06K	G08C	G11C	H01C	H01F	H01G	H01H	H01J	H01L	H04Q
ABB	0	2	4	0	0	2	0	5	18	6	36	0	47	0
Balluff	0	0	0	0	0	0	0	0	0	0	0	0	0	0
Beckhoff														
Endress+Hauser	9	0	2	1	0	6	0	0	2	0	1	0	3	0
Festo	0	0	0	0	0	1	0	0	1	0	0	0	3	0
Gemü														
ifm Electronic														
Leuze	1	0	1	0	5	0	0	0	0	0	0	0	0	0
Mesco														
Mitsubishi Electric	2	0	3	27	15	0	4	0	0	0	0	0	2	4
Omron	0	3	11	6	19	2	0	0	0	1	39	0	4	0
Pepperl+Fuchs	0	0	0	0	0	0	0	0	0	0	0	0	0	0
Phoenix Contact	0	0	2	1	0	0	0	0	0	0	0	0	0	0
Rockwell	1	0	3	1	1	0	0	0	1	0	2	1	14	5
Schneider Electric	2	8	2	0	0	0	0	0	3	0	48	0	2	0
Sensopart														
SICK	12	7	0	1	4	0	0	0	0	0	0	0	0	0
Siemens	31	0	48	119	59	4	96	4	39	7	111	12	437	115
Softing														
Technische Universität München														
Turck														
Wago Kontakttechnik	58	20	76	156	103	15	100	9	64	14	237	13	512	124

APPENDIX C. SUGGESTED KEYWORDS FOR FUTURE ANALYSES

Own Comment on Technology Fields	Technology Fields Related to Competence in Industrial Automation	Keywords
Includes architecture and functional patents	Industry solutions around PLC and industrial communications	"Factory automation," "process automation," "discrete automation," "industrial automation," "distributed control system," "fieldbus," "field bus," "industrial ethernet," "industrial process control," "industrial control system," "automation system," "condition monitoring," "automation control," "automation interface," "industrial controller"
	Industrial software	"Soft PLC," "SCADA," "manufacturing execution system," "automation software," "enterprise resource planning"
Includes primarily physical patents	Identification technologies	"RFID"[a] not "WiFi"
	Components (A&D), motion control and drives, wireless networks	"Motion control," "assembly automation," "drive control," ("WiFi" not "RFID"), "safety automation," "level measurement," "limit detection," "flow measurement"
	Sensors	("Sensor" and "automation"), ("sensor" and "bus"), ("sensor" and "interface")

[a]RFID is taken as a state-of-the-art contemporary technology example.

Architecture patents are those whose abstract describes how components are arranged in a system. Sub-architecture patents are those whose abstract describes how components are arranged in a subsystem. If the main content of the patent abstract describes functional behavior of a system ... we label patents as functional. Physical patents are those whose abstract concerns the physical description of an item or subsystem, i.e., what the system looks like (Brusoni et al., 2001, p. 606).

Patents which include "factory automation" or "process automation" in their abstract in general are related to a description of how the automation network shall be structured. Industrial process control equipment is necessary to realize controls system in industrial automation; patents should be thus related. As we know from qualitative in-depth study, system integrators – Siemens, Rockwell, Schneider Electric, Omron, and Mitsubishi Electric – shape the way how automation networks are structured. Functional patents in factory automation are related to the terms "motion control," "drive control," or "assembly automation." These are patents which describe what automation cells do, i.e., robots perform fast motions. However, we could not find sufficient key words for a detailed analysis on "process automation." Technology fields grouped under B and C are probably rather physical patents than architectural ones (terminology as to Brusoni et al., 2001, p. 606); they describe items or subsystems of automation system solutions.

CHALLENGES FOR DIFFERENTIATORS COMBINING MODULARIZATION AND COMPETENCE RENEWAL

Heike Proff

ABSTRACT

The growing modularization of complex products encourages the division of labor in industry. End product manufacturers outsource production of individual components to large module suppliers, saving on costs in the short term. In the medium term, however, they sacrifice competences. The competitive strategy they choose – either cost leadership or differentiation – determines how this conflict is resolved. This paper examines the shift in competences to module suppliers, and the likely reactions of end product manufacturers, particularly those pursuing a differentiation strategy. The discussion begins at a general level, and then focuses on the automotive industry as an example. The paper derives potential strategic actions going forward based on transaction cost theory and core competency theory, and conducts a content analysis to examine them empirically.

A Focused Issue on Identifying, Building, and Linking Competences
Research in Competence-Based Management, Volume 5, 143–174
Copyright © 2010 by Emerald Group Publishing Limited
All rights of reproduction in any form reserved
ISSN: 1744-2117/doi:10.1108/S1744-2117(2010)0000005009

INTRODUCTION

Modularization, defined as the breakdown of complex products into independent components (Sanchez & Mahoney, 2001; Fixson, 2002a; Langlois, 2002; Worran, Moore, & Cardona, 2002), is becoming increasingly important in many sectors. The practice is particularly widespread in the computer industry, and is also gaining ground in the automotive industry. This paper will be using the latter as a concrete example.

Modularization transforms the value chains of end product manufacturers and suppliers within an industry because dissecting products means defining interfaces between the modules (Sanchez & Mahoney, 1996; Baldwin & Clark, 1997; Thomke & Reinertsen, 1998; Mikkola, 2003; Ethiray & Levinthal, 2004). This in turn makes it easier to outsource component production to specialized suppliers. As modularization is essentially a decision between make and buy, it alters the firm's boundary (Dyer, 1996, 2000; Combs & Ketchen, 1999; Novak & Stern, 2003). Over time, this influences the distribution of competences between original equipment manufacturer (OEM) and module suppliers, since companies often cede competences when they outsource as a result of modularization. Modularization therefore also has an impact on the future distribution of profits between OEMs and suppliers (McGrath, MacMillan, & Venkatraman, 1995; Proff, 2007).

Modularization and the greater outsourcing of value-added activities that it allows means OEMs can *reduce costs in the short term*. This especially relates to labor costs, development costs from boosting development efficiency, sourcing and production costs from economies of scale, and investment costs as a result of lower investments (Milgrom & Roberts, 1990; Picot, Reichwald, & Wigand, 2007; Takeishi & Takahiro, 2001). If the number of parts that product development needs to design falls due to the use of standard modules, OEMs can also dramatically reduce development time (Thomke & Reinertsen, 1998; Robertson & Ulrich, 1998). These are termed efficiency or specialization advantages.

Over the medium term, however, modularization can also lead to a *drain* of end product manufacturer *competences* if capabilities are transferred to suppliers together with the outsourced parts (Dyer, 2000; Sheffi, 2006). Only few very efficient and specialized module suppliers are able to gain specialization advantages and competences from modularization. Many other module suppliers and smaller suppliers remain subordinate to the huge power of OEMs. This is demonstrated in the growing concentration of suppliers in many sectors (comparisons of concentration in the automotive industry, e.g., Mercer Management Consulting and Fraunhofer-Gesellschaft, 2003; McKinsey & Company & PTW, 2003). As a result, modularization leads to a shift in value creation and profitability between manufacturers and suppliers in a sector – not always to the benefit of suppliers.

The significance of competences and thus also of any loss of competence as a result of modularization also varies amongst end product manufacturers. The extent to which this differs depends on what their competitive strategy is: cost leadership or differentiation in their business segment (Porter, 1980, 1985).

Cost leaders aspiring to the lowest possible cost position need competences too, of course, such as efficient processes for developing and manufacturing products and their components to support their cost leadership strategy. However, they will outsource specific components to specialized suppliers, taking for granted a partial drain of competences under certain conditions. This is the case if the components are simple to split off, and manufacturers can quickly achieve cost savings via the specialization advantages of suppliers, who replace the mid-term cost advantages with capabilities (Milgrom & Roberts, 1990). However, these cost leaders do not always weigh up the short-term specialization advantages and mid-term disadvantages from their loss of competences (Deutsche Bank, 2002).

Firms that target a unique position from a customer perspective via a differentiation strategy require appropriate competences to be able to charge a price premium, such as superior product quality or (incremental) innovation. A price premium is a price above what the basic technical product would normally cost ("value for money"). It safeguards customer loyalty for goods that are purchased repeatedly (Rao & Monroe, 1996). Cost savings, though necessary, can never substitute for these competences (Deutsche Bank, 2002). As a result, differentiators have to be a lot more careful than cost leaders where modularization and particularly outsourcing are concerned. They are often too swift to reduce costs via outsourcing due to processes based on division of labor, without heeding the competence drain that this involves (Maxton & Wormald, 2004).

Research on modularization has not so far analyzed the impact of modularization depending on the competitive strategy the manufacturer is pursuing (Baldwin & Clark, 1997; Thomke & Reinertsen, 1998; Sanchez & Mahoney, 2001; Langlois, 2002; Worran et al., 2002; Mikkola, 2003).

This paper attempts to shed some light on this neglected area. It first analyzes the challenges of increasing modularization for end product manufacturers on a general level. It then examines the situation for differentiators, who are most strongly affected. In the second section, a focus on the automotive industry highlights the challenges, because they are particularly significant and apparent in this sector. We intend this to serve as an example for other industries. The third section provides an overview of the status of research on the efficient company boundary, and the impact of modularization on this boundary. We supplement the widespread transaction cost theory with core competency theory, discussing the opportunities – but also limits – of examining them jointly. The fourth section derives possible strategic reactions of end product manufacturers, and the fifth uses a content analysis of specialist articles to examine the plausibility of these hypotheses. The paper closes with an outlook.

CHALLENGES FROM MODULARIZATION USING THE EXAMPLE OF THE AUTOMOTIVE INDUSTRY

Modularization has existed in the automotive industry for over 20 years (Fixson, 2002a, 2002b). Two phases of greater modularization can be distinguished.

In the *first phase* through to the mid-1990s, modularization was a reaction of OEMs to innovation and cost pressure. Customers were demanding more for their money. Capital markets were also exerting pressure to achieve higher returns (Deutsche Bank 2002; Mercer Management Consulting & Fraunhofer-Gesellschaft, 2003). OEMs tried to use modularization to create the prerequisite for greater outsourcing of value-added activities. Their objective was to reduce costs and increase differentiation via greater product variety (Sanchez, 1995; Baldwin & Clark, 1997; Global Insights, 2003). This first phase of modularization was typified by Volkswagen requesting JIT delivery to their production line of the entire front section (bumper, headlights, and cooler module) for the mid-range segment (VW Golf) (Jürgens, 2003) from Hella AG, a lighting supplier. Since then, several OEMs have been sourcing these front sections from the Hella–Behr joint venture. This trend toward modules has also extended to other vehicle segments. OEMs are increasingly asking their suppliers to provide further services (in addition to production and assembly) such as R&D and systems integration.

The first phase of modularization put the module suppliers under extreme price, cost, and flexibility pressure (McKinsey & Company & ika, 1999). But it also offered them the opportunity to push on with modularization independently. Some of them have been doing this in the *second phase* of greater modularization since the beginning of the 21st century. Large module suppliers such as Johnson Controls, Bosch, or Hella–Behr grasped the initiative and developed more comprehensive modules. Hella–Behr, for example, entered into a joint venture with Plastic Omnium (HBPO), a French supplier of plastic components. The joint venture carries out design, development, production, and logistics for front-section modules that integrate electronic driver support systems. OEMs managed to reduce their costs by sourcing modules, but also sacrificed capabilities, especially to large module suppliers. The latter are keen to keep their activities highly (cost) intransparent to strengthen OEM dependency and drive up their own profit margin. Other suppliers who are unable to do this, however, remain under heavy price and cost pressure. They are dismissing staff or even being forced to exit the market. Only highly specialized parts suppliers are also able to achieve a high profit margin (Fig. 1a shows the concentration process among automotive suppliers; Fig. 1b highlights the differentiation of their returns).

Overall, modularization has initiated a change process in the automotive sector. The industry had long considered itself the hub of progress, but actually resembled more of an intractable dinosaur during the New Economy era. Business models from the computer industry – which has already outsourced most of its production activities to module suppliers – are now also being introduced in the automotive industry (Baldwin & Clark, 1997).

Large module suppliers tend to focus on strengthening four areas of competence to improve their competitive position (Proff, 2005a).

1. *Development and production competences* to create revenue latitude by increasing their independence from OEMs (Takeishi & Takahiro, 2001): These competences form the core of supplier activities, derived from specializing in individual products and manufacturing processes. This enables them to accumulate an overproportional amount of know-how relative to OEMs.
2. *Integration competences* to create further revenue leeway by increasing (cost) intransparency: Integration competences comprise the coordination of degrees of technical maturity, as well as the deadlines and budgets of individual (development) projects (Maxton & Wormald, 2004).
3. *Platform competences* to reduce costs via economies of scale: Module platforms are based on standardization strategies of the module suppliers that are already relatively extensive (Kurek, 2004).

a) Concentration among suppliers

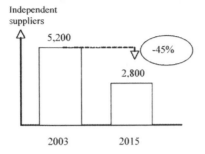

c) Falling share of OEM inhouse production

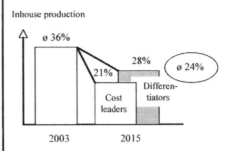

b) Differentiation of supplier returns

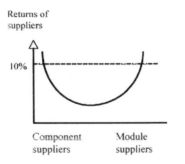

d) Declining development integration of OEMs

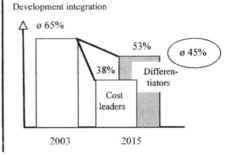

Fig. 1. Concentration, Returns, Inhouse Production and Development Integration in the Automotive Industry. *Source*: Deutsche Bank (2002), McKinsey & Company and PTW (2003), Mercer Management Consulting and Fraunhofer-Gesellschaft (2003).

4. *Change competences* by leveraging the lacking discipline and over-complexity in OEM development processes to generate further scope for increasing revenues: Change competences make it easier for module suppliers to handle late OEM changes, giving them greater latitude in follow-up negotiations (Mattes, Meffert, Landwehr, & Koers, 2004).

This means not all OEM competences are affected by modularization, only those in the fields of sourcing, logistics, production, and development. OEMs (both cost leaders and differentiators) still retain vital competences, such as in after-sales service – a key revenue source that makes a high contribution to profits – but these will not be discussed in this paper.

Forecasts on modular structure in the automotive industry back the supposition that the modularization trend will continue, with module supplier competences becoming ever stronger as a result (Kurek, 2004). Well-founded scenarios of changes in the module structure of an average car reveal the immense pressure on OEMs to take action. These scenarios indicate that in-house OEM production will fall from 36 percent in 2005 to around 24 percent in 2015, while their development integration will sink from 65 percent to 45 percent by the same year (cf. Fig. 1c and d). Falling in-house production and especially the heavy decline in OEM development integration will inevitably mean that OEMs lose capabilities, seeing them transferred to module suppliers (Dyer, 2000). Another sign of this is that OEMs are employing ever fewer engineers (Mercer Management Consulting & Fraunhofer-Gesellschaft, 2003), while suppliers are hiring them.

These development tendencies are particularly relevant to differentiators,[1] who have no choice but to demand price premiums. Price premiums are based on above-average product features, and can only be maintained long term if the company has competence advantages compared to competitors (Rao & Monroe, 1996). VW, Ford, and GM were forced to learn the hard way when they made excessive use of standard modules for their differentiating products – the Sharan, the Jaguar, and the Saab. The VW Sharan had problems from the outset differentiating itself from the similarly constructed but much cheaper vehicles Seat Alhambra and Ford Galaxy. Using the Ford Mondeo platform as the basis for a Jaguar brought Jaguar to the brink of disaster. Making use of the Opel Vectra platform for the Saab also had negative fallout for Opel. All three companies have since corrected these mistakes.

Forecasts therefore expect trends in the share of in-house production and development integration to vary depending on whether a company is a differentiator or cost leader. While only 21 percent vertical integration is expected for cost leaders in 2015, differentiators are likely to retain 28 percent (cf. Fig. 1c). Cost leaders will also increasingly surrender development to suppliers. They will only develop 38 percent themselves in 2015, while differentiators will still have a share of around 53 percent (cf. Fig. 1d).

OEMs are not at the mercy of large module suppliers despite the strident competency development of the latter. OEMs can use global sourcing to pit these suppliers against one another (Maxton & Wormald, 2004). This is particularly likely where change costs are low and investment in the supplier relationship is limited. However, the competence buildup of module suppliers does represent a strategic challenge for OEMs. Potential reactions to this challenge should therefore have a strong theoretical basis, and their impact on the automotive industry be investigated empirically.

RESEARCH STATUS

The challenge of modularization for OEMs is alteration of the company boundary. Differentiators particularly need to decide whether they should continue outsourcing to achieve short-term specialization advantages, or retain value creation within their company borders and even insource former or new competences to safeguard them in the mid term. Strategic reactions to greater modularization therefore have to take definitions of the efficient company boundary and outsourcing as their starting point. Transaction cost theory offers explanations of this kind. According to transaction cost theory, the decision whether to manufacture in-house or outsource depends – assuming imperfect contracts – on whether renegotiation is possible, and suppliers' own interests. Core competency theory also offers crucial advice. It explains the division of competences between OEMs and suppliers, and is especially relevant for end product differentiators. Both theories need to be used for a comprehensive explanation of the impact of modularization depending on the competitive strategy being pursued and possible strategic reactions (Argyres, 1996; Teece, 1996; Leiblein & Miller, 2003).

There is much controversy in academic circles on whether transaction cost theory and core competency theory are compatible (Sanchez, 2003). The two are often regarded as incompatible because the optimization of transaction costs requires an efficiency perspective, while capability development calls for a flexibility perspective. Companies are not considered capable of simultaneously maximizing efficiency and flexibility (Mette, 1999). This conflict between different options is also called incommensurability (Kieser, 1999; Scherer, 1995, 1999), and can be explained using opportunity costs. Flexibility incurs costs for activities such as maintaining quantitative and qualitative capacity reserves, or planning and supervising adjustment processes. This inevitably leads to efficiency losses. However, this kind of contradiction only arises in extreme cases: flexibility requirements need to be very high, and the corporate environment very dynamic, with frequent heavy fluctuations, such as in biotechnology or microelectronics. In most sectors – including the automotive industry – market change is not that dramatic or frequent. Within these constraints, the flexibility requirements for developing competences are not in contradiction to the efficiency requirements of low transaction costs (Proff, 2006).

This section will first describe the efficient boundary of a company and the impact of modularization according to transaction cost theory. It then goes on to incorporate core competence theory.

The Efficient Company Boundary as Postulated by Transaction Cost Theory

According to the traditional transaction cost theory of Williamson (Williamson, 1985; Riordian & Williamson, 1985), the efficient boundary of a company is influenced by transaction or governance costs, such as the costs of monitoring contracts. Williamson argues that a "representative" company can only produce intermediate products efficiently in-house if the investments in means of production exceed a critical specificity. Specificity is defined as "the fraction of its value that would be lost if it were excluded from its major use" (Milgrom & Roberts, 1992). Borrowing from Teece (1982), the specificity for investments in nonspecific nonmonetary capital, e.g., in a standard machine available on the market, is lower than for investments in specific nonmonetary capital, e.g., in a custom-made machine. It is highest for investments in human capital, i.e., in customized and especially complex company-specific know-how. The transaction cost disadvantages of coordination fall as the specificity (k) of investments in means of production rise. This especially applies to the coordination of transacting and monitoring activities at a company versus coordination in an increasingly imperfect market (ΔG). At the same time, production cost disadvantages at a company decline compared to perfect specialization advantages in the market (ΔC). Critical specificity (k^*) is achieved when internal transaction cost advantages balance out internal production cost disadvantages compared to the market (cf. Fig. 2).

An extended transaction cost perspective takes into account that high specificity of the investments when contracts are imperfect leads to a so-called "hold-up problem" in distributing the benefits of a contract. This is because this situation yields greater renegotiation opportunities and/or other dependencies (Grossman & Hart, 1986). The transaction costs of outsourcing rise as a result. In-house production tends to increase, and the company boundary is extended (insourcing). According to Teece (1996), value creation increases via the in-house production of intermediate products especially when three conditions are met: the internal costs of knowledge transfer and the central resources in the value creation process

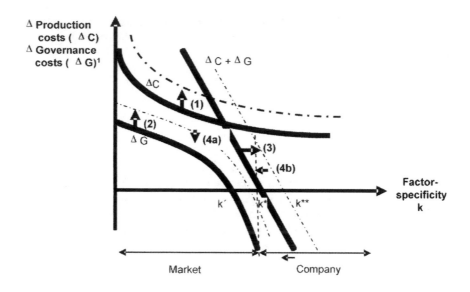

Fig. 2.   Impact of Modularization on the Efficient Company Boundary According
to Transaction Cost Theory.

are lower than they would be on the market, intellectual property is well
protected, and administration is efficient.

So what influence does modularization have on the efficient company
boundary according to transaction cost theory, and how will end product
manufacturers react (cf. Fig. 2)?

Traditional transaction cost theory explains that the breakdown of a
product into individual modules with clearly defined interfaces between
the modules creates the prerequisite for outsourcing. Standardization via
modularization eventually reduces the specificity of investments in means
of production. Suppliers with adaptable production units can leverage
specialization advantages, and offer intermediate products at lower
production costs (Milgrom & Roberts, 1990). It can be deduced from
transaction cost theory that the production cost advantage of the market
(the suppliers) increases versus that of the (end product) manufacturer due
to modularization. This is the reason why ΔC is shifting upwards in Fig. 2
(arrow (1)). In the automotive industry, a specialized seating manufacturer,
for example, can produce vehicle seats at a much lower price with lower pro
rata overheads and leaner structures than an OEM that is primarily focused

on the body, engines, and transmission. Another advantage is that the wage costs of seating module suppliers in Germany are lower because they belong to the Textile Workers' Trade Union, rather than the Metalworkers' Trade Union.

In parallel to this, the OEM's transaction and governance cost advantages versus suppliers described by Teece (1996) become less important because complexity of the administration and knowledge transfer processes declines as a result of standardization in the wake of modularization (graph ΔG shifts upwards, arrow (2) in Fig. 2). OEM administration and transfer costs, for instance, will fall if they only order complete seating groups, and no longer need coordination and agreement between the company's seating developers, engineers, and designers.

Critical factor specificity increases to $k^{**} > k^*$ (arrow (3) in Fig. 2) as a result of modularization. The OEM outsources that particular activity as a result, thus *constricting the company boundary.*

Extended transaction cost theory shows that having suppliers take on ever more complex value creation activities (Takeishi, 2002; Worran et al., 2002) accentuates the hold-up problem. Knowledge-intensive products using technologies that are hard to obtain on the global market are a case in point (Dyer, 2000). With products of this kind, suppliers who are pursuing their own interests can achieve a greater increase in their profit margin than OEMs who no longer have unlimited mastery of the production and development process, and have sacrificed competences. Late changes in the development process then become very expensive because OEMs can no longer evaluate the suppliers' changes. Neither do they have the option of integrating any further suppliers due to their own inertia in the development process. This reduces OEM returns, and increases OEM transaction costs on the market from their perspective compared with the transaction costs they would incur internally. ΔG therefore shifts downwards again (arrow (4a) in Fig. 2), which *extends the company boundaries again* (arrow (4b)). The costs of late changes are higher for differentiators than for cost leaders because the former change their products shortly before the start of production much more frequently to underline their independence (Pfaffmann, 1999).

Let us take the example of seat manufacture to examine the hold-up issue in greater detail. In the automotive industry, usually OEMs have purchasing power in the early development phase because they can use sourcing optimization to compensate for the suppliers' lower pro rata overheads, leaner structures, and less complex administration and knowledge transfer processes. However, if top management demands softer seats after a test drive, OEMs have no cost transparency – and also no further means of applying pressure. They are forced to bow to the price surcharges of the seat module suppliers. This is how large suppliers often make up (at the end) for the pressure OEMs applied at the beginning of the development process.

A comprehensive analysis of transaction costs therefore yields contradictory results on how company boundaries change with modularization (arrow (3) vs. arrow (4b) in Fig. 2).

However, relating transaction cost theory to a "representative company" is unrealistic because this assumes that all companies have the same vertical integration if they manage their business efficiently (Leiblein & Miller, 2003). This would mean that every company is affected by modularization in the same way. But there are firms that have differing efficiency levels at the same vertical integration, and others that have differing vertical integration at the same efficiency level. The core competency theory takes into account these structural differences between companies. This theory posits that specificity is due to unique competences: their distribution between suppliers and OEMs determines the optimally efficient company boundary (Hoopes, Madson, & Walker, 2003).

The Optimally Efficient Company Boundary Postulated Using Both Transaction Cost Theory and Core Competence Theory

Core competence theory bases a company's optimally efficient boundary on varying levels of or use of unique skills and competences (Prahalad & Hamel, 1990; Sanchez & Heene, 1996) or capabilities (Teece, Pisano, & Shuen, 1997). These variables lead to differing competitive advantages, vertical integration, and value creation (Teece, 1982; Hoopes et al., 2003).

Competences have to fulfill three key requirements: they should provide customer benefits, be hard for competitors to imitate, and align competitive dynamics to market dynamics (Barney, 1991; Peteraf, 1993). According to core competence theory, strategic management retains value creation within the company if it utilizes resources that provide customer benefits, are hard for competitors to imitate or substitute, and can be transferred within the company at lower costs than via the market. Core competence theory thus offers an explanation of specificity as the central factor in the transaction cost approach – something Teece (1982) merely classifies. As the competence becomes hard for competitors to imitate if *company-specific* resources evolve into practiced routines (Nelson & Winter, 1982) and become complex organizational resources (Dierickx & Cool, 1989; Barney, 1991;

Grant, 1991), core competence theory expands on traditional transaction cost theory. There have already been first attempts to combine the two approaches (Argyres, 1996). Competence considerations also amplify transaction cost theory extended by the inclusion of follow-up negotiations (the hold-up problem).

Extending Traditional Transaction Cost Theory by Core Competence Theory
The specificity of OEM products and components versus those of suppliers is due largely to company-specific routines in the development process (Sanchez & Heene, 2004). Argyres (1996), for example, shows that the efficient boundary of a company depends on the type of knowledge generated in the R&D process. His backing of this supposition is primarily competence oriented, and he distinguishes between knowledge generation from deepening competences, and from broadening them. Volberda and Baden-Fuller talk in this connection about improving competences by strengthening or upgrading existing competences, and developing new ones (Baden-Fuller & Volberda, 1997; Volberda & Baden-Fuller, 1998).[2]

Strengthening competences supposes a sequential R&D process that takes place in decentral structures, and continues to deepen a technological field. A renewal journey, in contrast, involves an R&D process that aims to unify the research approaches of differing technological fields using highly centralized structures. The results collated by central R&D have to then be quickly disseminated within the company. To do this, the company has to be very flexible and *agile* to actually leverage these competence advantages versus suppliers (Thomke & Reinertsen, 1998). Argyres supposes, referring to the transaction cost approach, that the specificity of investment in production is much higher with competence renewal stemming from centralized R&D than with the decentral improvement of competences. With the latter, the risk is that specificity decreases, the market catches up, and suppliers siphon off activities and functions from the OEMs. The company boundary shrinks as a result. Competence renewal with growing specificity, on the other hand, leads to expansion of the boundary.[3]

Modularization results in OEMs standardizing their development and production routines. This makes it easier for their competences to be imitated or substituted, and the *company boundary contracts due to outsourcing* (arrow (3) in Fig. 2). Companies that only strengthen their existing competences are affected more dramatically by contraction of their boundaries due to modularization than those pursuing reinvention of their competences. This is because standards facilitate imitation and substitution. Companies on a renewal journey change the standards by introducing new competences, and can thus counter the tendency toward narrowing company boundaries (arrow (4b) in Fig. 2).

Companies with a *differentiating competitive strategy* should therefore pursue *competence renewal*, while cost leaders need to focus on improving their competences.

Supplementing Extended Transaction Cost Theory with Core Competence Theory

The hold-up problem described in the extended transaction cost theory can also be substantiated by core competence theory. Renegotiations are harder for a company if its competences are drained off to a negotiation partner pursuing their own interests. The company has ever less to pit against the greater competences of its negotiating partner, and continues to lose negotiating power. OEMs try to limit the know-how advantage of suppliers by using supplier roadshows, where suppliers are asked to present their new ideas in advance of an request for proposal (RfP) (Clark, 2003).

The hold-up problem becomes even more prominent when transaction cost theory is extended by core competence theory. *Modularization* accentuates the hold-up issue for OEMs. Transaction costs on the market and the costs of late modifications continue to rise, which counters the greater outsourcing and contracted company boundary (arrow (4b) in Fig. 2).

According to traditional transaction theory (with and without the core competence perspective), the effect of modularization is to narrow the company boundary via outsourcing. This is counteracted by the growing market power and intransparency of module suppliers, especially when renegotiation takes place. Rising market intransparency due to module suppliers building up their competences is just as much of a challenge as the relative competence drain and loss of differentiation. (This is especially true for differentiators who often change their products shortly before production ramp-up, and who therefore incur higher change costs.) OEMs can confront both problems by embarking on a renewal journey. This is often neglected, however, due to the massive cost pressure operating in many markets. The next section therefore derives strategic reactions to modularization that trigger competency renewal.

Deriving Potential Strategic Reactions of OEMs

The starting point for renewing competences should be the core competence theory definition of how competences are developed. This states that competences are built from the (financial) resource base, if they fulfill three key requirements: they provide customer benefits, are hard for competitors to imitate or substitute, and are aligned to the company's market dynamics.

Core competence theory therefore posits that competence renewal is promoted by the following factors: First, *a good economic climate* improves the revenue situation, allowing *expansion of the resource base* (revenues fluctuate depending on the economic cycle (Jensen, 1989). Second, management *perception that competences have become inflexible*, and are providing *declining benefits for customers*, creates pressure for change. This pressure to acquire new competences arises when a unilateral improvement of existing resources results in rigid competences. If constant renewal has led to chaos, on the other hand, competences need strengthening (Huff, Huff, & Thomas, 1992; Leonard-Barton, 1992). Third, *know-how dispersion inevitably* increases (Pavitt, 1985; Langlois & Robertson, 1995) over time via publications, presentations, staff interviews, transfer of staff to suppliers, R&D cooperation (Mansfield, 1986), and contact networks (Appleyard, 1996). This makes it easier to imitate and substitute competences, which can only be countered by developing new competences. Fourth, *better alignment with market dynamics better cushions the firm from exogenous shocks, such as late changes in the development process*. Buffering a firm against shocks of this kind safeguards company profits, which can then be invested in the cost-intensive acquisition of new competences (Proff, 2005b).

Strategic reactions can be derived from these drivers of competence renewal, factoring in transaction cost theory. Differentiators (in particular) can use these strategic reactions to counteract the competence drain from growing modularization. We will now examine the corresponding research hypotheses for our empirical analysis:

1. The resource base/competences should be expanded via *investment in know-how* during periods when the economic climate is favorable. End product manufacturers often attempt to do this by insourcing competences that already exist on the market. Transaction cost theory outlines the following prerequisites for this: The new know-how can be legally protected to reduce the production cost advantages of the market and make imitation and substitution difficult. The company has good administrative processes compared to its competitors and suppliers, enabling it to process and disseminate the new know-how internally at relatively low transaction and governance costs (Teece, 1996).

These prerequisites are fulfilled if the firm insources cross-functional competences with multiple applications. In this case companies are more likely to make efforts to protect their intellectual knowledge and ensure good administrative processes than if the know-how is just for individual applications. Insourcing new competences is much more efficient than merely backsourcing technologies to fill unutilized production capacity that cannot be downsized. In the automotive industry, for example, OEMs are increasingly trying to insource capabilities in the field of automotive electronics and software – a technology opportunity they have largely missed out on. The problem is that almost 80 percent of innovations in the automotive industry are driven by the electronics and software arena, whether electrohydraulic brakes or infotainment systems. Vehicle electronics and the corresponding software are forecasted to have huge importance as a cross-divisional function to ensure comfort, communication, and safety. This field is also expected to deliver the greatest development progress and innovation. Electronic and software components will account for 35 percent of automotive value creation in 2015 (Mercer Management Consulting & Fraunhofer-Gesellschaft, 2003; McKinsey & Company & PTW, 2003). OEMs are likely to maintain their lead in overall vehicle construction, however, even compared to module suppliers. If they insourced electronics and software competences, they could therefore likely process these at relatively low costs and quickly create sound administrative processes. The first hypothesis is therefore:

Hypothesis H1. End product manufacturers react to the relative loss of competences to large module suppliers by insourcing new cross-functional capabilities to extend their resource base.

Another possibility (alongside insourcing) to prevent the loss of competences to module suppliers is to distribute competences among several parties. One dilemma is that insourcing runs the risk of over-investment. A solution may be for OEMs to request assistance from tier-2 suppliers or engineering service providers when building up their competences vis-à-vis module suppliers. This will allow them to reduce their existing competence disadvantages versus module suppliers, but at the same time to leverage the specialization advantages of the market in line with transaction cost theory. This would limit the OEM competence drain because most parts suppliers and engineering service providers do not have the integration and platform competences of module and tier-1 suppliers. This means they would only take on a restricted range of competences (Kurek, 2004).

The efficient management of an innovation-oriented supplier network is a core OEM skill in the automotive industry, as in many other sectors

(Dyer, 2000; Maxton & Wormald, 2004). OEMs need to bring together tier-2 suppliers of seating frames and upholstery and engineering service providers to create a customized seat (to take just one example), spreading the competences more broadly than if they were cooperating with one large module supplier of complete seating units. We can therefore frame two further hypotheses:

Hypothesis H2. End product manufacturers react to the relative loss of competence to large module suppliers by cooperating with tier-2 suppliers to expand their resource base.

Hypothesis H3. End product manufacturers react to the relative loss of competence to large module suppliers by cooperating with engineering service providers to expand their resource base.

2. *Action should be taken* if core rigidities become apparent. To confront this, a company has to be very open to external influences (Cohen & Levinthal, 1990), have very fast reactions (agility) internally, be flexible, and thus be capable of adaptation. Transaction cost theory specifies the prerequisites of agility as protection of *intellectual property* when renewing encrusted structures, to reduce external production cost advantages by increasing specificity, and make imitation or substitution difficult as well as good administrative (especially cross-functional) processes, compared to competitors and suppliers in order to be able to process and disseminate the new know-how internally at relatively low transaction and governance costs, and with little bureaucracy.

Only when these prerequisites are in place can a new competence developed in the company's R&D division (for instance) really be applied to the benefit of customers. OEMs have often developed technologies yet failed to use them themselves due to their rigid business systems, resulting in the loss of their competence lead over time. Examples are airbags and injection pumps developed jointly by Bosch and Daimler: today they are only produced by Bosch. This suggests a fourth hypothesis:

Hypothesis H4. End product manufacturers react to the relative competence drain to large module suppliers by strengthening the company's agility. They do this by reducing bureaucracy and developing cross-functional solutions. This enables them to swiftly utilize their competences to provide customer benefits.

3. *Knowledge diffusion should be curbed* if the know-how drain is heavy. Actions to keep the knowledge confidential are vital. Core competence theory argues that installing routines for the use of company-specific resources and developing them into complex organizational resources make imitation and substitution harder.

However, reengineering limits the extent to which this is possible. OEMs need to continuously discover new competences to maintain a know-how lead vis-à-vis suppliers, despite constant knowledge diffusion. Let us take production in the automotive industry as an example, where Toyota is considered a benchmark. Competitors would dearly love to imitate Toyota's production methods. But just cloistering off its manufacturing plants is not sufficient: Toyota is also continuously reinventing its competences, styling itself as a moving target always one step ahead of its imitators. Extended transaction cost theory also explains that the know-how edge of the market and thus the relative competence disadvantage of OEMs versus large module suppliers can be reduced if OEMs can siphon off market know-how.

This means creating situations where suppliers are forced to reveal their know-how. These may be idea competitions, specialist congresses, or "Supplier Days." Large module suppliers such as Bosch, ZF, or Mahle keep their know-how particularly close to their chest. This makes it all the more important that OEMs create supplier-to-OEM know-how diffusion. Supplier roadshows were developed in this sector for precisely this reason. They provide a platform for suppliers to present their latest innovations as a gateway for inclusion in an OEM's purchasing process. This gives OEMs an opportunity to wrestle back market power (or at least purchasing power), while also gaining a good overview of the status of technological development. Even major suppliers have no choice but to participate when invited by OEMs larger than them. The OEMs need to have specially trained staff and internal processes in place to absorb the know-how so they can implement it. This leads to the fifth hypothesis:

Hypothesis H5. OEMs react to the relative loss of competences to large module suppliers with idea competitions and supplier roadshows to make it harder for their competences to be imitated or substituted by module suppliers.

4. Exogenous shocks should be limited to achieve better alignment with market dynamics. This allows profits to be funneled into reinventing competences. Exogenous shocks from late changes are a particularly important factor for OEMs. Extended transaction cost theory indicates that reducing their incidence will restrict the opportunity of profitable

renegotiations for module suppliers, and avoid an excessive drain of know-how to module suppliers (always a risk if late changes mean agreed technology transfer levels have to be overstepped).

OEMs will see benefits from improving their change management when faced with exogenous shocks, and calculating change costs with greater precision as a basis for decision making. These adjustments will mean they can exert pressure on suppliers not just at the beginning of the development process, but also shortly before production ramp-up. This assumes, however, that they can plausibly threaten to integrate an alternative supplier into the development process at short notice. An unplanned late change in suppliers can lead to major quality problems in series ramp-up. DaimlerChrysler experienced this when it switched suppliers for its onboard electronics shortly before starting series production of the last E-Class. A further hypothesis on OEM reinvention of competences as a reaction to the loss of capabilities would therefore be:

Hypothesis H6. OEMs react to the relative loss of competences to large module suppliers by improving their change management in the event of exogenous shocks.

These six strategic reactions to the challenges of greater modularization will naturally generate costs. As a result, cost leaders will not necessarily take these steps. This highlights again how differently companies react to the wide spectrum of issues involved in greater modularization depending on their competitive strategy. Cost savings are one aspect. The loss of competences triggered by outsourcing is the other side of the coin. How strongly OEMs react will depend on whether they are a cost leader or differentiator. This yields a seventh hypothesis:

Hypothesis H7. Differentiators react more intensively to the actions of module suppliers than nondifferentiators, for fear of losing their differentiation potential.

EMPIRICAL ANALYSIS

Analysis Approach

The aim of the empirical analysis is to substantiate the relevance of our seven hypotheses. It should be seen as a plausibility test rather than as a rigorous test of the hypotheses. Content analysis is a methodology still not commonly applied in business management literature. It was used to subject the hypotheses on possible strategic reactions to a plausibility test that goes beyond individual case studies. (Conducting interviews would pose problems because the topic of these strategic reactions is so sensitive.)

We used longitudinal-cut content analysis as our empirical methodology. Content analysis is an "empirical method for the systematic, intersubjectively verifiable description of content-related and formal characteristics of communications." It was based on the research hypotheses, and systematically evaluated articles from two German specialist journals, *Automobil-Produktion* (automobile production) and *Automobil-Entwicklung* (automobile development) from 1995 to 1997 and from 2001 to 2003, on OEMs and module suppliers.

The content analysis assumed that the texts of both journals provide a reliable reflection of reality. This can be assumed in a sector like the automotive industry because it receives detailed and very differentiated media reporting. Experts consider the journals objective and independent of the interests of their advertisers. A similar analysis of the aviation industry by Chen/MacMillan (Chen & MacMillan, 1992) makes use of the specialist aviation journal *Aviation Daily* based on the same assumptions. The general business press usually does not go into the impact of modularization in sufficient detail, and was therefore not included. The journals provide equal coverage of differentiators and cost leaders. They are geared to the "automotive elite," which includes the top managers of all OEMs, and are widely distributed within the automotive industry.

The prime advantage of a content analysis versus interviews is that the evaluation is not of opinions that depend on interviewees' willingness to answer questions and their memory/ability to express themselves (Proff, 2006). The method is therefore applied in strategy research (D'Aveni & MacMillan, 1995; Chen & MacMillan, 1992; Kabanoff, Waldersee, & Cohen, 1995).

A structured content analysis was used to analyze a total of 285 commentary-style overview articles on the strategic interaction of OEMs and module suppliers (the appendix outlines the four steps of this analysis: planning, development, testing, and implementation). The characteristics gleaned from the articles were translated into data, keywords were recorded on a coding sheet, and coding units were derived from the seven hypotheses. As in many business management studies (Chen & MacMillan, 1992; D'Aveni & MacMillan, 1995; Kabanoff et al., 1995), the analysis is based on frequencies: the frequency of a mention is used as an indicator of significance.

The codings of the years 1995–1997 and 2001–2003 were summarized into one – medium frequency – to balance out slight distortions of the strategy-related statements due to the special effects of specific years (to the greatest extent possible). The significance of the changes between 1996 and 2002 were examined using a "dual-sample median value test" (Chen & MacMillan, 1992) that can analyze changes in the automotive industry. The breakdown into differentiators and nondifferentiators in the auto-motive industry was geared to the price premiums viable on the market: differentiators are able to demand much higher market prices (adjusting their models for fittings and add-ons) (Rao & Monroe, 1996; Proff, 2007). The calculation was made using the automotive prices per vehicle stated in the automotive catalog for 2003–2004, and the prices stated for the fittings.

The coding had to be made manually because it cannot be reliably standardized. It is therefore not appropriate to attempt a computer-based content analysis using a program such as "Textpack" from the Centre for Surveys, Methodologies and Analyses (ZUMA) in Mannheim (e.g., Mohler & Zuell, 1998). The coding was conducted by three coding specialists in parallel due to the leeway for interpretation. A deviation of 5 percent remained between the coding of the three specialists despite the test phase and coding test run. A final "master code" was determined for each of the 285 commentary-style overview articles after the joint review of an article.

A survey was then used to check the validity of the statements in the articles. To this end, 3 German OEMs and 10 module suppliers were interviewed in Germany in 2004. Interviewees expressed their opinions on the increasing shift in competence from OEMs to large module suppliers, and on the results of the content analysis regarding the OEMs' strategic reactions. Semistandardized questionnaires with a rating scale in seven categories from 1 (Do not agree) to 7 (Completely agree) allowed differentiated replies, as well as latitude for estimates and comments.

Results of the Analysis

The content analysis provides indications of the *strategic reactions of OEMs* to the competence drain elaborated on in sections "Challenges from Modularization Using the Example of the Automotive Industry" and "Research Analysis," and confirmed by the interviewees.[4] The results are summarized in Table 1.

The results of the analysis can be collated into five key conclusions.

Table 1. Strategic Reactions of OEMs to Growing Modularization.

Strategic Reactions of OEMs	Reactions to Module Supplier Challenges Using these Strategies 2002 (Relative Frequency of Responses, Percentage)		Tendency to More Intensive Reactions between 1996 and 2002[b] (α)	
	Differentiator OEMs[a]	Nondifferentiator OEMs	Differentiator OEMs[a]	Nondifferentiator OEMs
1. Insourcing	17	5	0.01	n.s.
2. Cooperation with tier-2 suppliers	20	10	0.01	n.s.
3. Cooperating with engineering service providers	15	8	0.01	n.s.
4. Improving the company's agility	2	5	n.s.	n.s.
5. Staging idea competitions/ supplier roadshows	7	7	n.s.	n.s.
6. Improving change management	1	3	n.s.	n.s.
7. Stronger reaction of differentiating OEMs ($\Sigma 1$–6)	62	38	0.01	n.s.

n. s., not significant.
[a]OEMs pursuing a differentiation strategy.
[b]Median values during the years 1995–1997 and 2001–2003.

First, OEMs pursing differentiation strategies and cost leaders resolve the conflict between cost savings and loss of competence from outsourcing (as a reaction to modularization) in different ways. The analysis yielded 1,320 mentions of strategic reactions; 62 percent of them related to differentiators, and 38 percent to cost leaders. The number of mentions of reactions aimed at renewal was significantly higher among differentiators than among nondifferentiators.

Second, differentiators intensified their strategic reactions to greater modularization between 1996 and 2002, while nondifferentiators reacted with less intensity. The tendency toward more intense reactions was only significant among the differentiators ($\alpha = 0.01$). A mindset shift is thus taking place at differentiators, while cost leaders are systematically continuing their pursuit of the lowest costs.

Third, differentiators are trying to strengthen their competences vis-à-vis module suppliers using investments in know-how, both via insourcing and cooperation with tier-2 suppliers and engineering service providers. They are attempting, for example, to squeeze module suppliers into a "sandwich position" that will positively impact OEM profits mid term via the spread of competences. Cost leaders take these measures much less frequently.

Fourth, differentiators primarily seek out and intensify reactions in the company's direct environment (insourcing and alliances). They tend to neglect internal process improvements, such as enhancing agility by reducing bureaucracy or developing cross-functional solutions, conducting idea competitions and "Supplier Days," or improving change management. This means that three key opportunities remain unleveraged: using competences to swiftly provide customer benefits, making sure it is hard for competitors to imitate or substitute their competences, and limiting the impact of exogenous shocks.

Fifth, OEMs following cost leadership strategies have to rely on continuous improvement processes to reduce the costs of all value creation activities. They therefore use a number of options more frequently than differentiators: internal process improvements to increase agility, idea competitions, and strengthening their change management.

The survey supports the findings of the content analysis. Differentiators are increasingly focusing on their competences and attempting to acquire them from within their company's environment. Their strategic reactions to the challenge of greater modularization aim to reduce costs in the short term, while attempting to prevent the loss of their competences to module suppliers in the mid term.

OUTLOOK

In the short term, modularization offers OEMs the opportunity to react to cost pressure on the market via outsourcing. In the long term, however, it jeopardizes OEM profitability. This is because the future distribution of profits between OEMs and suppliers depends on the division of competences, and outsourcing leads to a drain of competences to suppliers.

This paper therefore analyzed OEM reactions to modularization depending on their competitive strategy. The hypotheses were subjected to a plausibility test using the automotive industry as an example. Content analysis was the method applied – still relatively rare in strategy research. It substantiated the assertion that differentiators – in contrast to cost leaders – consider the loss of competence more important than short-term cost savings because they try much harder to renew their competences. Of the strategic reactions derived, they so far pursue only those that relate to their market, neglecting internal process improvements. This points to the huge improvement potential that needs to be tapped. Another factor driving this is the heavy capital market pressure, which generally demands higher margins from the automotive industry (Deutsche Bank, 2002).

The challenges of greater modularization for differentiators and their possible strategic reactions were highlighted and scrutinized focused on the automotive industry. The rationale was derived from a general viewpoint, however, and is thus transferable to other sectors. One example is differentiated (German) mechanical engineering companies, which are also increasingly pursuing modularization strategies to capture cost-reduction potential without jeopardizing their differentiation.

Supplementary analyses of other sectors could reveal the specificities of the automotive sector. These are driven for, example, by the industry's extreme cost pressure, or the market entity of an extensive oligopoly. These further analyses could reveal whether these factors are responsible for the unilateral efforts toward insourcing and cooperation.

Regional differences in the challenges and potential reactions could also be examined. There are signs that modularization is seen as more of a challenge in Japan and Western Europe than in the United States, and thus has a greater tendency to generate reactions (Takeishi & Takahiro, 2001).

Further research is needed on the individual strategic reactions. How far should the backsourcing of competences go? How can companies continuously reinvent their competences? How can a company catch up if it is lagging behind technologically?

The content analysis could also be supplemented by a comprehensive survey building on its results. This could also face up to any issues with the methodology, especially regarding reliability and comparability of the texts, and the limitations on statistical evaluation due to the ordinal-level data. This would also allow a sensitivity analysis. The problem would still remain that surveys evaluate views and opinions, which in turn depends on interviewees' willingness to respond, their memory, and their ability to express themselves. A more extensive content analysis could anchor this methodology more firmly in business management research.

Modularization intensifies the trend toward more economically efficient division of labor and thus to perfect competition in many industries. Companies have always tried to hold back this development because it squeezes their profits, and in extreme cases throttles them altogether.

The route they take depends – as this paper has shown – on the competitive strategy they select.

NOTES

1. Cost reductions of EUR 1,000–1,500 per vehicle are expected due to the changes in value creation and the increasing integration of production and R&D by module suppliers. These and similarly high savings from continuous productivity gains partially balance out the extra costs incurred by serial improvements to fittings and add-ons. Only a slight increase in prices is possible (merely making up for inflation).

2. They analyze competence development over time because nowadays a one-time effort to build up competences is no longer sufficient. Competences need continuous reinvention because changes in a company's internal and external environment jeopardize their competence advantages, and competences depreciate in value over time like all economic goods (McGrath et al., 1995).

3. There may be a target conflict between the creation of new know-how (competence renewal) and the use of existing know-how (competence improvement) (Argyres, 1996, p. 398) because very efficient central structures and flexible decentral structures are incompatible at a particular point in time (Mette, 1999). However, this only applies in an extremely dynamic environment, e.g., in microelectronics, and not in the largely stable automotive industry. This target conflict can also be overcome over time. According to Volberda and Baden-Fuller, competences can (cf. Schumpeter's process of creative destruction, 1942) only develop in an ongoing sequence of improvement and renewal (Baden-Fuller & Volberda, 1997; Volberda & Baden-Fuller, 1998).

4. The survey substantiates the *initial inference* of a growing shift of competences from OEMs to large module suppliers. Large module suppliers can build up competences, but are under enormous cost pressure (to almost the same extent as the other module suppliers), both from OEMs and component suppliers. They consider the cost pressure of cost leaders higher than that of differentiators, and see more of an opportunity to siphon off competences from cost leaders.

ACKNOWLEDGMENTS

I appreciate helpful comments and suggestions from participants at International Motor Vehicle Programme (IMVP) meetings at the Wharton school and the MIT (especially John Paul MacDuffie) and participants at the International Conferences of Competence-Based Management (ICCBM) and the Symposien Strategisches Kompetenz-Management (especially Ron Sanchez, Aimé Heene, and Jörg Freiling).

REFERENCES

Appleyard, M. (1996). How does knowledge flow? Interfirm patterns in the semi-conductor industry. *Strategic Management Journal, 17*(Winter Special Issue), 137–154.

Argyres, N. (1996). Capabilities, technological diversification and divisionalization. *Strategic Management Journal, 17*, 395–410.

Baden-Fuller, C., & Volberda, H. (1997). Strategic renewal in large complex organizations. A competence-based view. In: A. Heene & R. Sanchez (Eds), *Competence-based strategic management* (pp. 89–110). Chichester: Wiley.

Baldwin, B. Y., & Clark, K. B. (1997). Managing in an age of modularity. *Harvard Business Review, 75*, 84–93.

Barney, J. K. (1991). Firm resources and sustained competitive advantage. *Journal of Management, 17*, 99–120.

Chen, M. J., & MacMillan, I. (1992). Nonresponse and delayed response to competitive moves: The roles of competitor dependence and action irreversibility. *Academy of Management Journal, 35*, 539–570.

Clark, K. B. (2003). Project scope and project performance: The effect of parts strategy and supplier involvement on product development. In: M. A. Lewis & N. Slack (Eds), *Operations management: Critical perspective on business and management* (pp. 446–467). London: Routledge.

Cohen, W., & Levinthal, D. (1990). Absorptive capacity. A new perspective on learning and innovation. *Administrative Science Quarterly, 35*, 128–152.

Combs, J., & Ketchen, D. (1999). Explaining interfirm cooperation and performance: Towards a reconciliation of predictions from the resource-based view and organizational economics. *Strategic Management Journal, 20*, 867–888.

D'Aveni, R., & MacMillan, I. (1995). Crisis and the content of managerial communications. A study of the focus of attention of top managers in surviving and failing firms. *Administrative Science Quarterly, 35*, 634–657.

Deutsche Bank, (Ed.) (2002). *Global autos. The drivers how to navigate the auto industry.* Frankfurt: Deutsche Bank.

Dierickx, I., & Cool, K. (1989). A stock accumulation and sustainability of competitive advantage: Reply. *Management Science, 35*, 1514.

Dyer, J. (1996). Specialized supplier network as a source of competitive advantage: Evidence from the auto industry. *Strategic Management Journal, 17*, 271–291.

Dyer, J. (2000). *Collaborative advantage. Winning through extended enterprise supplier networks.* New York: Oxford University Press.

Ethiray, S., & Levinthal, D. (2004). Modularity and innovation in complex systems. *Management Science, 50*, 159–173.

Fixson, S. (2002a). *The multiple faces of modularity.* An analysis of a product concept for assembled hardware products. IMVP Working Paper 2002, Cambridge, MA.

Fixson, S. (2002b). *Linking modularity and cost: A methodology to assess cost implications of product architecture differences to support product design.* Ph.D. thesis, Massachusetts Institute of Technology, Cambridge, MA.

Global Insights, Inc. (Ed.) (2003). *Ragtops, race cars, and movie stars. The "nicheification" of the U.S. auto industry.* Frankfurt: Global Insights.

Grant, R. (1991). The resource-based theory of competitive advantage. Implications for strategy formulation. *California Management Review, 33*, 114–135.

Grossman, S., & Hart, O. (1986). The costs and benefits of ownership: A theory of vertical and lateral integration. *Journal of Political Economy, 94*, 601–719.

Hoopes, D., Madson, T., & Walker, G. (Eds). (2003). Guest editor's introduction to the special issue: Why is there a resource-based view? Towards a theory of competitive heterogeneity. *Strategic Management Journal, 24*, 889–902.

Huff, J. O., Huff, A. S., & Thomas, H. (1992). Strategic renewal and the interaction of cumulative stress and inertia. *Strategic Management Journal, 13*, 55–75.

Jensen, M. E. (1989). The eclipse of the public corporation. *Harvard Business Review, 67*, 61–75.

Jürgens, U. (2003). *Characteristics of the European automotive system. Is there a distinctive European approach?* Discussion paper SP III 2003-301, Wissenschaftszentrum Berlin für Sozialforschung, Berlin.

Kabanoff, B., Waldersee, R., & Cohen, M. (1995). Espoused values and organizational change themes. *Academy of Management Journal, 38*, 1075–1104.

Kieser, A. (1999). Anleitung zum kritischen Umgang mit Organisationstheorien. In: A. Kieser (Ed.), *Organisationstheorien* (3rd reedited and extended edition, pp. 1–30). Stuttgart: Kohlhammer.

Kurek, R. (2004). *Erfolgsstrategien für Automobilzulieferer.* Heidelberg: Springer.

Langlois, R. (2002). Modularity in technology and organization. *Journal of Economic Behavior and Organization, 49*, 19–37.

Langlois, R., & Robertson, P. (1995). *Firms, markets and economic change.* London: Routledge.

Leiblein, M., & Miller, D. (2003). An empirical examination of transaction- and firm-level influences on vertical boundaries of the firm. *Strategic Management Journal, 24*, 839–859.

Leonard-Barton, D. (1992). Core capabilities and core rigidities: A paradox in managing new product development. *Strategic Management Journal, 13*, 111–125.

Mansfield, E. (1986). How rapidly does new industrial knowledge leak out? *Journal of Industrial Economics, 34*, 217–223.

Mattes, B., Meffert, H., Landwehr, R., & Koers, M. (2004). Trends in der automobilindustrie: Paradigmawechsel in der Zusammenarbeit zwischen Zulieferer, Hersteller und Händler. In: B. Ebel, M. B. Hofer & J. Al-Sibei (Eds), *Automotive management. Strategie und marketing in der automobilwirtschaft* (pp. 18–38). Berlin: Springer.

Maxton, G., & Wormald, J. (2004). *Time for a model change.* Cambridge: Cambridge University Press.

McGrath, R., MacMillan, I., & Venkatraman, S. (1995). Defining and developing competence. A strategic process paradigm. *Strategic Management Journal, 16*, 251–275.

McKinsey & Company, & Institut für Kraftfahrwesen Aachen (ika), (Eds). (1999). *Profitable Wachstumsstrategien in der Automobilzulieferindustrie.* Frankfurt: VDA (Materialien zur Automobilindustrie, Nr. 20).

McKinsey & Company, & Institut für Produktionsmanagement, Technologie und Werkzeugmaschinen (PTW), (Eds). (2003). *HAWK 2015 – Wissensbasierte Veränderungen der automobilen Wertschöpfungskette.* Frankfurt: VDA (Materialien zur Automobilindustrie, Nr. 30).

Mercer Management Consulting, & Fraunhofer-Gesellschaft, (Eds). (2003). *Future automotive industry structure 2015.* Munich: Mercer.

Mette, M. (1999). *Strategisches Management im Konjunkturzyklus.* Wiesbaden: Gabler.

Mikkola, J. (2003). Modularity, component outsourcing, and inter-firm learning. *R&D Management, 33*, 439–454.

Milgrom, P., & Roberts, J. (1990). The economics of modern manufacturing. Technology, strategy, and organization. *The American Economic Review, 80*, 511–528.

Milgrom, P., & Roberts, J. (1992). *Economics, organization and management*. New York: Englewood Cliffs.

Mohler, P., & Zuell, C. (1998). *Textpack – Short description. Windows 95, NT*. Mannheim: Zentrum für Umfragen, Methoden und Analysen (ZUMA).

Nelson, R., & Winter, S. (1982). *An evolutionary theory of economic change*. Cambridge, MA: Belknap Press.

Novak, S., & Stern, S. (2003). Complementarity among vertical integration decisions. Evidence from automobile product development. Paper presented at the Wharton Technology Mini Conference, Philadelphia.

Pavitt, K. (1985). Technology transfer among the multinationally diversified advanced countries. An overview. In: N. Rosenberg & C. Frischtak (Eds), *International technology transfer* (pp. 3–5). New York: Praeger.

Peteraf, M. (1993). The cornerstones of competitive advantage. A resource-based view. *Strategic Management Journal, 14*, 179–191.

Pfaffmann, E. (1999). *Kompetenzbasiertes Management in der Produktentwicklung. Make-or-buy-Entscheidungen und Integration von Zulieferern*. Wiesbaden: Gabler.

Picot, A., Reichwald, R., & Wigand, R. (2007). *Information, organization and management: Expanding markets and corporate boundaries*. New York: Wiley.

Porter, M. E. (1980). *Competitive strategy. Techniques for analyzing industries and competitors*. New York: The Free Press.

Porter, M. E. (1985). *Corporate advantage. Creating and sustaining superior performance*. New York: The Free Press.

Prahalad, C. K., & Hamel, G. (1990). The core competence of the corporation. *Harvard Business Review, 88*, 79–91.

Proff, H. (2005a). *Challenges for modular suppliers from increasing modularization in the automotive industry*. International Motor Vehicle Program (IMVP) Working Paper, Boston.

Proff, H. (2005b). Outline of a theory of competence development. In: R. Sanchez & A. Heene (Eds), *Competence perspectives on managing internal processes*. Advances in applied business studies (Vol. 7, pp. 229–255). Oxford: Elsevier.

Proff, H. (2006). Using consistent corporate strategies to maximize value addition by the parent organization of diversified company. *International Journal of Learning and Intellectual Capital, 3*, 178–194.

Proff, H. (2007). Dynamic strategies: An attempt at a comprehensive explanation. *International Journal of Learning and Intellectual Capital, 4*, 170–189.

Rao, A., & Monroe, K. (1996). Causes and consequences of price premiums. *Journal of Business, 69*, 511–533.

Riordian, M., & Williamson, O. (1985). Asset specificity and economic organization. *International Journal of Industrial Organization, 3*, 365–378.

Robertson, D., & Ulrich, K. (1998). Planning for product platforms. *Sloan Management Review, 39*, 19–31.

Sanchez, R. (1995). Strategic flexibility in product competition. *Strategic Management Journal, 16*, 135–159.

Sanchez, R. (2003). Integrating transaction costs theory and real options theory. *Managerial and Decision Economics, 24*, 267–282.

Sanchez, R., & Heene, A. (1996). A systems view of the firm in competence-based competition. In: R. Sanchez, A. Heene & H. Thomas (Eds), *Dynamics of competence-based competition. Theory and practice of a new strategic management* (pp. 39–62). Oxford: Pergamon.

Sanchez, R., & Heene, A. (2004). *The new strategic management. Organization, competition and competence.* New York: Wiley.

Sanchez, R., & Mahoney, J. (1996). Modularity, flexibility, and knowledge management in product and organization design. *Strategic Management Journal, 17*(Winter Special Issue), 63–76.

Sanchez, R., & Mahoney, J. (2001). Modularity and dynamic capabilities. In: H. Volberda & T. Elfring (Eds), *Rethinking strategy* (pp. 158–171). London: Sage.

Scherer, A. G. (1995). *Pluralismus im strategischen Management. Der Beitrag der Teilnehmerperspektive zur Lösung von Inkommensurabilitätsproblemen in Forschung und Praxis.* Wiesbaden: Gabler.

Scherer, A. G. (1999). Kritik der Organisation oder Organisation der Kritik? Wissenschaftstheoretische Bemerkungen zum kritischen Umgang mit Organisationstheorien. In: A. Kieser (Ed.), *Organisationstheorien* (2nd reedited and extended edition, pp. 1–37). Stuttgart: Kohlhammer.

Schumpeter, J. A. (1942). *Capitalism, socialism, and democracy.* London: Allen and Unwin.

Sheffi, Y. (2006). *Worst-Case-Szenario. Wie Sie Ihr Unternehmen auf Krisen vorbe-reiten und Ausfallrisiken minimieren.* Landsberg, Lech: Moderne Industrie.

Takeishi, A. (2002). Knowledge partitioning in the interfirm division of labor. The case of automotive production development. *Organizational Science, 13*, 321–338.

Takeishi, A., & Takahiro, F. (2001). Modularization in the auto industry. Inter-linked multiple hierarchies of product, production, and supplier systems. *Tokyo International Journal of Automotive Technology and Management, 1*, 379–396.

Teece, D. (1982). Towards an economic theory of the multiproduct firm. *Journal of Economic Behavior and Organization, 3*, 39–63.

Teece, D. (1996). Firm organization, industrial structure, and technological innovation. *Journal of Economic Behavior and Organization, 31*, 193–224.

Teece, D., Pisano, G., & Shuen, A. (1997). Dynamic capabilities and strategic management. *Strategic Management Journal, 18*, 509–533.

Thomke, S., & Reinertsen, D. (1998). Agile product development: Managing development flexibility in uncertain environments. *California Management Review, 41*, 8–30.

Volberda, H., & Baden-Fuller, C. (1998). Strategic renewal and competence building: Four dynamic mechanisms. In: G. Hamel, C. K. Prahalad, H. Thomas & D. O'Neil (Eds), *Strategic flexibility. Managing in a turbulent environment* (pp. 371–389). Chichester: Wiley.

Williamson, O. (1985). *The economic institutions of capitalism. Firms, markets, relational contracting.* New York: Free Press.

Worran, N., Moore, K., & Cardona, P. (2002). Modularity, strategic flexibility, and firm performance: A study of the home appliance industry. *Strategic Management Journal, 23*, 1123–1140.

APPENDIX. PLANNING, DEVELOPMENT, TESTING, AND IMPLEMENTATION OF THE CONTENT ANALYSIS

Planning

The content analysis begins with forming the hypotheses and selecting the survey material (texts). In this case, the *hypotheses* were formulated such that the zero hypothesis can be both rejected and confirmed with equal probability. The *analysis material* was also determined in this phase. A decision was made to use overview articles from the German specialist automotive journals *Automobil-Produktion* and *Automobil-Entwicklung* from 1995 to 1997 and from 2001 to 2003.

Development

The second step begins with building a category system. This means determining subdimensions, categories, and indicators using open definition lists. Next, the registration unit and focus of the analysis are defined. *Theory-guided categories* link terms and research interest.

- Hypothesis H1 on "insourcing competences" was attributed the keyword "insourcing," as well as coding units such as "backsourcing," "acquiring competences by taking on new production tasks," "developing production competence," "taking on development competences," and "developing development competences."
- Hypothesis H2 on "cooperation with tier-2 suppliers" and H3 "cooperation with engineering service providers" were attributed coding units such as "cooperation," "division of labor," "joint development," "network activities" with component suppliers or tier-2 suppliers, engineering service providers, or "engineering service firms."
- Hypothesis H4 on "Improving the company's agility" was attributed the keyword "agility," as well as coding units such as "shorter decision paths in the development field," "faster application of know-how," "higher ability to absorb innovation," or "faster pace of development."
- Hypothesis H5 on "idea competitions and internal supplier roadshows" was attributed the keywords "idea competitions" and "supplier roadshows," as well as the coding units "Supplier Day," "innovation fairs," and "supplier fairs."

- Hypothesis H6 on "improving change managements" was attributed the keyword "better change management," as well as "accelerated reactions to change," "faster reactions to additional requests," or "faster reaction to development projects."

Keywords were selected as registration units. The reason was that (as in most business management studies (D'Aveni & MacMillan, 1995; Kabanoff et al., 1995) *frequencies* form the *focus of analysis*. The significance of a statement can be inferred from how often it is mentioned (Kabanoff et al., 1995). Deducing the significance of a strategic reaction from the frequency of the coding is, strictly speaking, only justified if all the articles were written by one or several people who is/are known for using frequency as an indicator of significance. Because this is unlikely to be the case, it could be contended that frequency reflects style rather than significance (similar to the length, i.e., the number of words or lines in a section of the text). Critics therefore usually argue that one should interpret the significance from qualifying words such as "uppermost goal" or "higher priority." However, these formulations can also be an expression of style. Insiders believe that significance can be inferred from the relative frequency of a keyword related to all the coded keywords. Frequencies replaced the nominal scale (pure classification). "The nominal categories were ordered according to the frequency of their occurrence by observing that category Y came up most frequently, for example, and category Z the most seldom (or not at all)." The results revealed an ordinal measurement scale. (Simple) statistical tests could only be conducted after this preparatory work was completed.

Testing

The preceding section covered all the empirically viable equivalents for the categories (at the level of the texts to be analyzed) that the coding specialist can add to the search. The specialist used his/her language competence to do this within the constraints of the definition. The coder's own interpretation was supposed to be "not entirely suppressed, but subordinated to the predetermined definition, and monitored in line with that."

Experience has shown that a certain contextual framework of reference for the keywords to be coded is unavoidable despite intensive attempts to achieve broad standardization. The code book with the coding instructions, category system, and coding sheet were examined in the test phase to ensure extensive comparability of the results in spite of this. The reliability was checked using test codings of 20 percent of the articles (selected at random). This provided evidence of both intracoder as well as intercoder reliability. A repetition of the coding of the same articles after four weeks with the same coding order on both occasions (also chosen at random) revealed a 95 percent correlation. Intercoder reliability was checked using the parallel coding of articles by three coding specialists. The coding specialists calculated the median value of correlated coding pairs. This demonstrated a consistency of 90 percent during the test coding.

Implementation

The actual coding is conducted in the implementation phase. The keywords are transferred to the coding sheet. A 5 percent deviation remained between the coding of the three coders despite the test phase and coding test run. A final "master code" was decided on for each company in each of the three years after joint review of an article.

RECURSIVE ADVANCEMENT OF COMPETENCE-BASED BUSINESS MANAGEMENT AND ITS CONCEPTUAL MODELING

Pekka Huovinen

ABSTRACT

An issue of managing a business (unit) as a whole successfully is perceived to belong to the fundamental issues within strategic management. This paper proposes that a business unit can be managed successfully in short and longer term in its focal contexts as a set of three recursive, competence-based, and process-based systems. Many elements of Stafford Beer's (1985) viable system model along the key competence-based theoretical bases are applied to this system design task. The outcome is an ideal, recursive template for advancing competence-based business management (CBBM) and its conceptual modeling. It is assumed that it is possible to design a business unit as a viable system that is capable of sustaining a separate existence at only three levels of hierarchy, as part of single or multi-business firms. Business-process

A Focused Issue on Identifying, Building, and Linking Competences
Research in Competence-Based Management, Volume 5, 175–202
ISSN: 1744-2117/doi:10.1108/S1744-2117(2010)0000005010

models and their redesign processes are chosen as the 2nd-order, focal system which produces a business unit's competitiveness and solves longitudinal CBBM problems. One level of recursion down includes a unit's value creating, capturing, releveraging, and respective processes that enable to solve cross-sectional problems. One level of recursion up includes a unit's existential foresights and their crafting processes that solve existential problems. Recursivity is designed inside each system in terms of three kinds of subsystems for (a) primary value releveraging, process-model redesign, and business-foresight crafting, (b) the management of varieties in releveraging, modeling, and foreseeing, and (c) the monitoring and probing of all three systems. Systemic competences are incorporated inside respective systems. Such competences possess three flexibilities of absorption, attenuation, and amplification. At each level of recursion, a competence-based process is a unit of conceptual modeling of CBBM. A business unit is defined as a set of its purposeful processes. No thing or one is left outside them. Viability is ensured by real-time interaction and the 1st-, 2nd-, and 3rd-order feedback loops between three systems. Overall, the suggested, recursive, 3-system template is intended to serve future, compatible modeling efforts among interested, pioneering firms, professional CBBM modelers, scholars, and alike. Its novelty is produced by choosing and designing the CBBM modeling as the 2nd-order system-in-focus with its two recursions, by designing and using systemic, competence-based processes as the units of conceptualization, and by choosing and drawing the figures to illustrate the 3-system template in the ways that allow also business managers comprehend and apply the suggested template in practice.

1. INTRODUCTION

Managing a single business (un)successfully is herein seen at the same time the most challenging and enduring level of strategic management within firms. Dynamism involves dynamic and static as well as global, international, and domestic businesses that firms co-create or find themselves in. Besides this author's prior contributions (e.g., Huovinen, 2005), one can find support for the primacy of business management (BM) from among the fundamental issues in strategic management (Rumelt, Schendel, & Teece, 1994), the empirical performance differentials evidence (e.g., McGahan & Porter, 2002), the launching strategy framework to pin down various positioning strategies (Mintzberg, 2005), and the recent systemic thinking about how to manage highly dynamic businesses (e.g., Doz & Kosonen, 2008).

In the same vein, *BM research* is perceived as the most important subfield within strategic management research. Business-specific effects are the most important factors explaining performance differentials among competing firms (e.g., Rumelt, 1991; McGahan & Porter, 2002). Business success and its problematic origins is one of Rumelt et al.'s (1994) fundamental issues. Indeed, Porter (1994) recalled that the issue of firm success or failure has implications for other fundamental issues such as why firms differ, how they behave, how they choose strategies, and how they are managed. He posited that to explain the success of firms, we need a theory of strategy that links environmental circumstances and firm behavior to market outcomes. Thus, the basic unit of analysis in a theory of strategy must ultimately be *a strategically distinct business*. Later, Hamel (1997) pointed out to "a dirty little secret" that the strategy industry did not have any theory of strategy creation either. It is herein posited that these white areas within strategy theorizing had not been filled in by the end of 2009. Encouragingly, many diverging flows of models, concepts, frameworks, and alike have emerged in the area of BM as follows.

Besides [business] strategy, an issue of managing a business as a whole successfully is perceived to belong to the fundamental issues within strategic management as well. Within BM research, many authors are repeatedly answering the question "What is (are) the primary way(s) of managing a firm's business that will enable managers to set challenging goals and also to attain them?" Thus, it is not surprising that *no mandate is left for (organizational) competence-based scholars* to act as the sole producer of new competence-based knowledge vis-à-vis successful BM. A pioneering review revealed that there are at least eight schools of thought on BM, i.e., (1) Porterian, (2) resource-based, (3) competence-based, (4) knowledge-based, (5) organization-based, (6) process-based, (7) dynamism-based, and (8) evolutionary BM. For this comprehensive review, the competence-based focus (competence is the primary element within a concept) was broadened to the competence-related inquiry (competence is at least one of the key elements within a concept). Overall, a population of 84 competence-related BM concepts has been published via books and articles between the years 1990 and 2002 (Huovinen, 2005, 2008b). In turn, the second review could identify 51 competence-related, international BM concepts that have been published via 20 journals between the years 1990 and 2006 (Huovinen, 2007).

The main aim of this paper is to design a novel, recursive, 3-system template for advancing the competence-based business management (CBBM) and its conceptual modeling. *The three subaims* are as follows:

- To report on the choices of the elements of Stafford Beer's (1985) viable system model (VSM) and the other competence-based theoretical bases as well as their application and correspondence to the elements of a novel, recursive, 3-system template (Section 2).
- To design the three recursive systems for addressing and capturing the fundamentals in the CBBM and its conceptual modeling in terms of managing a business unit's 1st-order value releveraging, 2nd-order business-specific model redesign, and 3rd-order foresight-crafting processes viably (Section 3).
- To make conclusions on the contribution of the recursive, 3-system template for advancing the CBBM and its conceptual modeling, the implications for practicing managers and further research as well as the deepening and testing of the suggested template (Section 4).

The outcome of this system design task is *an ideal, recursive template for advancing the CBBM and its conceptual modeling*. It is intended to serve future, compatible CBBM modeling efforts among interested, pioneering firms, professional modelers, scholars, and alike. Indeed, it is initially proposed that a business unit can be managed successfully in short and longer term in its focal contexts as a set of three recursive, competence-based, and process-based systems.

A BM model is herein recognized as a simplified representation of a real object with its properties and causal relationships, i.e., a BM team or a manager is leading its unit's operations in targeted global or (inter)national, highly dynamic, or static market contexts (aligning with Ghauri & Gronhaug, 2005, pp. 47–48). The term "model" is later used to refer broadly to models, concepts, and frameworks as the units of conceptualization of BM based on the competence perspective and the hard, non-mathematical systems thinking.

2. CHOICE OF THE THEORETICAL BASES FOR THE SYSTEM DESIGN TASK

This system designer would not have gotten very far if he had attempted to rely only on one of the eight schools of thought on BM, i.e., the competence-based school and its existing models. *The logic of any school of thought* is defined as being based on the limited range of reasoning and many framing assumptions that inform why this particular school's position to study and advance BM should be preferred, instead those of other schools. In other words, the founders of any school (or research tradition) have to make many trade-offs between the focal dimensions of BM (e.g., organizational competences) versus alternative, diverging dimensions (among the seven other schools). Inevitably, this involves the biased truth within any school's preferences vis-à-vis goals for advancing BM concepts and practices, a research agenda, primary contexts, research methods, etc. (applying Hart, 1998; Cooper, 1998).

Ex ante, a key condition was specified, i.e., to design a novel template as a synthesis of a neutral frame of reference and the theoretical competence-based bases. *The independent point of departure* for the redesign task was primarily sought from among the literature on systems thinking, design, and theory. In principle, both hard and soft systems methodologies allow the adding of "content" management dimensions. Several candidates were investigated and rejected. For this redesign task, Forrester's (1961, 1968) system dynamics is unnecessarily focused on simulation modeling (e.g., Lane & Schwaninger, 2008). Checkland's (1999) soft systems methodology (SSM) does not address the needed criteria of viability and how to take corrective action if necessary (e.g., Kinloch, Francis, Francis, & Taylor, 2008, p. 4). Espejo's (1999) recursive learning system is people focused and in part it is relying on Beer's (1985) VSM. The new St. Gallen Management Concept (Schwaninger, 2001) is unnecessarily comprehensive including normative management and its integrative systems methodology (ISM) is focused on enabling actors to communicate and to achieve requisite variety.

Instead, *Beer's (1985) VSM* is mainly relied upon for the following reasons. The VSM consists of five interacting subsystems that support a viable firm. The VSM is concerned with what defines a firm and enables it to maintain its viability. The VSM lays down a minimum set of necessary relations that must be obtained if a firm is to continue managing its dynamic business successfully. The VSM has been used for 40 years to diagnose organizational structures and communications so that the necessary and sufficient conditions for viability can be met (Leonard, 2000). Before his death, Beer (2002) emphasized that self-sustaining firms are autonomous within limits that are defined in terms of their own systemic structures and firms should be managed in real-time. Management should deal only with the information that changes their firms and act as teams building selective and immediate responses.

The recursive systems view (Beer, 1975, pp. 415–417) is herein preferred for trying to capture much of complexity of managing a global or (inter)national business unit in the short and longer term in targeted highly evolving (even chaotic) or less dynamic markets. Applying Beer (1985), it is assumed that it is possible to define a viable system, a business unit, which is capable of sustaining a separate existence *at only three levels of hierarchy*, as a single business firm or part of a multi-business corporation. At each level, there is one viable system that consists of many subsystems. The viability of the 1st-order system is enabled by the 2nd-order system and the viability of the 2nd-order system is in turn sustained by the 3rd-order system. This is a way of modeling a business unit (and a firm, an industry, an economy, and a society) like a series of "Chinese boxes." It is perceived that in particular *the following elements inherent in Beer's (1985) VSM* are necessary for this design task, i.e., (i) the independent, separate existence of a business unit, (ii) mutual interaction between a business unit and its environment or targeted markets, (iii) the development and exploitation of enabling attenuators and amplifiers, (iv) real-time management actions, (v) the coupling of organizational entities and necessary systems, (vi) embedded autonomy, and (vii) managing of complexity with requisite varieties.

In turn, *the corresponding, theoretical, competence-based bases* include a holistic view of firms as goal seeking, open systems, goals and closing of strategic gaps, higher-order and lower-order control loops, a virtuous circle of value creation and distribution, cognitive flexibility and management processes, managerial cognitions, organizational competences, five competence modes, and competence leveraging (Sanchez, Heene, & Thomas, 1996; Sanchez & Heene, 1996, 2004; Sanchez, 2004, 2008).

The key elements of the novel, 3-system template for the recursive advancement of the CBBM and its modeling as well as their correspondence to the selected elements of Beer's (1985) VSM and the theoretical competence-based and other bases are compiled in Table 1.

3. THREE RECURSIVE SYSTEMS FOR ADVANCING THE COMPETENCE-BASED BUSINESS MANAGEMENT AND ITS CONCEPTUAL MODELING

The CBBM is designed in a non-mathematical way along the recursive systems and competence-based dimensions as follows. The total CBBM problem is defined as three recursive management problems (Section 3.1).

Table 1. Elements of the Novel, Recursive 3-System Template for the CBBM and its Modeling as Well as Their Correspondence to the Selected Theoretical Bases.

Elements of a Novel, Recursive, 3-System Template	Corresponding Elements of Beer's (1985) VSM (Pages)	Corresponding Theoretical Bases in Other References
Three recursive, wicked CBBM problems and their solutions	Recursions, self-reference, and redesign (3–4, 13, 17)	Wickedness (Rittel & Webber, 1974, pp. 88–89)
Business unit as an open, viable goal-seeking system as part of a single or multi-business firm	To survive in a particular sort of environment; as part of a larger corporation (1)	Holistic view on firms as goal-seeking, open systems (Sanchez et al., 1996, p. 13)
Competence-based process as a unit of conceptual modeling	–	Five competence modes (Sanchez, 2004)
Business unit as 1st-, 2nd-, and 3rd-order, recursive systems	System-in-focus, recursions, self-reference, and connectivity (4–6)	A firm as an open system (Sanchez & Heene, 1996, p. 41)
1st-, 2nd-, and 3rd-order real-time managing of a business unit and its interaction with markets	4th principle of organization (55), infinite regression of self-images (116), Law of Cohesion (134)	Virtuous circle of value creation and distribution (Sanchez & Heene, 2004, pp. 23–24)
1st-order system of value releveraging	System 1 (19) and System 3 for inside-and-now (86)	Competence leveraging (Sanchez et al., 1996, p. 8)
2nd-order system of process-model design	System-in-focus (6), System 4 for outside-and-then (115), 2nd Axiom of Management (118)	Cognitive flexibility and management processes (Sanchez, 2008, p. 67, 71)
3rd-order system of foresight crafting	System 5 as mastermind (128), 3rd Axiom of Management (130)	Managerial cognitions (Sanchez & Heene, 1996, p. 47)
1st-, 2nd-, and 3rd-order purposes	What a system does (99)	Goals (Sanchez et al, 1996)
1st-, 2nd-, and 3rd-order viability	To maintain an existence (1) and System 3, 4, and 5 (86, 115, 128)	Managerial cognitions (Sanchez & Heene, 1996, p. 47)
1st-, 2nd-, and 3rd-order autonomy	Freedom to act (105)	Heterarchy (Hedlund, 1986)
1st-, 2nd-, and 3rd-order systemic competences	–	Organizational competences (Sanchez et al., 1996, p. 8)
1st-, 2nd-, and 3rd-order subsystems of managing varieties	Senior management, 1st Principle of Organization, requisite variety, attenuators, amplifiers (21–30, 39)	Goals and closing of strategic gaps (Sanchez et al., 1996, p. 9)

Table 1. (*Continued*)

Elements of a Novel, Recursive, 3-System Template	Corresponding Elements of Beer's (1985) VSM (Pages)	Corresponding Theoretical Bases in Other References
1st-, 2nd-, and 3rd-order subsystems of primary functions	System 1 (19), System 3 (86), and System 4 (115)	Primitive entities, including value creation (Sanchez, 2008, p. 47)
1-, 2nd-, and 3rd-order subsystems of monitoring, probing	System 2 (66), 3rd Principle of Organization, transduction (47), System 3 Star (86)	Goals and closing of strategic gaps (Sanchez et al., 1996, p. 9)
1st-, 2nd-, and 3rd-order feedback	2nd Principle of Organization, transmission channels (43–45)	Control loops (Sanchez & Heene, 2004, pp. 53–55)

The managing of a business unit is defined as the three recursive, competence-based, process-based systems with the help of the selected systemic and competence-based elements (Section 3.2). Each system with its subsystems is designed for managing a business unit viably in recursive, competence-based, and process-based ways (Sections 3.3–3.5).

3.1. Competence-Based Business Management as Three Recursive Problems

The competence-based management of a business unit is herein seen as *an open goal-seeking system*. Aligning with Rittel and Webber (1974, pp. 88–89), it is argued that CBBM and its modeling problems are inherently "*wicked.*" Information needed to understand a CBBM problem depends on one's idea for solving it. Problem understanding and resolution are concomitant notions. To find a problem is thus the same thing as finding a solution; a particular problem cannot be defined until a solution has been found. One cannot understand a CBBM (and its modeling) problem without defining its context. One cannot meaningfully search for information without the orientation of a resultant, viable model.

In other words, business unit managers are caught in the ambiguity of their causal business webs, i.e., these webs defy efforts to delineate their boundaries, to identify the causes of most business problems, and to expose their more or less wicked nature. Typically, many practicing business managers go on trying the solutions that have readily failed to work in the past, instead of attempting to pose their business problems in different and solvable ways (Beer, 1985, p. iii).

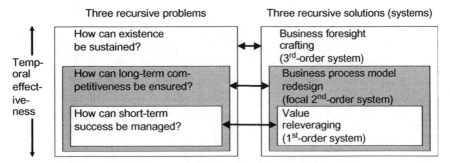

Fig. 1. Total CBBM Problem of a Business Unit Defined as Three Recursive Problems (the Left Side) Coupled Causally with Their Solutions (i.e., Recursive Systems, the Right Side).

In turn, a total CBBM problem facing business managers is herein divided into and stated as *three recursive management problems* (Fig. 1, the left side) coupled with their initial solutions (the right side) along the temporal dimension as follows:

- How can *the short-term success* of a business unit be managed? It is initially proposed that the aims attainment and the high operational performance can be based on the 1st-order system of managing a unit's value releveraging, its varieties, monitoring, and probing ("How to solve cross-sectional CBBM problems?").
- How can *the long-term competitiveness* of a business unit be ensured? It is initially proposed that the goals attainment and the superior competitiveness can be based on the 2nd-order system of managing a unit's business-process model redesign, its varieties, monitoring, and probing ("How to solve longitudinal CBBM problems?").
- How can *the existence* of a business unit be sustained? It is initially proposed that the existential goal attainment can be based on the 3rd-order system of managing a unit's business-foresight crafting, its varieties, monitoring, and probing ("How to solve existential CBBM problems?").

3.2. Competence-Based Business (Unit) Management as Three Recursive Systems

It is herein proposed that a business unit can be managed successfully in short and longer term in its focal contexts as a set of three recursive, competence-based, and process-based systems. The three embedded systems enable (a) to foresee and to produce highly advanced and highly applicable BM models that allow management teams and individual managers to reinvent their business ideas, offerings, strategies, competitive advantages, and management processes, (b) to achieve highly effective value creation, capturing, and releveraging processes, (c) to explain ex ante reasons for and ways to manage foreseeing, modeling, value releveraging, and (inter)acting with focal stakeholders (un)successfully in their contexts, and (d) to monitor, to probe, and to manage causes and path-dependencies for advantageous varieties in generic and contextual foreseeing, modeling, and releveraging between competing business entities (and stakeholders), processes, teams, and individuals. To this end, business-process models and their redesign processes are chosen as the 2nd-order, focal system which produces a business unit's competitiveness. One level of recursion down includes a unit's value creating, capturing, releveraging, and respective processes. One level of recursion up includes a unit's existential foresights and their crafting processes. Thus, the CBBM of a unit is conceptualized as three recursive systems that are named as follows:

- 1st-order system of value releveraging
- 2nd-order, focal system of business-specific process model redesign
- 3rd-order system of business-foresight crafting.

Recursivity and underlying invariances are designed inside each system as *three kinds of subsystems* for (a) primary value releveraging, process model redesign, and business foresight crafting, (b) the management of varieties in releveraging, modeling, and foreseeing, and (c) the monitoring and probing of the other subsystems and this subsystem itself (Fig. 2).

The selected elements of Beer's (1985) VSM cover the necessary aspects of recursive, viable systems as part of the system design task. Herein, each of them is applied to, re-stated, and incorporated, together with the corresponding competence-based bases, into *the seven elements of a recursive, 3-system template* of the CBBM and its modeling as follows.

(1) *Within a multi-business firm, a viable business unit* is a coherent whole that is capable of maintaining an existence independently of other business units or firms that interact (a) with clients and against each other as competitors in offering markets and (b) with suppliers on competitive and collaborative bases in resource markets. A business unit operates in its own right in an agreement with a firm's overall goals.

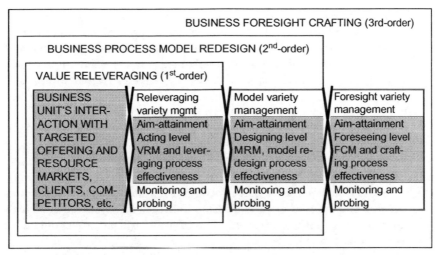

Fig. 2. CBBM Conceptualized as a Set of Three Recursive Systems Along a Temporal Dimension. *Key*: VRM refers to value releveraging management, MRM to model redesign management, and FCM to foresight crafting management.

(2) *Business unit–market interaction* takes place, i.e., a business unit and its offering and resource markets are interdependent and evolving through interactions, influences, and adjustments. A unit is influencing its two markets and vice versa. Offering markets and resource markets interact also through other units and stakeholders.

(3) *The 1st-order, 2nd-order, and 3rd-order systemic competences* are incorporated inside respective systems. Such a competence includes an ability to orientate toward and connect a business unit with its two markets. Each competence possesses three flexibilities of absorption, attenuation, and amplification. It guides and re-specifies technologies, knowledge, capabilities, and other resources (embedded in teams, individuals, management systems, and IT systems) that enable a (sub)system to think and (inter)act in pre-defined, emerging, or innovative ways that are needed for goals attainment (applying Huovinen, 2008a, p. 178).

At each level of recursion, *a competence-based process is a unit of conceptual modeling of CBBM*. A business unit is defined as a set of its purposeful processes. No thing or one is left outside them. In other words, a business unit's processes produce its external deliverables that are valued by clients and other stakeholders as well as its internal (sub)deliverables needed as inputs for internal stakeholders' (sub)processes. *Each competence-based process involves four kinds of subprocesses* as follows: (a) one management process with its internal manager(s), goals/aims, targeted, valuable deliverables, inputs, and resources, (b) internal operational subprocesses with their units/teams, subgoals/aims, valuable subdeliverables as well as related inputs and resources. In principle, any subprocess can be managed and performed fully internally or fully or in part externally as (c) partnered subprocesses with short/long-term partners, subgoals/aims, valuable subdeliverables as well as related inputs and resources, or as (d) outsourced subprocesses with their subcontracted performers, subaims, valuable subdeliverables as well as related inputs and resources (Fig. 3).

(4) *Real-time managing* takes place through a business unit's all processes that link internally the three systems and their subsystems as well as externally the business (sub)unit(s) with its (their) stakeholders in offering markets and resource markets.

(5) *Organizationally*, each subunit, subsystem, and element is coupled with a corresponding, systemic (sub)competence, inputs, and resources internally or a subunit can address any of them via subcontracting, partnerships, or networking.

(6) *Autonomy* is nurtured so that a business unit can cope effectively with market dynamism and its fluctuations. Each subunit, subsystem, and subprocess takes responsibility for co-evolving with its submarket. Each of them is empowered for goals/aims attainment. Systemic subcompetences enable them to self-reflect, to improve their states, or to renew attributes pro-/reactively according to changes. Development needs are also mapped onto each of them.

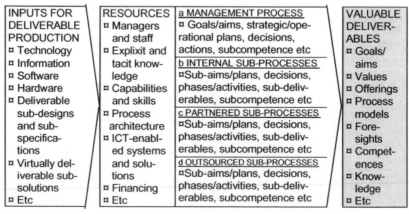

Fig. 3.   Competence-Based Process as a Unit of Conceptualization of the CBBM.

(7) *Managing of complexity* is ongoing within a dynamic, self-organizing business unit. Variety is used as a measure of complexity, because it counts a number of possible, comparable states of a system. A variety of any offering or resource market greatly exceeds that of a business unit's operational processes that serve or exploit it, which in turn greatly exceed a variety of a business unit's management processes that regulate or control them. Thus, a business unit seeks balance through *Ashby's law of requisite variety*, i.e., only variety can absorb variety. Based on the continuous loops of variety involvement, a business unit looks for assurances that the counter-balanced varieties of markets, operational processes, and management processes are roughly equal and, thus, a unit aims at doing so by designing the 1st-order variety in value releveraging, the 2nd-order variety in business-process modeling, and the 3rd-order variety in foreseeing, with a minimal damage to competitiveness (applying Beer, 1985, pp. 21–30). Each (sub)unit, subsystem, and element is competent of solving problems as close as possible to points where they occur by re-exploiting its subcompetences. Each (sub)competence enables to carry out a mix of adjustments, i.e., attenuators and amplifiers, in order to equate embedded dynamism. Roles differ in serving the attainment of key goals/aims and the achievement of valuable deliverables.

A business unit as a vertical trio of the 1st-order, 2nd-order, and 3rd-order systems represents an enabling mechanism for the adoption and mastery of recursive CBBM. It is herein argued that a competent observer must be able to impute the purpose of each of these recursive systems from its actions and, thus, from its states at any point in time. Hence, *the purpose of a viable business unit* is "what it does [successfully]," i.e., a sum of the highly valuable deliverables of all the business-specific processes that are managed inside each of three recursive systems. There is, after all, no point in claiming that the purpose of a business unit is to do what it consistently fails to do (applying Beer, 1985, p. 99).

3.3. Recursive, Competence-Based, 1st-Order System of Viable Value Releveraging to Clients by Using Business-Process Models and Managing Releveraging Variety

The purpose of the recursive, competence-based, 1st-order system is to enhance the real-time viable management of a business unit's value releveraging to clients in its contexts, i.e., varieties in value releveraging, high contextual value levels, and the effective performance levels of *value releveraging management (VRM) processes* and operational processes, in part based on the 1st-order monitoring and probing as well as inward loops with the 2nd-order and 3rd-order systems. All this enables a business unit to achieve the superior performance and to solve its cross-sectional, short-term problems. Externally, clients and other stakeholders are willing to buy or order, receive, and exploit a business unit's deliverables as well as to pay well for the leveraging of them. Internally, a unit's process owners and actors appreciate their renewed or reinvented processes that enable them to perform better.

In Fig. 4, the three subsystems of the 1st-order system of a business unit's real-time value releveraging as well as their key elements and causal interaction are illustrated in the left-side boxes and with the two broad arrows. In turn, the higher-order, inward feedback loops connecting the 1st-order system with the 2nd- and 3rd-order ones are illustrated with the three narrow arrows. The primary advantageous uses of such real-time,

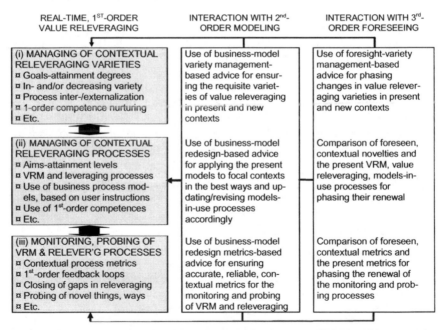

REAL-TIME, 1ST-ORDER VALUE RELEVERAGING	INTERACTION WITH 2nd-ORDER MODELING	INTERACTION WITH 3rd-ORDER FORESEEING
(i) MANAGING OF CONTEXTUAL RELEVERAGING VARIETIES ¤ Goals-attainment degrees ¤ In- and/or decreasing variety ¤ Process inter-/externalization ¤ 1-order competence nurturing ¤ Etc.	Use of business-model variety management-based advice for ensuring the requisite varieties of value releveraging in present and new contexts	Use of foresight-variety management-based advice for phasing changes in value releveraging varieties in present and new contexts
(ii) MANAGING OF CONTEXTUAL RELEVERAGING PROCESSES ¤ Aims-attainment levels ¤ VRM and leveraging processes ¤ Use of business process models, based on user instructions ¤ Use of 1st-order competences ¤ Etc.	Use of business-model redesign-based advice for applying the present models to focal contexts in the best ways and up-dating/revising models-in-use processes accordingly	Comparison of foreseen, contextual novelties and the present VRM, value releveraging, models-in-use processes for phasing their renewal
(iii) MONITORING, PROBING OF VRM & RELEVER'G PROCESSES ¤ Contextual process metrics ¤ 1st-order feedback loops ¤ Closing of gaps in releveraging ¤ Probing of novel things, ways ¤ Etc.	Use of business-model redesign metrics-based advice for ensuring accurate, reliable, contextual metrics for the monitoring and probing of VRM and releveraging	Comparison of foreseen, contextual metrics and the present metrics for phasing the renewal of the monitoring and probing processes

Fig. 4. Recursive, Competence-Based, 1st-Order System of Highly Effective Value Releveraging Including Variety Management and Interaction with the 2nd- and 3rd-Order Systems. *Key:* VRM refers to value releveraging management.

higher-order feedback are presented in the three middle boxes and the three right-side boxes.

The three 1st-order subsystems (i, ii, and iii) are designed as follows. (i) *A subsystem of contextual value releveraging varieties management* involves the setting of demanding variety-specific goals and also attaining them through the integration of the three 1st-order subsystems. Ideally, variety managers and decision makers can make use of real-time, higher-order feedback, i.e., the 2nd-order, model varieties-based advice for ensuring the viability of releveraging varieties and in-/decreasing any particular variety as well as the 3rd-order, foresight varieties-based advice for the phasing of the changes of the present releveraging varieties. In turn, proactive and pre-emptive value releveraging varieties enable a business unit and its stakeholders to excel in the actual releveraging of values to targeted clients in their contexts.

(ii) *A subsystem of contextual value releveraging management (VRM)* involves the setting of demanding aims for turnover, profitability, offerings, value levels, and the performance levels of value creation, capturing, and releveraging as well as also attaining such aims based primarily on (a) highly competent managers and process teams and (b) the effective use of the 2nd-order business-process models and self-learning through model-specific user instructions. Flexible models accommodate the realization of requisite varieties even in chaotic contexts. Ideally, VRM can make use of the 2nd-order, model design-based advice and the 3rd-order, foreseen, contextual novelties for applying the present business-process models in the best ways and updating or revising operational, models-in-use plans vis-à-vis evolving contexts.

(iii) *A subsystem of the monitoring and probing of contextual VRM and operational releveraging processes* involves the setting of aims for covering and anticipating major internal and external factors (e.g., novelties, risks, changes, complexities) that are causally impacting on each transaction, client-value level, VRM process, and operational process as well as detecting any gaps occurring between the targeted and realizing states of such acting. The attainment of these aims is primarily based on (a) highly competent releveraging performance monitoring managers and teams as well as (b) the effective use of the monitoring-process models and self-learning through model-specific user instructions. Advanced monitoring and probing process models track down requisite variety boundaries even for chaotic contexts. Ideally, monitoring and probing managers and teams can make use of the 2nd-order, model redesign-based metrics as advice and the 3rd-order, foreseen, contextual metrics as pointers for ensuring the re-use or redesign of the accurate, reliable metrics vis-à-vis VRM and operational processes on a rolling basis.

The recursive, 1st-order viability implies that a business unit can continuously reinvent, renew, cut off, or sell one, many, or all of its value releveraging processes such as marketing, selling, procurement, logistics, service, financial, administrative, legal, and expertise-based processes. On the other hand, managers as well as internal and external parties, teams, and individuals embedded within processes are also so autonomous that any of them can leave and try to continue similar operations as part of a new, existing business unit or to establish a new business unit of their own (applying Beer, 1985, p. 100). In addition, process models-in-use accommodate *a high variety of alternative ways* to make decisions and to conduct VRM process and operational processes in focal contexts.

3.4. Recursive, Competence-Based, 2nd-Order System of Viable Business-Process Models Redesign by Using Redesign Process Models and Managing Model Variety

The purpose of the recursive, competence-based, 2nd-order system is to advance the real-time management of a unit's generic and contextual, viable business-process models, i.e., varieties in modeling, highly advanced, generic and contextual models, and the effective performance levels of *model redesign management (MRM) processes* and operational processes, in part based on the 2nd-order monitoring and probing as well as inward loops with the 3rd-order and 1st-order systems. All this produces a business unit's core competitiveness and enables the unit to solve its longitudinal problems.

In Fig. 5, the three subsystems of the 2nd-order system of a business unit's real-time business-process modeling as well as their key elements and causal interaction are illustrated in the middle boxes and with the two broad arrows. In turn, the lower-order inward feedback loops connecting the 1st-order system and the higher-order loops connecting the 3rd-order system with the 2nd-order system are illustrated with the four narrow arrows. The primary advantageous uses of such real-time, higher-order feedback are presented in the three right-side boxes and those of such real-time, lower-order feedback are presented in the three left-side boxes.

The three 2nd-order subsystems (iv, v, and vi) are designed as follows. (iv) *A subsystem of generic and contextual business-process model varieties management* involves the setting of demanding variety-specific goals and also attaining them through the integration of the three 2nd-order subsystems. Ideally, variety managers and decision makers can make use of the 1st-order, releveraging variety-based feedback for ensuring the

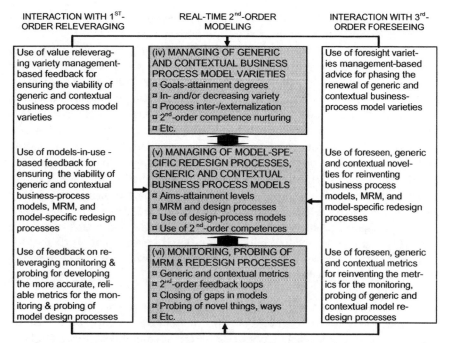

INTERACTION WITH 1ST-ORDER RELEVERAGING	REAL-TIME 2nd-ORDER MODELING	INTERACTION WITH 3rd-ORDER FORESEEING
Use of value releveraging variety management-based feedback for ensuring the viability of generic and contextual business process model varieties	**(iv) MANAGING OF GENERIC AND CONTEXTUAL BUSINESS PROCESS MODEL VARIETIES** ¤ Goals-attainment degrees ¤ In- and/or decreasing variety ¤ Process inter-/externalization ¤ 2nd-order competence nurturing ¤ Etc.	Use of foresight varieties management-based advice for phasing the renewal of generic and contextual business-process model varieties
Use of models-in-use -based feedback for ensuring the viability of generic and contextual business-process models, MRM, and model-specific redesign processes	**(v) MANAGING OF MODEL-SPE-CIFIC REDESIGN PROCESSES, GENERIC AND CONTEXTUAL BUSINESS PROCESS MODELS** ¤ Aims-attainment levels ¤ MRM and design processes ¤ Use of design-process models ¤ Use of 2nd-order competences	Use of foreseen, generic and contextual novelties for reinventing business process models, MRM, and model-specific redesign processes
Use of feedback on re-leveraging monitoring & probing for developing the more accurate, reliable metrics for the monitoring & probing of model design processes	**(vi) MONITORING, PROBING OF MRM & REDESIGN PROCESSES** ¤ Generic and contextual metrics ¤ 2nd-order feedback loops ¤ Closing of gaps in models ¤ Probing of novel things, ways ¤ Etc.	Use of foreseen, generic and contextual metrics for reinventing the metrics for the monitoring, probing of generic and contextual model re-design processes

Fig. 5. Recursive, Competence-Based, 2nd-Order System of Viable Business-Process Model Redesign Including its Variety Management and Interaction with the 3rd-Order and 1st-Order Systems. *Key*: MRM refers to model redesign management.

viability of their generic and contextual model varieties as well as the 3rd-order, foresight varieties-based advice for phasing the renewal of present model varieties. In particular, self-renewing, highly viable business-process model varieties enable business-process model designers to become leaders in respective model classes and contexts.

(v) *A subsystem of generic and contextual MRM* involves the setting of demanding aims for the levels of generic models, contextual models, and redesign process performance as well as also attaining such aims based primarily on (a) highly competent model redesign managers, CDM teams, and individual designers as well as (b) the effective reliance on model class-specific redesign process models and innovative self-learning through process model-user instructions. Flexible redesign process models accommodate the realization of requisite varieties even related to chaotic contexts. Ideally, MRM and model designers can make use of the 1st-order, value releveraging-based, model-user feedback for ensuring the viability of business-process models and the 3rd-order, foreseen, generic, and contextual novelties for reinventing any of their models on time.

(vi) *A subsystem of the monitoring and probing of generic and contextual MRM and operational redesign processes* involves the setting of aims for covering and anticipating major internal and external factors (e.g., novelties, risks, changes, complexities) that are causally impacting on the advancement level of particular models and each model design task as well as detecting any gaps occurring between the targeted and realizing states of models and processes. The attainment of such aims is primarily based on (a) highly competent modeling-performance monitoring managers and teams as well as (b) the effective use of the monitoring-process models and self-learning through model-specific user instructions. Advanced monitoring and probing process models track down requisite variety boundaries even for chaotic contexts. Ideally, monitoring and probing managers and teams can make use of the 1st-order, value releveraging-based, contextual feedback for ensuring the accuracy and reliability of the present modeling monitoring metrics and of the 3rd-order, foreseen, generic, and contextual metrics for reinventing such metrics.

The recursive, 2nd-order viability implies that a business unit can continuously reinvent, renew, cut off, or sell one, many or all of its business-process models that, by design, enable to compete successfully in relevant, targeted contexts, e.g., markets, sectors, segments, and competitive arenas. In the case of divestments, a particular business-process model and/ or its modeling organization may be sold together with the 1st-order value releveraging organization. On the other hand, managers as well as the internal and external parties, teams, and individuals embedded within modeling processes are also so autonomous that any of them can leave and try to continue their modeling work without their left-behind-models or they can negotiate on the buy-out of them. In addition, redesign process models accommodate *a high variety of alternative ways* to make decisions and to conduct model redesign work.

3.5. Recursive, Competence-Based, 3rd-Order System of Viable Business-Foresight Crafting by Using Crafting Process Models and Managing Foresight Variety

The purpose of the recursive, competence-based, 3rd-order system is to advance the real-time management of a business unit's viable business foreseeing, i.e., varieties in foreseeing, highly robust, generic and contextual foresights, and the effective performance levels of *foresight crafting management (FCM) processes* and operational processes, in part based on the 3rd-order monitoring and probing as well as inward loops with the 2nd-order and 1st-order systems. All this enables a business unit to sustain its viability and to solve its existential problems.

In Fig. 6, the three subsystems of the 3rd-order system of a business unit's real-time foreseeing as well as their key elements and causal interaction are illustrated in the right-side boxes and with the two broad arrows. In turn, the lower-order inward feedback loops connecting the 1st-and 2nd-order systems with the 3rd-order one are illustrated with the three narrow arrows. The primary advantageous uses of such real-time, lower-order feedback are presented in the three middle boxes and the three left-side boxes.

The three 3rd-order subsystems (vii, viii, and ix) are designed as follows. (vii) *A subsystem of generic and contextual business foresight varieties*

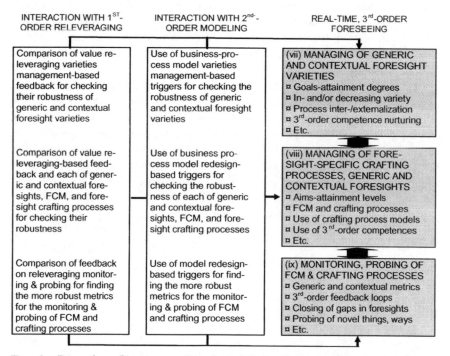

Fig. 6. Recursive, Competence-Based, 3rd-Order System of Robust Business-Foresight Crafting Including Variety Management and Interaction with the 2nd-Order and 1st-Order Systems. *Key*: FCM refers to foresight crafting management.

management involves the setting of more and more demanding variety-specific goals and also attaining them through the integration of the three 3rd-order subsystems. Ideally, variety managers and decision makers can make use of the 2nd-order, model varieties-based triggers and the 1st-order, value releveraging varieties-based feedback for checking the robustness of their generic and contextual foresight varieties. In turn, such highly robust varieties enable a business unit even to launch major advances that help sustain its existence.

(viii) *A subsystem of generic and contextual FCM* involves the setting of demanding aims for the robustness levels of a unit's generic and contextual foresights and foresight crafting performance as well as also attaining such aims based primarily on (a) highly competent foresight crafting managers, FCM teams, and individual foreseers as well as (b) the effective reliance on foresight type-specific crafting process models and innovative self-learning through foreseeing instructions. Flexible crafting process models accommodate the realization of requisite varieties even related to chaotic contexts. Ideally, FCM and foreseers can make use of the 1st-order, value releveraging-based feedback and the 2nd-order, modeling-based triggers for checking the robustness of each generic and contextual foresight and any of their crafting process models.

(ix) *A subsystem of the monitoring and probing of generic and contextual FCM and operational crafting processes* involves the setting of aims for covering and anticipating major internal and external factors (e.g., emerging driving forces and trends) that are causally impacting on each foresight and its (re)crafting process as well as detecting any gaps occurring between the targeted and realizing states of foresights and processes. The attainment of such aims is primarily based on (a) highly competent foreseeing monitoring managers and FCM teams as well as (b) the effective use of the monitoring-process models and self-learning through model-specific user instructions. Advanced monitoring and probing models track down requisite variety boundaries even for chaotic contexts. Ideally, monitoring and probing managers and teams can make use of the 1st-order, value releveraging-based, contextual feedback and the 2nd-order, model redesign-based triggers for finding a more robust metrics of foresight-specific monitoring and probing.

The recursive, 3rd-order viability implies that a business unit can continuously reinvent, renew, throw away, or sell one, many, or all of its business foresights that, by design, enable to sustain a business unit's existence through the future phases of the re-foreseen evolution of markets, globally or (inter)nationally viable business models as well as management philosophies, innovations, and processes. Dynamism involves the management of a business unit as a set of multiple competence-based subsystems and processes at the three recursive levels. On the other hand, valuable foresights are embodied inside key thinkers, their cognitive teams, and networks inside and outside a focal business unit. Such "foresight competence carriers" are also so autonomous that any of them can leave and try to implant and nourish a new set of their recursive business foresights elsewhere on the most attractive ground. In addition, crafting process models accommodate *a high variety of alternative ways* to make choices or trade-offs and to conduct foresight crafting work. However, no business manager or a team of them can rule out "fatal uncertainty," i.e., it remains to be possible that a particular business unit as a whole or its part(s) will be divested or distinguished based on internal and/or external causal developments.

4. CONCLUSIONS ON THE RECURSIVE ADVANCEMENT OF COMPETENCE-BASED BUSINESS-MANAGEMENT MODELS

Herein, the contribution and implications of the template are discussed. Thereafter, the author discloses his intent to apply some additional elements of Beer's (1985) VSM as part of the competence-based conceptualization and the explorative testing of the template in the future.

(i) *The contribution* of the suggested recursive, 3-system template to advance the conceptual modeling of CBBM is obviously based on its correspondence to the selected elements of Beer's (1985) VSM. These elements could be applied to such high degrees of correspondence that allow the determination of the necessary conditions for the viability of the CBBM and its modeling. Varieties disposed by offering markets and resource markets are always much greater than that available to business units. The template allows to amplify the variety of a 3-system business unit to deal with external varieties inherent in targeted markets and attenuate its internal varieties so as to releverage value to clients most effectively. For any applications, some sufficient, contextual conditions are to be added and specified inside the core template to cope in particular with external, 1st-, 2nd-, and 3rd-order varieties that each of recursive, 3-system business units must handle.

The novelty of the recursive template lies in its 3-system structure that enables the design of particular CBBM models comprehensively along (a) the primary dimension of releveraging value, designing models, and crafting foresights, (b) the dimension of managing complexity and balancing internal and external varieties, and (c) the dimension of monitoring and probing. Alternatively, CBBM modelers can focus on and proceed only along one of these three dimensions. Indeed, the modeling plane of CBBM (or corporate management) itself may now for the first time be preferred and designed as the 2nd-order system-in-focus.

It seems that *the prior applications* of the VSM to a sphere of managing and planning (of businesses) either address the partial aspects or areas of managing effectively (e.g., Hoverstadt, 2008) or are all-encompassing versions of the VSM safeguarding its systemic nature and its ways of illustrating the levels, parts, and functions of firms (e.g., Stephens & Haslett, 2009). In comparison with these kinds of applications, the suggested, recursive, 3-system template is designed in a novel way. In the same vein, *a thought-provoking proposition* underlying this template is that a business unit can be managed successfully in short and longer term in its focal contexts as a set of three recursive, competence-based, and process-based systems. The three embedded systems enable (a) to foresee and to produce highly advanced and highly applicable BM models that allow management teams and managers to reinvent business ideas, offerings, strategies, competitive advantages, and management processes, (b) to achieve highly effective value creation, capturing, and releveraging processes, (c) to explain ex ante reasons for and ways to manage foreseeing, model redesigning, value releveraging, and (inter)acting with focal stakeholders (un)successfully in their contexts, and (d) to monitor, to probe, and to manage causes and path-dependencies for advantageous varieties in generic and contextual foresee-ing, redesign, and releveraging between competing business entities (and other stakeholders), processes, teams, and even individuals.

In addition, the suggested hard template can be used as *a basis for soft conversations, group discussions, team-based events, and alike.* In order to maximize the learning and understanding, some interpretative systems approaches (e.g., SSM of Checkland, 1999) or the emancipatory ones (e.g., the critical systems heuristics of Ulrich, 1987) may be relied upon despite their content-based rules and restrictions. In addition, interested parties may rely on Team Syntegrity that does not provide any content-based restrictions (Mejia & Espinosa, 2007, p. 33). Beer invented Team Syntegrity process as a companion to the VSM (Leonard, 2008, p. 644).

(ii) *The major implication for managerial practice* is the guiding principle designed inside the suggested, recursive, 3-system template. Namely, *the focus on the 2nd-order CBBM modeling* coupled with the 3rd-order foreseeing guides (teams of) business managers to pay necessary attention to strategic external and internal issues that happen in the near and longer term. This preference should result in the higher effectiveness of the 1st-order value releveraging, too. Indeed, the handling of present threats should not anymore overcome an axiom-like insight to manage emerging, future issues and to pre-empt them with present, recursive means.

Admittedly, *similar partial insights* are embedded in many recent management and strategy concepts. For example, Doz and Kosonen (2008, pp. 14–21) stress the (2nd-order like) critical insight complemented with the (3rd-order) foresight and coupled with (the 1st-order) integrated value creation logics in managing strategically agile firms in fast strategy games. The fast imperative is the continuous redirection and/or reinvention of a corporation's core business without losing momentum. New businesses can be developed on their own conditions until they can be scaled up fast to have a noticeable impact at the corporate level. Hamel and Breen (2007) emphasize the (2nd-order like) management, strategy, and business innovations. [Business] strategy life cycles are shrinking and it is today possible to ramp up a new business faster than ever before. But the more rapidly a business grows, the sooner it fulfills the promise of its original business model, peaks, and enters its dotage. In turn, Kim and Mauborgne (2005) focus on the (1st-order like) realization of blue ocean strategies, i.e., (i) to create uncontested market spaces, (ii) to make competition irrelevant, (iii) to create and to capture new demand, (iv) to break value/cost trade-offs, and (v) to align whole activity systems in pursuit of differentiation and low cost.

It is herein boldly advocated that *interested business managers* start with a self-diagnosis of the viability of her, his, or their business (unit) management as a trio of (a) value releveraging processes, (b) business modeling processes, and/or (c) cognitive-foresight crafting processes. The purpose of such a diagnosis is to assess the current degrees of any enabling recursions inside the existing business unit as well as to proceed with foreseeing its future boundaries and, thereafter, with redesigning this business unit in order to succeed in evolving competition within targeted, attractive offering markets and resource markets. Unfortunately, neither generic guidelines, nor the contextual ones exist yet for the experimentation and adoption of the suggested, recursive, competence-based, and process-based BM modeling.

However, diagnosing, designing, and managing a business unit according to the suggested 3-system template – not to speak about all the principles of the VSM – is *not a guarantee* that this business unit will survive. Each business unit is threatened by deficiencies and dangers in interrelated offering markets and resource markets, but it is less likely that a unit will fail due to a lack of internal cohesion and communication (aligning with Leonard, 2008, p. 644). Typically, if a monitoring system and its feedback loops do not facilitate the arrival of the key information within the window of time in which effective value releveraging, model redesign, or foresight recrafting action is possible, emerging new variety cannot be matched (applying Leonard, 2006).

(iii) *Some implications for further research* on the CBBM and its modeling are put forth as follows. The outcome of this system design task is intended to serve as *a shared template* for future, compatible CBBM modeling efforts among interested, pioneering firms, professional modelers, scholars, and alike. In particular, researchers, developers, and practitioners belonging to *the 3rd competence-based school of thought on BM* – among the eight concerning and diverging schools – are encouraged to re-direct their research agendas along recursive, competence-based dimension and to cover a seemingly vast "white" space of the conceptual, non-mathematical modeling of the CBBM. It is assumed that a high degree of systemic recursivity is one of the necessary attributes of any model that will be proven to be highly applicable to managing a dynamic business unit in reality (Huovinen, 2008a, 2008b). Such R&D efforts can be coupled with the principles and the existing concepts of competence-based management as a whole (e.g., Sanchez, 2008).

For the time being, *the ownership of a business unit*, ownership process models, and related competences are still outside the suggested recursive, 3-system template. The same applies to *the competence-based principle of organizing* which is also left fully open for a myriad of highly flexible, both proven and emerging solutions.

In the future, more competence-based models and the hard systems methodology of Beer's (1985) VSM can be coupled. In addition, *such competence-based, systemic fusions* can be enlarged and connected to forebears in systems thinking (e.g., Ashby), contemporaries (e.g., sympathizers in systems and cybernetics), emergent ideas and theories (e.g., complexity theory), other areas of application (e.g., risk management), and other approaches contributing to BM (aligning with Adams, Beer, & Wasilevski, 2004).

(iv) *The future development of the suggested semi-Beerian template* may involve the application of some additional insights, axioms, and principles of Beer's (1985) VSM. It is admitted that the present template for advancing CBBM modeling is not conceptually complete. In other words, *some complementary, deeper explanations* are needed vis-à-vis its internal, causal, 3-system (and 9-subsystem) structure as well as internal and external connections, i.e., a business unit's interaction with its targeted offering markets and resource markets. The management of a business unit in various contexts could be further dynamized by applying such models as management of complexity (through four principles of organization), variety engineering ("in action, there is a group of variety generators, attenuators, and amplifiers in continuous production of systemic states, so organized as to absorb each other's profileration of variety"), homeostasis, and oscillation.

It seems that the redesign task of the present template resembles much the one of Hedman and Kalling's (2003) component model of a business model, i.e., Shaw (2008) considers it to be the most theoretically sophisticated (2nd-order like) model that is available because of its theoretical basis in several reference disciplines. However, this component model has no underlying theoretical basis in terms of its completeness, causal structure, external connections, and user instructions.

The 3-system template can also serve as *a shared framework for diagnoses and discussions* of what highly advanced CBBM models and practices may look like. Such joint planning would be facilitated by Beer's Team Syntegrity process (aligning with Leonard, 2008, p. 644), the SSM approach, or one of the other interpretive tools.

(v) *The first explorative, empirical inquiries* may be coupled with the contextualization and testing of the suggested, recursive, 3-system template. Answers are needed to many relevant questions such as "How to stipulate relationships among recursive causes inside a business unit with more rigor?" and "How to test empirically internal chains of causalities that explain (ex post) or enable to manage (ex ante) a business unit's success, competitiveness, and existence?" and "How to detect and to differentiate reliably to what degrees focal business units are being managed along any of the three recursive levels of conceptual CBBM modeling?" The statistical testing of the myriad recursive system elements and their complex dynamic interactions over time is difficult, to say the least (aligning with Porter, 1994, p. 430).

REFERENCES

Adams, D., Beer, H., & Wasilevski, S. (2004). The Stafford Beer connections. Available at http://www.metaphorum.org/links.htm (accessed on 28 April 2004).

Beer, S. (1975). On heaping our science together. In: C. W. Churchman (Ed.), *Systems and management annual* (pp. 469–484). New York: Petrocelli/Charter.

Beer, S. (1985). *Diagnosing the system for organizations*. Chichester: Wiley.

Beer, S. (2002). What is cybernetics. *Kybernetes, 31*(2), 209–219.

Checkland, P. (1999). *Systems thinking, systems practice. Soft systems methodology: A 30-year retrospective*. Chichester: Wiley.

Cooper, H. (1998). *Synthesizing research* (3rd ed.). Thousand Oaks, CA: Sage Publications.

Doz, Y., & Kosonen, M. (2008). *Fast strategy – How strategic agility will help you stay ahead of the game*. Harlow: Wharton School Publishing (Pearson Education).

Espejo, R. (1999). Aspects of identity, cohesion, citizenship, and performance in recursive organizations. *Kybernetes, 28*, 640–658.

Forrester, J. W. (1961). *Industrial dynamics*. Cambridge, MA: MIT Press.

Forrester, J. W. (1968). *Principles of systems*. Cambridge, MA: MIT Press.

Ghauri, P., & Gronhaug, K. (2005). *Research methods in business studies – A practical guide* (3rd ed.). Harlow: Financial Times Prentice-Hall (Pearson Education).

Hamel, G. (1997). Killer strategies that make shareholders rich. *FORTUNE*, June 23, 1997.

Hamel, G., & Breen, B. (2007). *The future of management*. Boston, MA: Harvard Business School Press.

Hart, C. (1998). *Doing a literature review*. London: Sage Publications.

Hedlund, G. (1986). The hypermodern MNC – A heterarchy? *Human Resource Management, 25*(Spring), 9–35.

Hedman, J., & Kalling, T. (2003). The business model concept: Theoretical underpinnings and empirical illustrations. *European Journal of Information Systems, 12*, 49–59.

Hoverstadt, P. (2008). *The fractal organization: Creating sustainable organizations with the Viable System Model*. Hoboken, NJ: Wiley.

Huovinen, P. (2005). (Un)successful management of a firm's dynamic business: Whereto should competence-based concepts be advanced? In: R. Sanchez & A. Heene, (Eds), *Competence perspectives on managing internal processes, Advances in applied business strategy* (Vol. 7, pp. 257–290). Oxford: Elsevier Science.

Huovinen, P. (2007). Competence-related international business management concepts and dynamism-based reinvention – Based on the review of the volumes of 42 journals published between the years 1990–2006. In: Larimo, J. (Ed.), *Proceedings of the 9th Vaasa Conference on International Business*, University of Vaasa, Vaasa, 19–21 Aug 2007.

Huovinen, P. (2008a). Moderate systemic inference in organizational learning: A "semi-Beerian" perspective. In: A. Heene, R. Martens, & R. Sanchez (Eds), *Competence perspectives on learning and dynamic capabilities, Advances in applied business strategy* (Vol. 10, pp. 173–210). Oxford: Elsevier Science.

Huovinen, P. (2008b). Platform for advancing research in competence-based business management: A population of 84 concepts published between the years 1990–2002. In: R. Sanchez (Ed.), *A focused issue on fundamental issues in competence theory development, Research in competence based management* (Vol. 4, pp. 175–218). Bingley, UK: Emerald Publishing.

Kim, W. C., & Mauborgne, R. (2005). *Blue ocean strategy*. Boston, MA: Harvard Business School Press.

Kinloch, P., Francis, H., Francis, M., & Taylor, M. (2008). Supporting crime detection and operational planning with Soft Systems Methodology and Viable System Model. *Systems Research and Behavioral Science, 26*, 3–14.

Lane, D. C., & Schwaninger, M. (2008). Theory building with system dynamics: Topic and research contributions. Guest editorial. *Systems Research and Behavioral Science, 25*, 439–445.

Leonard, A. (2000). The viable system model and knowledge management. *Kybernetes, 29*(5/6), 710–715.

Leonard, A. (2006). System Model and Team Syntegrity to explore distinctions. A paper presented at 4th Metaphorum Conference. John Moore University, Liverpool, 4–5 May 2006. Available at http://www.metaphorum.org/fourthmetafor.htm (accessed on 28 September 2009).

Leonard, A. (2008). Integrating sustainability practices using the Viable System Model. *Systems Research and Behavioral Science, 25*, 643–654.

McGahan, A. M., & Porter, M. E. (2002). What do we know about variance in accounting profitability? *Management Science, 48*(7), 834–851.

Mejia, A. D., & Espinosa, A. (2007). Team Syntegrity as a learning tool: Some considerations about its capacity to promote critical learning. *Systems Research and Behavioral Science. 24*, 27–35.

Mintzberg, H. (2005). Launching strategy. In: H. Mintzberg, B. Ahlstrand & J. Lampel (Eds), *Strategy bites back* (pp. 103–118). Harlow: Financial Times Prentice Hall (Pearson Education).

Porter, M. E. (1994). Toward a dynamic theory of strategy. In: R. P. Rumelt, D. E. Schendel, & D. J. Teece (Eds), *Fundamental issues in strategy* (pp. 423–461). Boston, MA: Harvard Business School Press.

Rittel, H. W. J., & Webber, M. M. (1974). Dilemmas in a general theory of planning. In: R. L. Ackoff (Ed.), *Systems and Management Annual 1974* (pp. 219–233). New York: Petrocelli.

Rumelt, R. P. (1991). How much does industry matter? *Strategic Management Journal, 12*, 167–185.

Rumelt, R. P., Schendel, D. E., & Teece, D. J. (1994). Fundamental issues in strategy, Introductions to parts I–IV, Afterword, and Appendix A. In: R. P. Rumelt, D. E. Schendel, & D. J. Teece (Eds), *Fundamental issues in strategy* (pp. 14–39, 49–53, 225–228, 291–296, 419–422, 527–555, 557–576). Boston, MA: Harvard Business School Press.

Sanchez, R. (2004). Understanding competence-based management: Identifying and managing five modes of competence. *Journal of Business Research, 57*, 518–532.

Sanchez, R. (2008). A scientific critique of the resource-base view (RBV) in strategy theory, with competence-based remedies for the RBV's conceptual deficiencies and logic problems. In: R. Sanchez (Ed.), *A focused issue on fundamental issues in competence theory development, Research in competence based management* (Vol. 4, pp. 3–78). Bingley, UK: Emerald Publishing.

Sanchez, R., & Heene, A. (1996). A systems view of the firm in competence-based competition. In: R. Sanchez, A. Heene & H. Thomas (Eds), *Dynamics of competence-based competition* (pp. 39–62). Oxford: Pergamon (Elsevier Science).

Sanchez, R., & Heene, A. (2004). *The new strategic management – Organization, competition, and competence.* New York: Wiley.

Sanchez, R., Heene, A., & Thomas, H. (1996). Introduction: Towards the theory and practice of competence-based competition. In: R. Sanchez, A. Heene, & H. Thomas (Eds), *Dynamics of competence-based competition* (pp. 1–35). Oxford: Pergamon (Elsevier Science).

Schwaninger, M. (2001). System theory and cybernetics. *Kybernetes, 30*, 1209–1222.

Shaw, D. R. (2008). A business model architecture: Observation problems and solutions in modelling businesses and their networks. In: J. Wilby (Ed.), *Proceedings of the 52nd*

Annual Meeting of the International Society for the Systems Sciences, ISSS 2008 (pp. 1–17). Available at http://www.isss.org (accessed on 28 September 2009).

Stephens, J., & Haslett, T. (2009). The application of Stafford Beer's viable system model to strategic planning. In: J. Wilby (Ed.), *Proceedings of the 53rd Annual Meeting of the International Society for the Systems Sciences, ISSS 2009* (pp. 1–25). Available at http://www.isss.org (accessed on 28 September 2009).

Ulrich, W. (1987). Critical heuristics of social systems design. In: R. Flood & M. Jackson (Eds), *Critical systems thinking: Directed readings* (pp. 103–115). Chichester: Wiley.

AN EXPANDED VIEW OF "MANAGEMENT PROCESSES" IN THE SYSTEMS VIEW OF ORGANIZATIONS

Adriana Priyono, Denis Tejada and Ron Sanchez

ABSTRACT

This paper draws on the conceptual and theoretical premises of the Competence-Based Management (CBM) approach to strategic management in elaborating the role of Management Processes in implementing a firm's Strategic Logic. We suggest how the CBM conception of Management Processes enables the integration of essential functional and support activities. We address these activities by characterizing Management Process as broadly concerned with marketing, strategy, *and* organization *issues, and elaborating ways in which Management Processes can and should address these issues. In this regard, the paper essentially proposes a normative model of what "Management Processes" must do to enable an organization to function as a sustainable open system for value creation and distribution.*

A Focused Issue on Identifying, Building, and Linking Competences
Research in Competence-Based Management, Volume 5, 203–227
Copyright © 2010 by Emerald Group Publishing Limited
All rights of reproduction in any form reserved
ISSN: 1744-2117/doi:10.1108/S1744-2117(2010)0000005011

1. THE COMPETENCE-BASED APPROACH

Competence-Based Management (CBM) theory represents organizations as open systems of resources and resource flows that are deployed and coordinated in processes for value creation and value distribution. In effect, organizations must be designed and managed as goal-seeking open systems (Sanchez & Heene, 1996, 2004). There are four perspectives that should be attentively considered in the CBM approach to designing and managing organizations. These four perspectives are known as the "Four Corner-stones" of competence theory: Dynamic, Systemic, Cognitive, and Holistic (Sanchez & Heene, 1996, 2004). This discussion considers the ways in which each of these cornerstone perspectives has substantial implications for the nature of effective Management Processes in organizations as open systems.

The Dynamic cornerstone refers to changes in a firm's environment that affect an organization's efforts to create and distribute value and in so doing to manage its resources, both tangible and intangible. Thus, as a market changes, an organization's Management Processes must continually monitor what is happening outside the firm (external analysis) and within the firm (internal analysis). The primary aim of this process is to maintain an organization's ability to create value by constantly improving its existing resources and capabilities and developing or accessing new resources and capabilities – what is known in CBM as "competence building and maintaining."

The Systemic cornerstone refers to the idea that an organization works as a system of interdependent elements that collectively share some goals for creating and distributing value through their interactions. These inter-dependent actors include entities in product markets, resource markets, strategic groups, and industry players. Management Processes must be designed to carry out an organization's Strategic Logic in ways that recognize and manage an organization's system properties – its systemic way of functioning and maintaining continuous flows of critical resources from resource markets and to product markets.

The next cornerstone is the Cognitive perspective. In order to identify new product or resource market opportunities, organizations' Management Processes need to include activities that evaluate external and internal environments continuously in an effort to understand the complex and dynamic environment in which an organization is competing. In order to successfully implement a current Strategic Logic, and to help identify and design future Strategic Logics, an organization's Management Processes must build, draw on, and fully use the collective intelligence of all participants. A particular challenge to strategic managers in designing

Management Processes is the need to learn how to manage their own cognitive processes (Sanchez & Heene, 1996).

The fourth cornerstone of the CBM approach is the need to adopt a Holistic perspective on Management Processes. The Holistic view demands that in order to function sustainably as an open system, a firm must be designed so that *all* its interdependent elements work together in pursuing the goals of the organization and so that value created is appropriately distributed to all participants. To be sustainable, an organization must have Management Processes that recognize and adequately serve the interests of all providers of essential resources in the organization's value-creation processes. Management Processes consistent with the holistic approach to organizing stress the reciprocal, mutually dependent relationships between an organization and its resource providers to achieve more effective collaboration among the organization's stakeholders.

1.1. Strategic Management

In the Competence-Based framework, the objective of strategic management is the creation of an organization that is competent in creating value in its product markets and distributing the value it creates to all providers of resources essential to sustaining the value-creating activities of the organization. Strategic management therefore includes the design and execution of both a Strategic Logic for competing and Management Processes to implement a Strategic Logic by gathering and deploying the resources and capabilities needed to sustain an organization's activities. The Management Processes adopted in an organization will significantly influence how an organization will be composed, structured, and coordinated in pursuing its Strategic Logic for value creation and distribution (Sanchez & Heene, 2004).

1.2. Organizational Competence

Organizational competence refers to the ability of an organization to sustain coordinated deployments of resources in ways that help the organization to achieve its goals. Creating a competent organization requires a Strategic Logic and derived Management Processes capable of sustaining simultaneous processes of building, maintaining, and leveraging organizational competences. *Competence Building* occurs when firms acquire or develop and learn how to use new and qualitatively different resources, capabilities, and ways of coordinating that expand the range of product offers it can create and realize. An organization's prior and ongoing competence building determines the scope of its current strategic options and its derived strategic flexibilities to respond to opportunities and threats in its environment (Sanchez, 1993, 1995). *Competence Leveraging* occurs when an organization brings product offers to markets in ways that do not involve qualitative changes in the resources, capabilities, or modes of coordination used by the firm. In leveraging its competences, an organization "exercises" and puts into action one or more of the strategic options created by its competence building.

A firm's Management Processes must support both its competence-building and its competence-leveraging activities. There are several basic concerns in the process of managing an organization's competence building and leveraging. The organization must manage several kinds of interactions across its boundaries with resource markets and product markets. To ensure that the organization accesses the best possible resources as inputs that sustain its value-creation processes, the value a firm creates through its product market interactions must be distributed in the right forms and amounts to all essential resource providers. In so doing, the organization's managers must determine the right "strategic balance" in allocating resource flows to competence-building and competence leveraging processes. By achieving the right strategic balance in allocating resources to its Competence Building and Competence Leveraging processes, an organization may create a sustainable "virtuous circle" of Competence Building and Leveraging, as shown in Fig. 1 below.

1.3. Model of an Organization as a Goal-Seeking Open System

The model of an organization as a goal-seeking open system summarizes the essential elements of an organization as an open system and the key interactions among them that Management Processes must coordinate in processes of competence building and leveraging. This model, presented in Fig. 2, has as its main elements an organization's Strategic Logic, Management Processes, tangible and intangible assets, operations, product markets, resource markets, and competitors in both product and resource markets.

At the core of a system design for an organization is the organization's Strategic Logic, which is defined as an organization's operative rationale for achieving its goals through coordinated deployments of resources and capabilities (Sanchez & Heene, 1996). In other words, the Strategic Logic

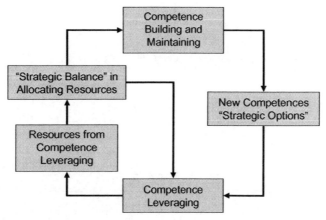

Fig. 1. Sustainable "Virtuous Circle" of Competence Building and Leveraging (From Sanchez & Heene, 1996, 2004).

represents the shared ideas of the people in the organization about the nature of the organization's goals for creating value, the resources needed to achieve those goals, the essential ways in which resources will be coordinated in creating capabilities to pursue those goals, and how the value created by the organization will be distributed to the various providers of resources to the organization. In effect, the Strategic Logic expresses the essential system elements and interactions that managers of the organization believe will enable the organization to achieve its goals for value creation and distribution.

To distinguish this conception of a firm's strategy from other interpretations of what a firm's strategy might mean, the CBM perspective uses the term *Strategic Logic* to refer to the goals that an organization sets for itself and to the activities through which the organization believes it can best achieve its goals. Moreover, the CBM approach holds that the Strategic Logic of an organization must be clearly understood and fully supported by all essential participants in the organization's value-creation processes. In order to identify clearly its targeted product market(s) and the way(s) it will create value for its targeted markets, an organization's Strategic Logic must have an adequately defined Business Concept, Organization Concept, and Core Processes, as shown in Fig. 3.

The Business Concept defines the market segments the organization will try to serve, the Product Offers it will bring to its markets, and the Key Activities it must perform in bringing its product offers to its targeted

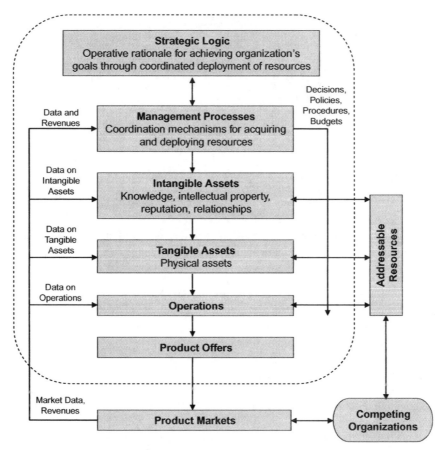

Fig. 2. Model of an Organization as a Goal-Seeking Open System (From Sanchez & Heene, 1996, 2004).

market segments. The Organization Concept defines the resources the organization will need to use to carry out its Business Concept, the organization design it will adopt for coordinating its resources, and the controls and incentives it will put in place to monitor and motivate its resources. The Core Processes define the product creation, product realization, stakeholder development, and any transformative processes the organization must undertake in carrying out its Business Concept. Once defined by strategic managers, these three essential aspects of an organization's Strategic Logic will determine the specific kinds of system

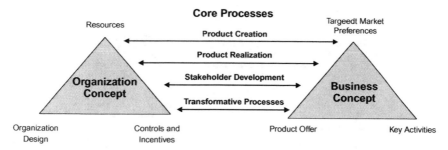

Fig. 3. Strategic Logic (From Sanchez & Heene, 2004).

elements the organization's Management Processes will undertake to put in place in its efforts to create value for its targeted market segments.

2. MANAGEMENT PROCESSES IN THE ORGANIZATION AS AN OPEN SYSTEM: MARKETING, STRATEGY, AND ORGANIZATION

According to Sanchez and Heene (2004), an organization's Management Processes include the essential processes for putting the organization's Strategic Logic into action through the creation and coordination of its other system elements (tangible and intangible resources and operations). Management Processes start with *gathering data* about an organization's product markets, its resource markets, the larger industry and macroenvironment, as well as its current resources, capabilities, and operations. The next step is the process of *interpreting data* in assessing the condition of the organization's external environment and internal system elements. The last step includes the process of *making decisions, setting policies, defining standard operating procedures* for coordinating resources, and *allocating budgets* for gathering, using, replenishing, retiring, and replacing resources (Sanchez & Heene, 2004).

Fig. 4 describes the main activities involved in sustaining these processes as an organization puts its current Strategic Logic into action and as it seeks to identify future Strategic Logics for the organization. The primary and secondary activities of Porter's value chain model (Porter, 1985) have been integrated into this open-system model to suggest how the activities described by this well-known model of value creation can be related to the open-system view of firm processes. As Fig. 4 suggests, the value chain's supporting activities are primarily related to the resources and capabilities

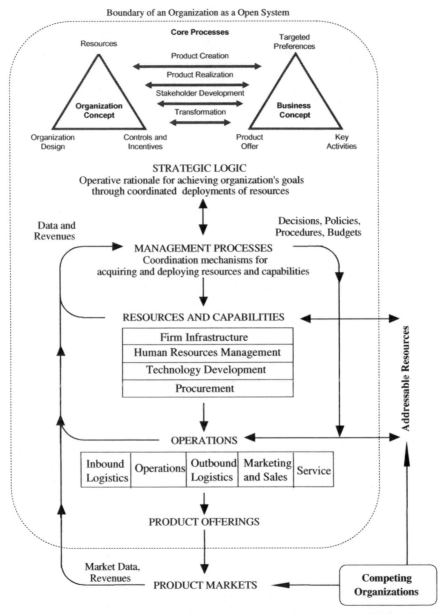

Fig. 4. Combined Open System and Value Chain Framework for Elaboration of Management Processes.

elements of an organization as a system, and the primary activities of the value chain are related to its operations system element. The model provides an elaborated representation of the essential interactions between an organization's system elements that must be initiated by Management Processes, and how the data generated from these interactions may be gathered and interpreted for making decisions, setting policies, defining standard procedures, and allocating budgets for gathering, using, replenishing, retiring, and replacing resources.

In the process of *gathering data*, an organization must gather data from all its system elements as well as from its external environment. In CBM terminology, these feedback channels are called *control loops* (Sanchez & Heene, 1996, 2004). *Lower-order control loops* gather data from the lower part of the model of an organization as an open system – i.e., from its tangible resources, operations, and product markets. The lower-order control loops typically gather and disseminate quantified operational data. By contrast, *higher-order control loops* gather data on system elements in the upper part of the model, including an organization's intangible assets (e.g., knowledge, relationships, and reputation), Management Processes, and Strategic Logic. These data typically consist of qualitative observations, although some quantifications may be possible. Management Processes must also include ways of *interpreting the data* the organization gathers.

Different areas within the Management Processes generate, gather, and interpret different kinds of data. Both data-gathering and data-interpreting activities can be considered more closely by elaborating the nature of Management Processes within three activity domains: marketing, strategy, and organization.

The *marketing* area is responsible for gathering data coming from the organization's product markets in order to identify new market opportunities, assess current marketing strategies, and discover the best way of communicating to intended customers. Marketing strategies are influenced by market forces; therefore, a firm's marketing activities should gather data on the organization's macroenvironment, its industry, and product market factors affecting the life cycle of products.

The *strategy* process of course considers product market data, but also considers data from inside the organization and from resource markets. Two kinds of internal data are involved in strategic internal analysis. First, using lower-order control loops, data are gathered from an organization's current operations and tangible resources, which Fig. 4 links to the primary activities defined by Porter's model of the value chain. Second, using higher-order control loops, data are gathered on the organization's intangible resources, Management Processes, and Strategic Logic, which include the "support activities" identified in Porter's model of the value chain that are needed to successfully perform a firm's "primary activities." Because these kinds of data are often qualitative and may rely extensively on subjective judgments, managers engaging in the strategy process must take care to *explicitly manage their own cognitive processes* (Sanchez & Heene, 1996, 2004) to avoid introducing unwarranted personal biases in identifying resources and ways of coordinating resources that can be effective in building and leveraging competences.

In processes for *interpreting data*, an organization must assess how effectively and sustainably its current Strategic Logic is creating and distributing value, as well as identify future strategic logics that could enable the organization to create and distribute value effectively in the future. In this process, managers must essentially try to identify *strategic gaps* (Sanchez & Heene, 1996) between the current states of the organization's system elements and the desired states needed to compete effectively in carrying out its Strategic Logic. The Management Processes a firm uses play a crucial role in determining how perceptions and evaluations of strategic threats and opportunities are generated within a firm, how a firm perceives strategic gaps, and how a firm decides to respond to perceived threats and opportunities by deploying and coordinating available resources and capabilities. As we discuss further below, planning scenarios that can be created through competence building can be used to develop alternative visions, to identify attractive strategic options (Sanchez, 2003), and to define possible future Strategic Logics. Planning scenarios also provide opportunities for an organization to review its prior interpretations, policies, decisions, and outcomes previously considered valid for specific situations, thereby encouraging and reinforcing strategic-level learning processes in the organization. The processes that managers use to interpret the organization's environment will of course influence the goals it adopts and the ways it seeks to achieve them, leading to new or modified Business Concepts and shaping future Strategic Logics.

The Management Processes for *making decisions, setting policies, defining operating procedures* and setting budgets largely determine the *organizational* approach that will be used to implement an organization's Strategic Logic, including how performance will be defined, monitored, and rewarded. This aspect of the strategy process, which determines which resources will be used and how they will be *coordinated and motivated*, fundamentally determines whether a given Organization Concept will be effective in carrying out a Business Concept. A key objective here is therefore to identify strategic resources and capabilities that will enable the organization to perform the

Key Activities in its Business Concept – i.e., the tasks with significant impacts on customer perceptions of the value offered by an organization's Product Offer that should therefore be considered top Management Process priorities. Management Processes must make these priorities clear and assure that these priorities are followed in utilizing its resources and capabilities in carrying out its Business Concept. The organization must also define Controls and Incentives that monitor and reward providers of key resources and capabilities to assure committed and motivated action consistent with the Business Concept. Making an organization's Business Concept clear throughout the organization helps to provide the whole organization with the information needed to effectively put all aspects of its Strategic Logic into action. *Controls* should then monitor the extent to which current Management Processes are successfully enabling the organization to leverage its current competences and build new competences needed for carrying out future Strategic Logics.

The foregoing activities within the three areas of Management Processes can be elaborated into three sets of strategically interrelated subprocesses that are typically carried out in different activity areas within a business unit, as suggested in Table 1.

3. THE MARKETING PROCESS

The main objective of the marketing process, as suggested in Fig. 5, is to identify and choose opportunities to create and realize mutually beneficial product offers for targeted customers. To do so successfully, an organization must undertake processes for identifying, evaluating, selecting, and

Table 1. Main Activities in Management Processes.

Marketing	Strategy	Organization
External market analysis	Competence assessment	Resource identification and governance
Evaluation of market attractiveness	Planning scenarios	
	Identification of possible new business concepts	Organization design
Defining product offers		Controls and incentives
Pricing policy		
Market communications		

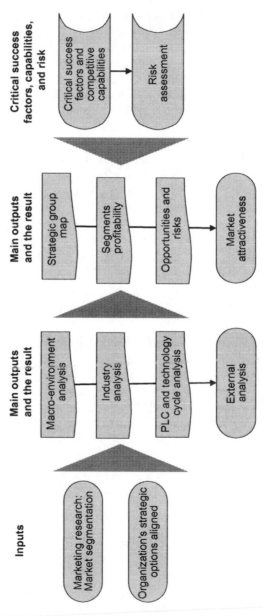

Fig. 5. Marketing Activities in Management Processes.

satisfying clearly defined and targeted customer preferences. We suggest that these processes must include external market analysis, evaluation of (relative) market attractiveness, defining (viable) product offers, setting pricing policy, and market communications.

3.1. External Market Analysis

The process for analyzing the external market environment begins with two fundamental inputs. The first input is an organization's marketing research and resulting segmentation of markets that enable the organization to understand both current and emerging needs, preferences, and resulting perceptions of value in relevant product markets. This view of an organization's potential markets must then be compared to the broad, long-term goals of the organization's stakeholders – the second key input – to identify those market opportunities that are best aligned with the kinds of value-creating activities the organization has (or can create) the competences and motivation to pursue. This comparison should lead to a "short list" of market opportunities that can then be evaluated in greater detail through three frameworks for analyzing key aspects of markets at the macroenvironment, industry, and product market levels.

A *macroenvironmental analysis* examines the environmental factors that are beyond the ability of any organization to influence directly. This analysis should include evaluations of the key drivers of change in the macro-economy, the demographic trends in markets of interest, sociocultural trends, political–legal developments (often predicted by sociocultural trends), and technology trajectories. In particular, the technology embedded in product offers may follow cyclical changes over time, including technology diffusion that can affect rewards to cumulative effort and/or technological discontinuities (Schilling, 2005). A firm's marketing processes therefore should monitor and analyze the evolution of relevant new technologies, identify current and future technologies, and determine the current technology cycle stage of its product offers in order to start building new capabilities and skills that will enable the organization to bring to market attractive product offers tailored to its targeted customers' needs and preferences.

Industry-level analysis focuses on identifying the competitive pressures from actual and potential competitors, suppliers, customers, substitute products, and new entrants (Porter, 1985). In addition, marketing processes should undertake to identify opportunities for creating mutual gain through cooperation that can transform competitive pressures into competitive advantages for the organization (Sanchez & Heene, 2004).

The product life cycle(s) for an organization's current and potential product markets should be analyzed to identify the specific challenges the organization will face in each stage of each product's life cycle. An organization must understand how its products could be developed and realized throughout their lifetimes and must identify and plan to develop capabilities and resources needed to compete effectively in current and future stages of the product life cycle (Sanchez & Heene, 2004; Sanchez, 2008).

3.2. Evaluation of Market Attractiveness

The foregoing external market analyses provide the basis for a market attractiveness evaluation, in which the first step is to identify how both current and potential competitors are allocating their resources to creating similar, updated, or new product offers. Analyzing competitors' patterns of resource allocation should suggest the "strategic balances" (Sanchez & Heene, 1996) they are seeking between their competence-building and -leveraging activities, and indicate which competitors belong to continuing, converging, or diverging competence groups (Gorman, Thomas, & Sanchez, 1996). Based on these assessments, a *strategic group map* can be developed to describe the current competences of each competitor as well as the direction of future competences they are trying to build. The market segment(s) each strategic group intends to serve in the future may be inferred from the analysis of their ongoing competence-building activities. The evaluation of the relative strengths of competitors within identified strategic groups and of each market segment's size and potential growth will suggest the potential *profitability* of each market segment and help to identify which segments the organization could profitably target.

Selection of market segments to target should be made after consideration of both long-term capabilities requirements and risks in pursuing specific market segments. Managers should identify *critical success factors* and derived competitive capabilities required to compete profitably in each market segment. A *risk assessment* must identify potential market and financial risks and also lead to consideration of contingency plans to address identified risks with the highest probability of occurrence and with the greatest impacts on the organization (both negative and positive).

3.3. Defining Product Offers

After analyzing the external environment, evaluating the attractiveness of identified market segments, and targeting the market segments in which a firm should be able to sustain profitable operations, the next step in the strategy process is defining, designing, and developing an organization's product offers (as suggested in Fig. 6). Creating product offers involves creating perceived value and managing perceived costs for customers with the kinds of market preferences the firm has decided to serve. The goal of product creation is to define and develop product offers in which perceived value and perceived costs are optimized so that Net Delivered Customer Value (NDCV) is maximized (Kotler, 2002). In the Kotler NDCV framework adopted by Sanchez and Heene (2004), perceived value may be derived from (i) a product's functions, features, and performance levels, (ii) services provided, (iii) the image value the product gives to users, and (iv) personal interactions. Perceived costs relate to (i) financial costs, (ii) time costs, (iii) energy costs, and (iv) psychic costs.

For organizations with modular design and development capabilities (Sanchez, 1995, 2004a), evaluation of alternative products may be done through real-time market research (RTMR) (Sanchez & Sudharshan, 1993) to give the organization fast feedback on customer preferences without incurring high marketing research and time costs. RTMR brings different prototypes of new products to targeted product markets to let customers decide which product versions they prefer. RTMR allows an organization to introduce real product models instead of (or in addition to) investing time and resources in traditional marketing processes for forecasting and predicting demand (Sanchez, 1999).

Feedback from a firm's interactions with targeted market segments and its marketing research processes provide an essential means for tracking market evolution and identifying emerging market preferences (Sanchez & Heene, 2004). Ongoing marketing research is thus a centerpiece of any organization's two-way communication between the firm as provider and its intended customers as users or consumers.

3.4. Pricing Policy

An organization's pricing policy fundamentally determines how much of the value offered by its products is distributed to its targeted customers and how much will be retained by the firm for distribution to its other resource

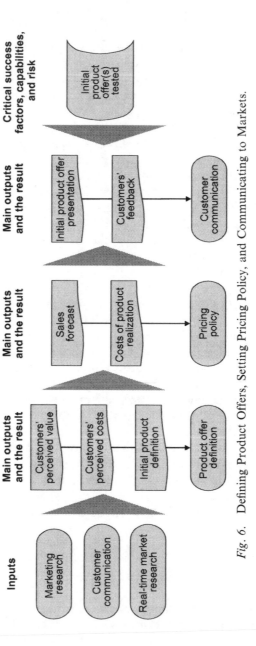

Fig. 6. Defining Product Offers, Setting Pricing Policy, and Communicating to Markets.

providers (suppliers, employees, investors, community). The process of defining a pricing policy should estimate total demand, forecast potential sales, estimate the costs of realizing (producing and delivering) the forecast quantity of products, and anticipate prices that competitors are likely to offer. Other elements to be considered in setting a pricing policy include the price elasticity of demand for the firm's product offer(s) and alternative approaches to engineering the life-cycle cost stream for the firm's customers. Once a pricing policy has been adopted, targeted customers' perceptions of NDCV should be monitored to identify opportunities to make any adjustments that may lead to greater value creation and/or more effective value distribution for both the organization and its targeted customers.

3.5. Market Communications

Finally, communications between the firm and its targeted customers should be defined and designed to effectively communicate the NDCV the firm hopes to create for its targeted customers (its overall value proposition) and to receive feedback on targeted customers' perception of the NDCV the firm is offering.

4. THE STRATEGY PROCESS

The strategy process within an organization's Management Processes has three main objectives. First, to define the strategic role of resources, capabilities, and Management Processes in creating organizational competences and competitive advantages (Sanchez, 2003). Second, to establish strategic organizational learning cycles through subprocesses like scenario planning and evaluations of market feedback. Third, on an ongoing basis to fine-tune and, when desirable, to redefine the Business Concept of the organization through targeting new market preferences, defining new product offers that will be presented to targeted market segments, and reprioritizing the key activities that must be performed in order to be effective in realizing new product offers for targeted market segments.

The strategy process for achieving these objectives involves both assessments of an organization's relative competences to establish and maintain specific kinds of value-creation activities, and the elaboration of alternative planning scenarios that may lead to the identification of viable new Business Concepts for an organization.

4.1. Competence Assessment

The assessment of an organization's competences to establish and maintain alternative competitive positions, as suggested in Fig. 7, starts with the identification of the expectations of customers in alternative targeted market segments with respect to the activities and processes required to create NDCV through the organization's product offers. Once those expectations are clarified, the next step is to identify the *resources and capabilities* whose use individually or in combination can enable the organization to deliver the required forms and levels of performance. Both firm-specific and potentially firm-addressable resources and capabilities should be identified and evaluated. However, since the mere possession of strategic resources cannot itself be a source of competences or competitive advantage, alternative organizational approaches to achieving the *effective use* of strategic resources and capabilities must also be evaluated (Sanchez, 2003.)

In order to evaluate an organization's capabilities – and to identify any deficiencies in its capabilities – required to serve various market segments, *patterns of action* that can lead to the effective use of strategic resources must also be identified and evaluated. Capabilities arise from organizational routines – the *repeatable patterns of action* in the way a firm uses its resources (Sanchez, Heene, & Thomas, 1996; Sanchez, 2003). An organization must understand the capabilities that it can currently deliver on demand, as well as the trajectory of development of future capabilities in its competence-building activities.

Organizational competences are created when an organization can deploy and coordinate its resources and capabilities in ways that enable the organization to undertake market initiatives that help a firm achieve its goals. Thus, ongoing organizational competence assessment is a critical element of the strategy process within Management Processes. This assessment should give the organization a clear understanding of the ways in which its resources and capabilities can be deployed and coordinated, what current and new market initiatives those resources and capabilities make possible, and what new coordination processes may be needed to use current resources and capabilities effectively to respond to new opportunities and threats.

The analysis of strategic resources, capabilities, and Management Processes for deploying and coordinating resources and capabilities can only lead to a real understanding of an organization's competences and potential competitive advantages when the three analyses are undertaken within a *dynamic, systemic, cognitive and holistic view* of a firm as a competence-building and -leveraging entity. Such an assessment should help

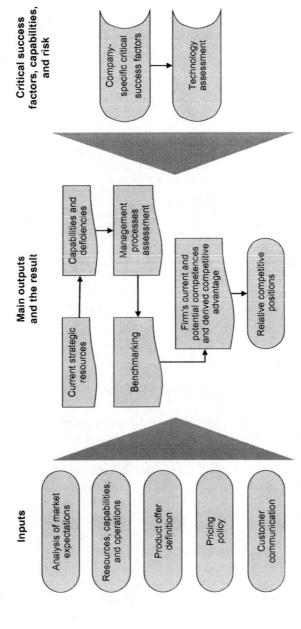

Fig. 7. Competitive Assessment Leading to Prediction of Relative Competitive Positions.

to clarify the *strategic flexibility* that an organization has to acquire, access, and redeploy strategic resources and capabilities in new uses; the speed with which an organization can acquire new resources and capabilities; and the effectiveness with which it can hope to deploy new combinations of resources and capabilities to meet new opportunities and threats (Sanchez, 1995, 2004b).

Following such analyses of current and potential competences, the next step is to consider the *strategic balance* of the organization – i.e., the relative emphasis the organization should place on leveraging existing competences versus building new competences. The current strategic balance of an organization may then be compared against the strategic balances of current and potential competitors, in order to assess more fully the potential threats from current and future competitors.

Once the organization has assessed its current and potential competences and determined its associated strategic balances, critical success factors should be identified for the various competences an organization may decide to pursue. The organization's ability to meet or exceed the critical success factors for the competences required for alternative value-creating activities should be benchmarked against those of current and likely competitors. These comparisons should clarify an organization's competitive advantages and disadvantages in alternative value-creating activities, and thus enable prediction of an organization's relative competitive positions among imagined alternatives.

4.2. Planning Scenarios

To more fully understand and interpret changes and developments in an organization's external environment, organizations may use planning scenarios to explore possible futures and to review past experiences. The scenario planning process should aim to stimulate an organization's managers to reexamine their assumptions, to "think the [normally] unthinkable" (Choo, 1998), and to bring to light the deep assumptions on which an organization's current Strategic Logic and Management Processes have been based. Of course, a planning scenario process cannot predict the future, but it can help to clarify managers' perceptions of the nature and dynamics of the forces that are shaping the environment (Choo, 1998.) In this sense, the planning scenario process can encourage an organizational learning process and help to convert tacit knowledge of individuals into explicit organizational knowledge (Sanchez, 1997, 2001). Likely scenarios can then be subjected to financial assessment, identification of potential strategic benefits and risks, and potential entry and exit strategies. Planning scenarios may thereby generate primary inputs to the strategy process by suggesting new strategic logics and supporting guidelines, policies, control systems, and resource allocations.

4.3. Identification of Possible New Business Concepts

The strategy process for defining, redefining, or continuing a Strategic Logic seeks to identify sustainable competitive positions in both product and resource markets that can result in fulfillment of stakeholder expectations. The planning scenario process can help an organization to align the mental maps of its managers in identifying and ranking the best perceived opportunities for the firm, and finally to select the Business Concept(s) the organization will pursue. The next steps are then to identify the strategic resources needed to create new product offers, the organizational capabilities that will lead to the most effective use of those strategic resources, and the individual and group skills and knowledge required to enable the required organizational capabilities. Once the strategic resources, capabilities, and individual and group skills and knowledge have been determined, the managers should compare them with the ones that the organization already has, in order to identify any *resource and capabilities gaps*.

Identified resource and capabilities gaps should then become part of the organization's critical success factors for implementing new Business Concepts by bringing new product offers to market. For these and other critical success factors, *key activities* must be determined to assure those factors are achieved. The last step of this procedure is to identify the way the organization will allocate its resources to each prioritized key activity in a manner consistent with its intended "strategic balance" in allocating the organization's resources.

The effort expended in this analysis will help to identify the strategic resources, capabilities, and Management Processes that must be put in place in order to effectively create value through new product offers. The identification of new strategic resources and capabilities, and of new ways of deploying them can enhance an organization's ability to build new competences in the long term, while creating value through effective use of the organization's current strategic resources and capabilities. This strategy process should be a vital part of an organization's strategic learning process by systematically reflecting on past experience and the new understanding it has acquired through its strategy process.

5. ORGANIZATION

After selecting its Business Concept(s), an organization must then focus on defining in detail the best Organization Concept(s) to carry out the new Business Concept(s). The Organization Concept must identify fully the new resources and capabilities needed to bring new product offers to targeted customers, an organization design that offers the best ways of coordinating both firm-specific and firm-addressable resources and capabilities, decide appropriate controls and incentives for monitoring and motivating the organization's resource providers, and elaborate ways of building required new competences from new and existing resources and capabilities.

5.1. Resource Identification and Governance

Identifying new resources and deciding the best mode of governance for those resources involves several steps. Starting with *resource and capabilities gap identification*, an organization should assess the relative advantages of using flexible resources versus specific-use resources. The relative advantages to be gained from specific-use versus flexible strategic resources and capabilities will be critical in deciding whether to internalize them (i.e., make them *firm-specific resources*) or to address them through market transactions, such as outsourcing or strategic alliances (i.e., access them as *firm-addressable resources*). For any resources and capabilities that the organization will internalize, there must be a clear and convincing rationale as to why those resources, capabilities, and resulting processes need to be internalized in order to create any intended competences and competitive advantages.

The last step of this process is to assess the Management Processes needed to effectively acquire, use, and coordinate necessary strategic resources and capabilities (Sanchez, 2004b). In some cases, this may involve a merger or acquisition (M&A) process. If so, an organization must first define clearly which resources, capabilities, and processes are being sought through M&A, and then define the processes for post M&A integration or other forms of coordination for the identified resources, capabilities, and processes.

In identifying resources and capabilities and evaluating alternative forms of governance for them, strategic managers must carefully consider the relative strengths and weaknesses of the strategic resources and capabilities that can and should be developed internally compared to those that can be accessed through outsourcing or strategic alliances. The understanding obtained from such analyses should make explicit the interactions between various resources and capabilities that must be achieved and maintained by the organization in order to create new competences and sustain any derived competitive advantages.

5.2. Organization Design

The first step in organization design is the *definition and allocation of tasks and subtasks* required to bring new product offers to targeted markets. These tasks and subtasks must be allocated and coordinated in ways that will create the capabilities and competences that the organization wants to achieve. The *hierarchy of task allocations* – especially the tasks that are given to the most senior managers – should focus firm resources on the activities that are most critical to achieving effective implementation of the Business Concept. Authority must then be distributed so that all managers allocated specific tasks have the authority necessary to acquire and allocate the resources needed to perform each allocated task. Finally, information flows must be designed to assure that the managers who have been allocated tasks will have the information needed to perform those tasks effectively.

In allocating tasks, distributing authority, and distributing information, the various processes that will implement the Business Concept(s) of the organization must be defined as to their specific goals, essential inputs, intended outputs, required resources, the sequencing of activities that must be performed, and the specific contributions of each process to creating value for targeted customers. A further process to be designed is the continuous evaluating, updating, and improving of organizational processes for maintaining the organization's competences.

5.3. Controls and Incentives

Control loops are the information flows that provide essential feedback to an organization's Management Processes. In order to make sure that key activities are being performed in the desired way, the design of control loops must include control mechanisms that enable measurement of current performance by each part of an organization. What a firm measures in monitoring its internal processes and interactions with product and resource markets will both reflect and shape its managers' priorities for developing and using resources and capabilities in implementing its Business Concept (Sanchez, 2003.)

An organization must also motivate desired behaviors through effective incentive design. Incentives must be aligned with performance measurements so that managers and employees concentrate their efforts on the critical success factors in the effective performance of the firm's key activities, leading to the kinds of interactions between strategic resources and capabilities that sustain the organization's competitive advantages.

A clear definition of what good performance means for each process in the organization, together with clear and well-aligned performance measures and appropriate incentives, should encourage the specific behaviors needed to achieve intended outcomes. The control system may include *market and output control mechanisms* that are quantitative in nature, as well as *bureaucratic and culture control mechanisms* that are more qualitative in nature.

6. CONCLUSION

In this discussion we have tried to suggest the essential steps involved in implementing the competence-based approach to strategic management, including defining viable Strategic Logics and implementing a chosen Strategic Logic through effective Management Processes. The steps outlined here of course need to be elaborated to define specific processes and techniques for monitoring, evaluating, and deciding. In the competence approach, the varying capabilities of firms in defining and implementing their Strategic Logics is an integral part of the "contest between managerial cognitions" (Sanchez et al., 1996) that largely determines competitive outcomes. In effect, the tasks we have outlined here constitute the means through which managers can contribute to their organization's strategic success.

REFERENCES

Choo, C. W. (1998). *Information management for the intelligent organization: The art of scanning the environment*. Medford, NJ: Learned Information.

Gorman, P., Thomas, H., & Sanchez, R. (1996). Industry dynamics in competence-based competition. In: R. Sanchez, A. Heene & H. Thomas (Eds), *Dynamics of competence-based competition*. Oxford: Elsevier Pergamon.

Kotler, P. (2002). *Marketing management*. Upper Saddle River, NJ: Prentice Hall.

Porter, M. (1985). *Competitive advantage*. New York: Free Press.

Sanchez, R. (1993). Strategic flexibility, firm organization, and managerial work in dynamic markets: A strategic options perspective. *Advances in Strategic Management, 9*, 251–291.

Sanchez, R. (1995). Strategic flexibility in product competition. *Strategic Management Journal,* *16*(Summer special issue), 135–159.

Sanchez, R. (1997). Managing articulated knowledge in competence-based competition. In: R. Sanchez & A. Heene (Eds), *Strategic learning and knowledge management* (pp. 163–187). Chichester: Wiley.

Sanchez, R. (1999). Modular architectures in the marketing process. *Journal of Marketing,* *63*(special issue), 92–111.

Sanchez, R. (2003). Integrating transactions costs theory and real options theory. *Managerial and Decision Economics, 24,* 267–282.

Sanchez, R. (2004a). Creating modular platforms for strategic flexibility. *Design Management Review, 15*(1), 58–67.

Sanchez, R. (2004b). Understanding competence-based management: Identifying and managing five modes of competence. *Journal of Business Research, 57*(5), 518–532.

Sanchez, R. (2008). Modularity in the mediation of market and technology change. *International Journal of Technology Management, 42*(4), 331–364.

Sanchez, R. (Ed.) (2001). *Knowledge management and organizational competence.* Oxford: Oxford University Press.

Sanchez, R., & Heene, A. (1996). A systems view of the firm in competence-based competition. In: R. Sanchez, A. Heene & H. Thomas (Eds), *Dynamics of competence-based competition* (pp. 39–62). Oxford: Elsevier Pergamon.

Sanchez, R., & Heene, A. (2004). *The new strategic management: Organization, competition, and competence (textbook).* New York: Wiley.

Sanchez, R., Heene, A., & Thomas, H. (Eds). (1996). *Dynamics of competence-based competition.* Oxford: Elsevier Pergamon.

Sanchez, R., & Sudharshan, D. (1993). Real-time market research: Learning-by-doing in the development of new products. *Marketing Intelligence and Planning, 11*(August), 29–38.

Schilling, M. (2005). A "small-world" network model of cognitive insight. *Creativity Research Journal, 17,* 131–154.

PART II
THE INTELLECTUAL STRUCTURE
OF THE COMPETENCE-BASED
PERSPECTIVE

THE INTELLECTUAL STRUCTURE OF THE *COMPETENCE-BASED MANAGEMENT* FIELD: A BIBLIOMETRIC ANALYSIS

Frédéric Prévot, Bénédicte Branchet, Jean-Pierre Boissin, Jean-Claude Castagnos and Gilles Guieu

ABSTRACT

The purpose of this paper is to carry out a bibliometric analysis of the Competence-Based Management (CBM) field. From the first books dedicated to CBM (Hamel & Heene, 1994; Sanchez, Heene, & Thomas, 1996; Heene & Sanchez, 1997) to more recent publications, the CBM field experienced a significant development. As the International Conferences on Competence-Based Management is a place for exchange and development of new ideas and applications, it appears to be central to the consolidation of the field. The conferences are followed by the publication of a series of books and a journal (Research in Competence-Based Management). Therefore it seems particularly adapted to use these publications in order to analyze the CBM field. We identified 12 books and 3 journal issues published between 1994 and 2005. This corresponds to a total of 185 papers written by 213 different authors, and a total of

A Focused Issue on Identifying, Building, and Linking Competences
Research in Competence-Based Management, Volume 5, 231–258
Copyright © 2010 by Emerald Group Publishing Limited
All rights of reproduction in any form reserved
ISSN: 1744-2117/doi:10.1108/S1744-2117(2010)0000005012

7,958 references cited in these papers. We present the results of our research in three steps. First, we analyze the profile of the authors of the papers. This leads to the identification of the most prominent authors and the identification of the authors' country of origin. Second, we analyze the content of the papers. We identify the type of the papers (theoretical or empirical), the main methodology (qualitative or quantitative), and the keywords. Third, we analyze the references. This allows the identification of the most frequently cited references, and their historical structure. In order to deepen the latter analysis, we perform a co-citation analysis to identify networks of references. The overall results lead to a better understanding of the organization of the CBM field.

INTRODUCTION

Drawing upon fundamental concepts of Resource-Based Theory (RBT) and extending the ideas proposed in the seminal article by Prahalad and Hamel (1990), the field of Competence-Based Management (CBM) has emerged as a fundamental stream of research in strategy. According to Rumelt (1994), the concept of competence developed at the beginning of the 1990s and contributed to filling a gap in Strategic Management research. Sanchez and Heene (1997) underline that the articles by Hamel and Prahalad (1989) and Prahalad and Hamel (1990, 1993) initiated the CBM approach. They place its origins at around 1992 and they identify the first attempts to build a new theory for CBM in papers presented in international workshops which appear at that time. The first books disseminating the CBM conceptual framework were published by Hamel and Heene (1994), Sanchez, Heene and Thomas (1996), and Heene and Sanchez (1997). Sanchez and Heene (1997) published a paper in their book identifying that strategy theory based on industrial organization economics and the RBV had come to an epistemological impasse. This was mainly due to the limits of ex-post theoretical explanation based on positivist theory building. In order to overcome these limits, Sanchez and Heene (1997) proposed a holistic approach. Therefore, they underlined that the main objective of the CBM approach is to reconnect strategy theory and practice by integrating dynamic, cognitive, and systemic aspects in strategy research. The CBM field is in continuous evolution. It has a strong foundation and is structured in different subfields. This structure originated from the books by Sanchez et al. (1996) and Sanchez and Heene (1997) who propose definitions and perspectives for further research. A growing number of scholars develop their research using these perspectives. After almost six years of theoretical and empirical development of the CBM, a consolidation of the conceptual basis was proposed in the book edited by Sanchez and Heene (2000). Therefore, in this paper, we propose organizing our analysis of the evolution of the most cited references in the CBM field into two periods: before and after 2000. The Competence perspective is still developing, and has been the subject of numerous publications, the topic having become a central issue (Freiling, Gersch, & Goeke, 2008) in the field. Top journals and conferences on Strategic Management have provided extensive exposure to the approach. Among these, the International Conference on Competence-Based Management has strongly supported broad dissemination of the Competence perspective. Thanks to seven conferences organized between 1992 and 2005, and a symposium in 2006, a large number of contributions have been published in a growing body of literature. Several books and a peer-reviewed journal have also been dedicated to this perspective.

As a result of these focused publications, a bibliometric analysis of works on CBM is now possible. Bibliometric analysis is a recognized and efficient tool for scanning and interpreting the structure of a research field (Callon, Law, & Rip, 1986; White & McCain, 1998; Boissin, Castagnos, & Guieu, 2001; Ramos-Rodriguez & Ruiz-Navarro, 2004; Nerur, Rasheed, & Natarajan, 2008). The purpose of the research presented in this paper is to study the structure of the field of CBM. We analyze the contributions to the field at three levels. First, we study the authors in order to identify those who are the most prominent. Second, we analyze the papers, identifying the different methodologies used and the keywords (this enables us to highlight the subfields in the general CBM field). Third, we analyze the references cited by the authors in their papers. This third level of analysis leads to the identification of the most influential references in the CBM field. This references study is then completed by an identification of the networks of references (references cited together) and an analysis of the evolution of these networks over time. The results of this study will lead to a better understanding of the stakes and forces at work in the field, and will help build future avenues for research in CBM.

We propose an analysis of the contents, authors, and references of papers gathered in the "Competence Perspectives Series" and the journal "Research in Competence-Based Management." Thus, the contents of the database are papers extracted from 12 books published between 1994 and 2005 stemming from the International Conference on Competence-Based Management and from the three issues of "Research in Competence Based

Management" (see appendix). This corresponds to a sum of 185 papers written by 213 different authors. In the reference lists of these 185 papers, we extracted 7,985 references from which we eliminated 27 (websites, forthcoming articles…). We have thus retained 7,958 references drawn from the works of 3,378 different authors.

In building our paper database we have recorded the title, author(s) (name, institution, and country), and the keywords and references (name(s) of the author(s) and the year). We also created two variables to qualify each paper. The first defines the type of paper as either theoretical or empirical, the second defines the methodology used in the paper as being qualitative or quantitative.

We analyzed our database at three levels: authors, papers, and references. In the following sections, we present the results of our analysis. The section concerning authors gives an overview of the population. We particularly analyze the prominent authors (number of papers published by each author), the country of origin, and each author's institution. In the section entitled "The Papers," we analyze papers by their type and by their methodology. A cluster analysis then enables us to build a typology of the papers based on keywords. The third section presents an analysis of the references. We first make three analyzes based on citation count: we identify the most cited references, we study the historical distribution of these references (according to the year of publication) and we look at the changes in the intellectual structure of the CBM field (this means that we compare most cited references in CBM publications during two different periods). We then build a co-citation matrix. This enables both the identification of repeated pairs of references (references frequently cited together in different papers) and the drawing of network maps (these are representations of the main links between most cited references: a link is a co-citation).

The following figure presents the design of our study (Fig. 1).

THE AUTHORS

Among the 213 authors we studied, 77% of them have only written one paper. Sixteen percent have written two. Three percent have written three, and 4%, four or more. Only nine different authors wrote about 30% of the papers. This means that 4.2% of the authors contribute to 30% of the production in terms of number of papers. The most prominent authors are listed in Table 1.

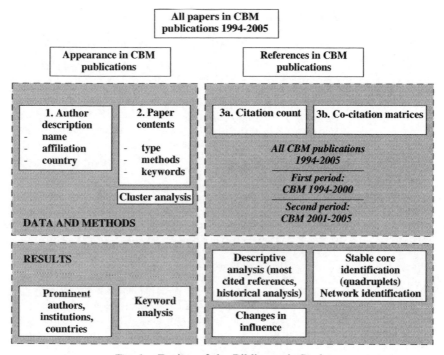

Fig. 1. Design of the Bibliometric Study.

Identification of country of origin was possible for only 207 of the 213 authors. The country of origin is the country where the institution with which the author is affiliated is situated (and we consider the time the author wrote the paper). The institutions are located in 21 different countries (cf. breakdown in Table 2). The five most represented countries account for 57% of the authors. If we then take the nine most represented countries, we obtain 78% of the authors. Considering 13 countries, we have 90% of the authors, and taking into account 15 countries, 95% of the authors.

We identified 139 different institutions. Contrary to what we observed for the countries, the repartition among institutions is very broad: The highest number of authors belonging to a single institution is 12 (Erasmus University) but this institution represents only 5% of the authors. This means that there is no institution leading the field of CBM. Furthermore, no group of authors comes from a single institution.

Table 1.   The Most Prominent Authors.

Authors	Affiliations	No. of Papers	Percent of Total Number of Papers ($n = 185$)
Sanchez, Ron	University of Illinois at Urbana-Champaign (US), University of Western Australia (Aus), IMD Lausanne (Swi), Lund University (Swe), Copenhagen Business School (DK), National University of Singapore (Sin)	19	10.3
Heene, Aimé	De Vlerick School of Management (B), Ghent University (B), Antwerp University (B)	16	8.6
Vandenbosch, Frans AJ	Erasmus University Rotterdam (NL)	9	4.9
Volberda, Henk	Erasmus University Rotterdam (NL)	7	3.8
Black, Janice	Michigan State University (US), New Mexico State University (US)	6	3.2
Thomas, Howard	University of Illinois at Urbana-Champaign (US)	5	2.7
Chiesa, Vittorio	Politecnico di Milano (It)	4	2.2
Elfring, Tom	Erasmus University Rotterdam (NL)	4	2.2
Freiling, Jörg	Ruhr-Universitat Bochum (Ger), University of Bremen (Ger)	4	2.2
Wallin, Johan	Synocus Oy (Fin)	4	2.2
Baden-Fuller, Charles	City University Business School (UK)	3	1.6
Lorino, Philippe	Université Paris-X and ESSEC (F)	3	1.6
Manzini, Raffaela	Politecnico di Milano (It), Libero Universita Carlo Cattaneo Castellanza Varese (It)	3	1.6
McKelvey, Bill	UCLA (US)	3	1.6
Meschi, Pierre-Xavier	Université Aix-Marseille and Euromed (Fra)	3	1.6
Stein, Johan	Stockholm School of Economics (Swe)	3	1.6

Table 2.   The Most Represented Countries ($n = 207$).

Country	Absolute Frequency	Relative Frequency (%)	Country	Absolute Frequency	Relative Frequency (%)
USA	35	17	Italy	12	6
Netherlands	27	13	Finland	12	6
Belgium	23	11	Sweden	10	5
UK	17	8	Germany	10	5
France	17	8	Denmark	8	4

THE PAPERS

Types of Papers and Their Methodology

We worked with 185 papers. There are, on average, 1.8 authors per paper. Thirty-seven percent of the papers have a single author. Forty-nine percent of the papers were written by two authors, and 11% by three.

For each paper, we identified whether it was theoretical or empirical. An empirical paper is based on empirical data, whereas we classified a paper as theoretical if it lacked empirical data. One hundred and four papers (57%) are empirical and 76 papers (43%) theoretical. In order to gain insight on the evolution of the research, we identified the proportion of empirical papers for each of the 15 volumes of CBM publications. Fig. 2 gives the percentage of empirical papers.

The number of each volume refers to the list in the appendix. The general trend is an increase in the number of empirical papers. Three volumes are mainly theoretical: Vol. 1, Competence-Based Competition, published in 1994; Vol. 6, Theory Development for Competence-Based Management, published in 2000; and Vol. 9, A Systems View of Resources, Capabilities and Management Processes, published in 2002. Volume 1 (1994) defines the basis of CBM, and explains its theoretical content. Volume 9 (2002) initiates a new period in theory building. On the basis of these results, we decided to split the database into two subsamples (publications from 1994 to 2000 and

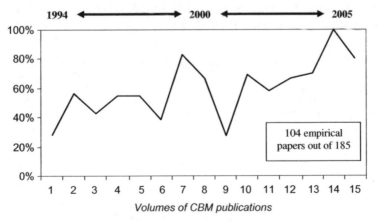

Fig. 2. Evolution of the Percentage of Empirical Papers in CBM Publications. *Note:* See appendix for the years of publication of CBM volumes.

publications from 2001 to 2005) in order to perform some additional analysis (see part 3: The References).

We also identified the dominant methodology of the empirical papers by their qualitative or quantitative nature: 65% are qualitative.

Keywords

In our database, no keywords are supplied by authors of the different papers. We found that an analysis of keywords is very interesting in order to study the content of the papers and to define the different subthemes in the field of CBM. We thus chose to attribute keywords to each paper. We assumed that the keyword "competence" could fit any of the 185 papers. Therefore, this keyword was not attributed. We first associated between two and four keywords to each paper on the basis of the most frequent words written in the abstracts by the authors themselves. As a result, we had 311 different keywords. We grouped the keywords and obtained 20 main keywords. We then reattributed these keywords to each paper. We attributed on average 2.8 keywords per paper, which means that in total we analyzed 507 keywords. Table 3 gives the frequency of occurrence of the keywords.

Two keywords "structure and organization" and "competitive advantage" represent 21% of the occurrences. The distribution of keywords is quite concentrated. If we consider the first six keywords, we reach 51% of the occurrences. Twelve keywords correspond to more than 80% of the occurrences and 16 to more than 95% (Fig. 3).

Table 3. The Most Frequently Used Keywords ($n = 185$).

Keyword	No.	%	Keyword	No.	%
Structure and Organization	56	11	Innovation	25	5
Competitive advantage	50	10	Marketing	23	5
Learning	49	9	Modularity	21	4
Systems view	41	8	Network	15	3
Knowledge	34	7	Environment	14	3
Sector study	33	7	Human resources	11	2
Change	29	6	Growth	8	2
Decision making	28	6	SME	6	1
Interfirm relations	26	5	Stakeholders	5	1
Methodology and Theory	25	5	Entrepreneurship	5	1

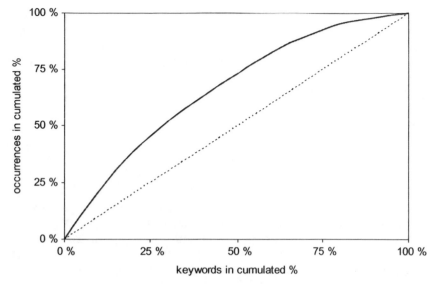

Fig. 3. Keyword Distribution.

In order to study the structure of the papers we performed a multi-dimensional analysis (Multiple Correspondence Analysis). In this analysis, we considered different variables defining each paper: the volume in which it was published, authors, kind of paper (theoretical/empirical), methodology (qualitative/quantitative), keywords (see above for details), and the number of references. In the first step of the analysis, the papers were projected on a subspace with the least possible deformation (minimization of error). The axes of this subspace structure the primary data. The axes are sorted by order of importance and they can thus be interpreted as linear combinations of the original variables. In the second step of the analysis, a hierarchical and ascending classification analysis was performed for grouping into clusters (i.e., categories) papers with similar "features." These clusters were then characterized by the initial variables. We chose the 16 most frequent keywords as active variables.

We found three main axes structuring the papers. The first axis concerns the level of analysis, and it opposes sector analysis and firm analysis. It differentiates the papers that have "sector study," "environment," and "change" as keywords (sector) from those having "inter-firm relations," "knowledge," and "competitive advantage" as keywords (firm). The second axis differentiates the study approach of the internal firm structure: analytical view or systems view. In terms of keywords, this means an opposition between "decision making," "environment," "structure and organization," and "marketing" (analytical) on the one hand, and "innovation," "modularity," "systems view," and "production" (systems) on the other. The third axis differentiates two relational approaches: internal ("modularity") and external ("network," "sector analysis," "inter-firm").

We then performed a cluster analysis based on the results of this factor analysis. The clusters group the 185 papers of the CBM publications. Clusters are differentiated according to the axes resulting from the factor analysis. Each cluster defines a subfield in the CBM field. Based on a study of the characteristics (mainly the keywords) of the papers included in the clusters, we named the first subfield "Organizing for identifying competences" (42% of the papers are included in this cluster, with keywords being "structure and organization," "systems view," and "innovation"), the second subfield is "Inter-firm relations" (21% of the papers belong to this cluster, with keywords being "inter-firm relations," "network," and "marketing"), the third "Change management" (18% of the papers are included in this cluster, with keywords of "change," "sector studies," "decision making," "sector and organization," and "environment"), the fourth "Innovation" (13% of the papers belong to this cluster, with keywords being "innovation," "learning," and "network"), and finally the fifth subfield is titled "Human resources" (6% of the papers are included in this cluster, with "human resources" as the main salient keyword).

The conclusion drawn from this analysis is that we can describe the CBM field as being organized around three main axes and divided into five main subfields (see Fig. 4).

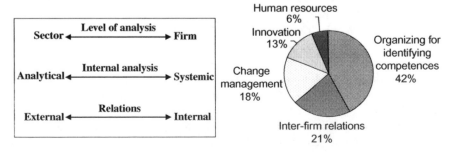

Fig. 4.   CBM: Axes and Subfields ($n = 185$).

THE REFERENCES

Number of References

In our database, 182 papers (98% of the papers) have a reference list. In total, there are 7,958 citations. There is an average of 44 references per paper. The number of references per paper ranges from 3 to 121. As can be seen in Fig. 5, 18% of the papers have fewer than 25 references, 21% have between 50 and 75 references, and 11% have more than 75 references.

As can be noted in Fig. 6, the average number of references per paper increases (the numbers refer to the CBM volumes as listed in the appendix). There are two possible explanations for this increase. First, there has been a common trend in all management journals and conferences to cite more references since the 1990s. Second, there is an accumulation of the number of references in the CBM field, therefore more references to be cited. The analysis of the structure of the CBM field (see above) shows that it covers different subfields. The increasing number of references per paper tends to prove that these subfields are interconnected. These are characteristic of an "evolving" research field leading to internal debates (an increase in the number of citations correlates with the existence of subfields).

Most Influential Authors

From an initial 4,363 different references we arrive at a total of 7,958 reference citing. Table 4 gives the most frequently cited references.

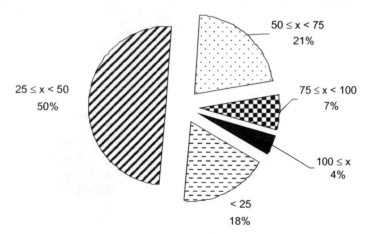

Fig. 5. Number of Citations by Paper (*n* = 185).

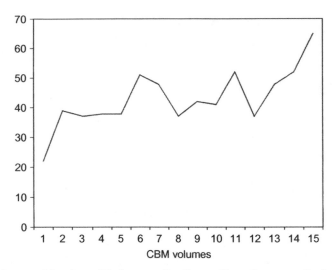

Fig. 6. Average Number of References Per Paper. *Note:* See appendix for the years of publication of the CBM volumes.

Table 4. The Most Frequently Cited References (*n* = 182).

Year	Authors	No. of Occurrences	Relative Frequency in Total 182 papers	Ranking in *SMJ* 1994–2000
1996	Sanchez, Heene, Thomas	127	0.70	–
1997	Heene, Sanchez	82	0.45	–
1990	Prahalad, Hamel	82	0.45	10
1991	Barney	67	0.37	2
1989	Dierickx, Cool	64	0.35	6
1984	Wernerfelt	63	0.35	3
1996	Sanchez, Heene	60	0.33	–
1959	Penrose	47	0.26	8
1986	Barney	47	0.26	13
1980	Porter	41	0.23	1
1997	Sanchez, Heene	39	0.21	–
1994	Hamel, Heene	39	0.21	–
1993	Peteraf	38	0.21	15
1982	Nelson, Winter	36	0.20	5
1993	Amit, Schoemaker	35	0.19	–
1985	Porter	35	0.19	4
1991	Grant	34	0.19	–
1995	Sanchez	34	0.19	–
1994	Hamel, Prahalad	33	0.18	–
1996	Sanchez	33	0.18	–

The major cited references are the seminal references of the field. CBM is well structured around these references. In fact, the level of occurrence of the most important references is very high. This means that the central paradigm is strong and shared by researchers in the field (e.g., Sanchez et al., 1996 is cited in 70% of the papers). CBM is clearly a subfield of Strategic Management: among the 20 most cited references in the CBM field, 10 are in the top 20 most cited references in the *Strategic Management Journal*. There are then two kinds of references: central references in Strategic Management and references defining the specificity of the CBM field.

Historical Structure of the References

Over the whole sample, only 1% of the total number of observed citations date before 1950. Twelve percent were written between 1950 and 1980, 61% between 1990 and 2000 (55% date from before 1994). Fig. 7 gives reference date distribution. We consider the references that are cited more than 10 times and which represent, for a given year, more than 30% of the references for this year.

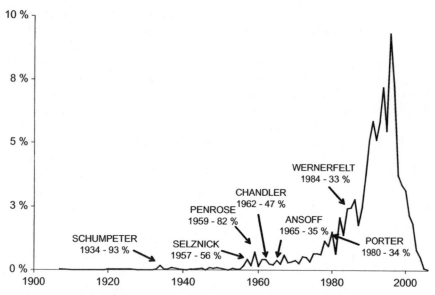

Fig. 7. Historical Distribution of References (*n* = 4,363 Different References).

Among the 4,363 references, 82 (2% of the total number of references) are papers from the CBM publications. In addition, among the different cited authors, 176 (i.e., 5%) are authors of papers in CBM publications. This is a high level and means that there is a strong, but open, identity in the CBM field.

The Central Structure of the CBM Field: A Co-Citation Analysis

We intend to define the central structure of the CBM field. That is to say, we seek *n*-tuples of citations that we find together in more than one paper. Because we are interested in the most frequently cited groups of citations, and in order to speed up the convergence of the algorithm, we consider only citation references which are cited 10 times or more in the whole sample. We then build, step-by-step, all possible ordered pairs (co-citations).

McCain (1990) proposes different computer techniques to identify the intellectual structure of a discipline, among these, one finds network mapping. This consists of building maps in order to analyze the structure of the reference co-citations. Main reference clusters are represented on a map. In this study, we chose to build three maps. The first map gives the intellectual structure of CBM research gathered from 1994 to 2005 (Fig. 8). Two additional maps represent the networks of the two subperiods defined above: 1994–2000 (CBM publications 1–8, see appendix) and 2001–2005 (CBM publications 9–15). In order to identify networks of references within the data and draw maps, we used *Grimmersoft Wordmapper* software.

For each reference, we give the number of citations in the database. The number with the link between two references indicates the number of co-citations (number of papers citing these references together). Exiting links between references contributes to defining a network. A network does not necessarily means that all references in the same network belong to the same school or argue for the same theory. On the contrary, some groupings could be dialectical ones. The conceptual opposition between reference A and reference B is often used by an author to structure his/her reasoning. Then, in the same article, an author could simultaneously refer to Sanchez et al. (1996) and Porter (1980). The author refers to the first reference to position his/her work in the CBM field, and refers to the second reference because "Porter's *Competitive Strategy* became the foundation for much of the strategy curriculum and marked a transition from the reliance on toolkits developed by consulting firms (such as the BCG matrix) to a

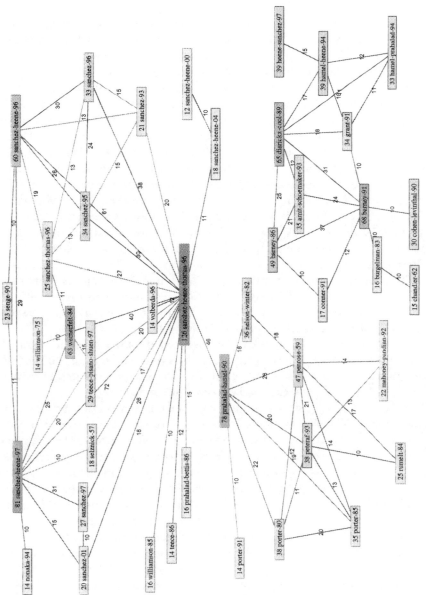

Fig. 8. Most Cited References (≥ 14), and Co-Citations (≥ 10) in CBM 1994–2005.

systematic, theoretical analysis of firm-level strategy" (Nerur et al., 2008, pp. 319–320).

There are three main references networks. The first one centers on the paper by Sanchez et al. (1996), including other works by Sanchez and Heene (1996, 1997), Sanchez (1995), Wernerfelt (1984), and Teece, Pisano, and Shuen (1997). This network represents the core of the CBM references. These are mainly authors specialized in competence literature with links to the foundations of Strategic Management literature (Williamson, Selsnick, Teece). The second network groups references from the fundamentals of industrial analysis in strategic management (Porter, 1980, 1985, 1991) and the foundations of Resource-Based View (Penrose, 1959; Peteraf, 1993). This network illustrates the transition in strategic management research from dominance of industrial economics to the emergence of the RBV. The co-citation of Prahalad and Hamel (1990) with Sanchez et al. (1996) makes the link between this pool of references and the CBM-specialized references (first and second network). The third network is not linked to the other two networks. It mainly groups references from the RBV field (Barney, 1991; Dierickx & Cool, 1989).

This map (Fig. 9) presents the most cited authors (this means more than 10 occurrences) and the highest co-citation rates (more than 10, i.e., 10% of the papers as there are 101 papers published in this period) in the papers of the CBM publications between 1994 and 2000.

This map (Fig. 10) presents the most cited authors (more than 10 occurrences) and the highest co-citations rates (more than 8, i.e., 10% of the papers as there are 81 papers published in this period) in the papers appearing in CBM publications between 2001 and 2005.

We can identify the evolution in the reference networks between the two periods. The first network, organized around Sanchez et al. (1996) representing specialized CBM-references is quite stable. The network representing the foundations of RBV is dissociated from the references of industrial analysis (Porter) and these last tend to disappear in the second period. The network grouping RBV-specialized references tends to remain stable. In spite of the apparent stability of the networks, some authors tend to be less frequently cited, whereas others tend to emerge. In order to more specifically analyze these changes, we calculated and compared the relative number of occurrences of each reference in the first and second periods (see Fig. 11).

The references defined as CBM-specialized (first network) are very stable: the most cited references in the first period remain the most cited references in the second period. Nevertheless, there is a slight change in the proportion

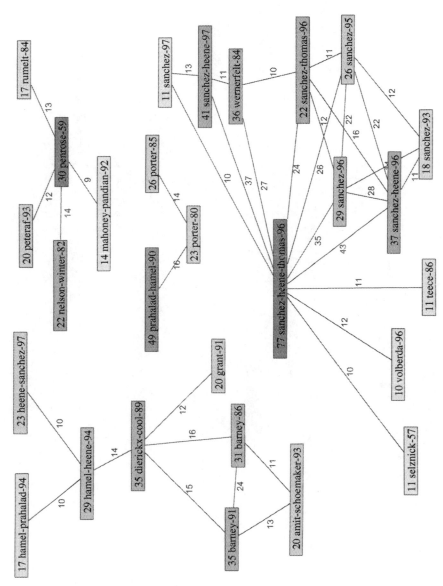

Fig. 9. Most Cited References (≥10), and Co-Citations (≥10) in CBM 1994–2000.

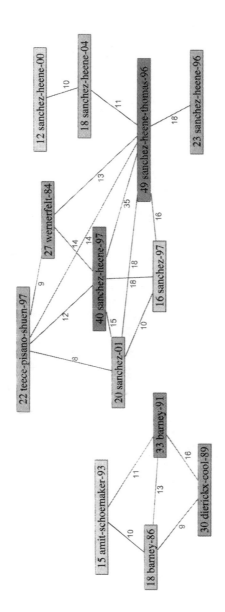

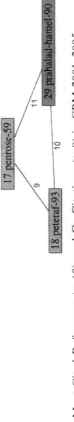

Fig. 10. Most Cited References (≥10), and Co-Citations (≥8) in CBM 2001–2005.

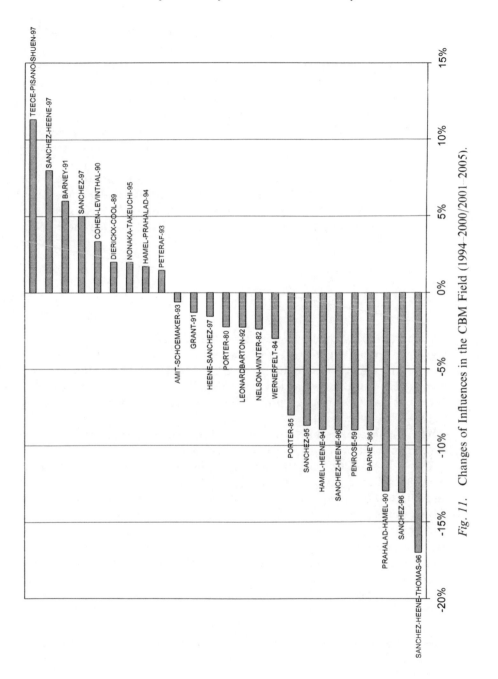

Fig. 11. Changes of Influences in the CBM Field (1994–2000/2001–2005).

of occurrences. Some references are relatively more cited (Sanchez & Heene, 1997; Sanchez, 1995), and tend to be substituted for other works by the same authors. Among the RBV references, there is a substitution phenomenon. The influence of Hamel and Prahalad (1994), Teece et al. (1997), Barney (1991), Dierickx and Cool (1989), and Peteraf (1993) increases relatively, whereas the influence of Prahalad and Hamel (1990), Barney (1986), Penrose (1959), Wernerfelt (1984), Grant (1991), and Amit and Schoemaker (1993) decreases. These two sets of substitutions occur within the same framework (respectively CBM and RBV).

Another trend is the substitution of one framework for another. For example, references to "Influence of Industrial Analysis and Evolutionary Economics" (Porter, 1980, 1985; Nelson & Winter, 1982) gives way to references dealing with knowledge and learning (Nonaka & Takeuchi, 1995; Cohen & Levinthal, 1990).

Identification of Groups of References

For the following analysis, we eliminated the pairs (co-citations) which appeared fewer than three times and we combined the remaining pairs to add an element and to build all possible triplets. We retained the triplets that are cited twice or more and we repeated the process. We performed 17 iterations (i.e., there is no group of 18 citations that are cited simultaneously in two different papers).

The number of n-uplets we obtained is represented in Fig. 12. The maximum is reached for n-uplets of seven elements.

Two n-uplets with 17 citation references (with 16 shared citations) appear twice in two different papers. We studied the n-uplets (n between 6 and 18) and retained the most frequently cited (they are all 6-tuples). In total, 14% of the n-tuples appear only once, 77% twice, 6% three times, 2% four times, and only 1% five or more times. For a given n, all the n-uplets we built are not necessarily independent: they may have areas of cross-over (a same citation reference can belong to many different n-uplets). For this analysis, we hypothesized that the studied field is structured around independent stable cores. We thus are interested in independent n-uplets (for all of the stable cores found, each citation reference is listed only once). Because we are looking for stable cores of the field, we only studied the most frequently cited n-uplets (more than four occurrences). Because we want these stable cores to be homogeneous and to be large in order to constitute real stable

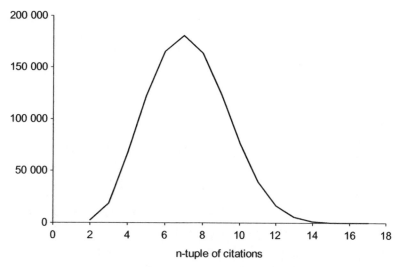

Fig. 12.   Number of *n*-Uplets in References Lists.

cores of the field, we consider the quadruplets. Table 5 presents the main characteristics of the identified quadruplets.

The quadruplets represent the groups of four references cited together in different papers. The number of occurrences represents the number of papers citing the four references together. We attributed a name to each group of references in order to define the nature of the group. Most of these groupings reveal the competitive structure of the works in CBM. Authors simultaneously cite paradigms that are in competition, which we could call "odd couples" like CBM- and RBV-core or origins, CBM and industrial analysis. The first group (Sanchez et al., 1996; Barney, 1991; Dierickx & Cool, 1989; Wernerfelt, 1984) is named CBM-core and RBV-core. In fact, the first paper is the most cited in our database, and can be considered as representing the core of the CBM approach; the three other papers are among the most cited in the RBV (Ramos-Rodriguez & Ruiz-Navarro, 2004; Acedo, Barroso, & Galan, 2006) and are cited together with Sanchez et al. (1996) in opposition. The name of the second group is CBM-origins (Prahalad & Hamel, 1990; Grant, 1991) and RBV-origins (Barney, 1986; Penrose, 1959). The third group is clearly pure CBM (Sanchez, 1993, 1995, 1996; Sanchez & Heene, 1996). Papers dealing with knowledge form the fourth group (Grant, 1996; Kogut & Zander, 1992; Cohen & Levinthal, 1990; Nonaka, 1994). In the fifth group, one finds papers conceptualizing RBV (Peteraf, 1993; Rumelt, 1984; Amit & Schoemaker, 1993;

Table 5. Characteristics of the Quadruplets.

Quadruplets (References)			Citing Papers (Text)	
Name	Authors	No. of occurrences	Keywords	Dates
CBM-core and RBV-core	Sanchez, Heene and Thomas (1996) Barney (1991) Dierickx and Cool (1989) Wernerfelt (1984)	24	Methodology and Theory (5) Structure and Organization (5) Systems view (4) Competitive advantage (4) Interfirm relations (3) Knowledge (1) Learning (1)	1996 (2) 1997 (6) 2000 (5) 2001 (1) 2002 (4) 2005 (6)
CBM-origins and RBV-origins	Prahalad and Hamel (1990) Grant (1991) Barney (1986) Penrose (1959)	10	Methodology and Theory (3) Interfirm relations (2) Structure and Organization (2) Competitive advantage (2) Marketing (1)	1994 (1) 1996 (3) 1997 (1) 2000 (2) 2005 (3)
CBM	Sanchez (1993) Sanchez (1995) Sanchez (1996) Sanchez and Heene (1996)	8	Methodology and Theory (6) Interfirm relations (1) Learning (1)	1996 (2) 1997 (5) 2002 (1)
Knowledge	Grant (1996) Kogut and Zander (1992) Cohen and Levinthal (1990) Nonaka (1994)	7	Knowledge (3) Structure and Organization (2) Interfirm relations (2)	2001 (2) 2005 (5)
RBV	Peteraf (93) Rumelt (1984) Amit and Schoemaker, (1993) Mahoney and Pandian (1992)	6	Competitive advantage (3) Interfirm relations (2) Methodology and Theory (1)	1997 (2) 2000 (1) 2004 (1) 2005 (1)
CBM and Industrial Analysis	Sanchez and Heene (1997) Teece et al. (1997) Porter (1980) Porter (1985)	5	Competitive advantage (2) Methodology and Theory (1) Marketing (1) Innovation (1)	2000 (2) 2005 (3)

Mahoney & Pandian, 1992). The last group is named CBM (Sanchez & Heene, 1997; Teece et al., 1997) and Industrial Analysis (Porter, 1980, 1985). The authors cited these references together to place them in opposition, as seen above in the first grouping.

We studied the papers citing the quadruplets in order to analyze the main keywords and dates of publication. This enables us to associate keywords and dates to each group of references (i.e., each quadruplet). For each keyword and each date of publication, we give the number of citing papers associated to this keyword and date (then, the sum of the numbers in brackets gives the number of occurrences). The group of references associated with CBM-core and RBV-core is represented mainly by keywords such as Methodology and Theory, Structure and Organization, Systems View, Competitive Advantage, and Inter-firm Relations. Methodology and Theory, Inter-firm Relations, Structure and Organization and Competitive Advantage represent the group CBM-origins and RBV-origins. The group of authors associated with pure CBM theory is logically represented primarily by the keyword Methodology and Theory. For the remaining groups, there is no real dominant keyword. We notice that the keyword Knowledge is logically associated with the group named Knowledge. The keywords Methodology and Theory, Structure and Organization and Inter-firm Relations are associated with different groups. This may be explained by the fact that the papers dealing with methodology, Theory and Structure and Organization generally contain more references than other types of papers. Another explanation is that dealing with these subjects leads to creating links between different theoretical fields. This same reason explains why the keyword Inter-firm Relations is associated with many different groups. "Inter-firm relations" appears to be a transversal theme in the CBM field, as it is referred to by all the different groups of authors. This underlines the importance of this theme and shows that it is a main direction for future research in the field (Sanchez & Heene, 2005; Prévot, 2008; Martens, Heene, & Sanchez, 2008).

Concerning the dates, there is no concentration of publications citing the groups of authors representing CBM-core and RBV-core, CBM-origins and RBV-origins, and RBV. Papers citing the groups of authors representing Knowledge are concentrated in 2001 and 2005 and the papers citing the groups of authors representing CBM and Industrial Analysis are concentrated in 2000 and 2005. This means that these themes are included in what we defined as the second period of publication. Papers citing the authors of the group CBM are concentrated in 1997.

CONCLUSION

The purpose of this research was to conduct a bibliometric analysis of the CBM field based on the study of 185 papers from 12 books and 3 issues of the review *Research in Competence Based Management* published between 1994 and 2005 following the International Conferences on Competence-Based Management (ICCBM). We identified the most prominent authors, we analyzed the contents of the papers (methodology and keywords) and we studied the 7,958 references cited in the papers. In the study of the references we identified co-citations and then built networks of references. These networks give an interesting view of the structure and evolution of the CBM field. In the analysis of the papers published between 1994 and 2001, we identified four clusters of co-citations. Even if it is not possible to completely differentiate each cluster from the others (some authors appear in multiple clusters), there seems to be a dominant character for each cluster. One cluster is organized around Dierickx and Cool (1989) and mainly groups RBV references together. Another is organized around Penrose (1959) and makes a link between RBV references and Nelson and Winter (1982). Another cluster links Porter (1980, 1985) and Prahalad and Hamel (1990). Still another cluster, the largest one in terms of number of co-citations is organized around Sanchez et al. (1996) and group references that can be considered as being core-CBM references. In the papers published between 2001 and 2005, mapping shows that there are three clusters and a reduction of the number of papers in the list of co-citations (i.e., fewer authors in the networks). One cluster groups four RBV seminal references (Barney, 1986; Dierickx & Cool, 1989; Barney, 1991; Amit & Schoemaker, 1993). Another cluster groups Penrose (1959), Peteraf (1993), and Prahalad and Hamel (1990). The most important cluster in terms of number of authors groups core-CBM references around two seminal papers: Sanchez et al. (1996) and Sanchez and Heene (1997). That means that CBM field tends to be organized around core references directly associated to the field itself. This illustrates that the field has reached a level of maturity and has clearly defined its differences with other fields (in particular RBV). It is interesting to compare this evolution of CBM to the evolution of RBT. In their research, Acedo et al. (2006) made a co-citation analysis of RBT, their results showing that RBT is divided in three subfields: resource-based view, knowledge-based view, and relational view. In RBT there is a tendency to split the literature into subfields, whereas in CBM the co-citation networks show a trend to unify and to focus on core-CBM papers. This unification corresponds to a maturing of the field and indicates a clarification and strengthening of the foundations of the field. This unification does not imply a reduction in the diversity of the topics studied. In fact, our keyword analysis clearly underlines the diversity in the topics related to CBM. However, at the same time, this is a growing need to differentiate from other research fields in strategy.

The results of the research presented in this paper are useful for anybody seeking a better understanding of the CBM field. They help explain the structure of the field and provide an analysis of its evolution. Scholars in the field can use these results to position their research and to identify avenues for new theoretical or empirical developments. Scholars who are less familiar with CBM may use the results of this research to gain knowledge about this field and to better understand the main stakes in its development. We can, however, identify certain limits to this research. The main limit is related to the fact that we only focused on papers published in books and in issues of the RCBM following the ICCBM. This allowed us to focus our research on a homogenous sample of papers. However, this approach ignores important CBM papers published outside the ICCBM. An interesting extension of our research would be to expand this bibliometric analysis to a larger number of papers from different journals in Strategic Management.

ACKNOWLEDGMENT

The authors would like to thank the anonymous reviewers for helpful comments on earlier versions of this paper, and Sarah Setton for her help in the final editing of this paper.

REFERENCES

Acedo, F. J., Barroso, C., & Galan, J. L. (2006). The resource-based theory: Dissemination and main trends. *Strategic Management Journal, 27*, 621–636.

Amit, R., & Schoemaker, P. (1993). Strategic assets and organizational rent. *Strategic Management Journal, 14*, 3–46.

Barney, J. (1986). Strategic factor markets: Expectations, luck, and business strategy. *Management Science, 32*, 1231–1241.

Barney, J. (1991). Firm resources and sustained competitive advantage. *Journal of Management, 17*, 99–120.

Boissin, J.-P., Castagnos, J.-C., & Guieu, G. (2001). Ordre et Désordre dans la Recherche Francophone en Stratégie. In: A.-C. Martinet & R.-A. Thiétart (Eds), *Stratégies: Actualités et futurs de la recherché* (pp. 27–42, Chapter 2). Paris: Vuibert.

Callon, M., Law, J., & Rip, A. (Eds). (1986). *Mapping the dynamics of science and technology*. London: Macmillan.

Cohen, W., & Levinthal, D. A. (1990). Absorptive capacity: A new perspective on learning and innovation. *Administrative Science Quarterly, 35*, 128–152.

Dierickx, I., & Cool, K. (1989). Asset stock accumulation and sustainability of competitive advantage. *Management Science, 35*, 1504–1511.

Freiling, J., Gersch, M., & Goeke, C. (2008). On the path towards a competence-based theory of the firm. *Organization Studies, 29*, 1143–1164.

Grant, R. M. (1991). The resource-based theory of competitive advantage: Implications for strategy formulation. *California Management Review*, 114–135.

Grant, R. M. (1996). Towards a knowledge-based theory of the firm. *Strategic Management Journal, 17*, 109–122.

Hamel, G., & Heene, A. (Eds). (1994). *Competence-based competition*. New York: Wiley.

Hamel, G., & Prahalad, C. K. (1989). Strategic intent. *Harvard Business Review, 67*, 63–76.

Hamel, G., & Prahalad, C. K. (1994). *Competing for the future*. Boston, MA: Harvard Business School Press.

Heene, A., & Sanchez, R. (1997). *Competence-based strategic management*. London: Elsevier Pergamon.

Kogut, B., & Zander, U. (1992). Knowledge of the firm, combinative capabilities, and the replication of technology. *Organization Science, 3*, 383–397.

Mahoney, J. T., & Pandian, J. R. (1992). The resource-based view within the conversation of strategic management. *Strategic Management Journal, 13*, 363–380.

Martens, R., Heene, A., & Sanchez, R. (Eds). (2008). *Competence-building and leveraging in interorganizational relations – Advances in applied business strategy* (Vol. 11). Oxford: Elsevier.

McCain, K. W. (1990). Mapping authors in intellectual space: A technical overview. *Journal of the American Society for Information Science, 41*, 433–443.

Nelson, R. R., & Winter, S. (1982). *An evolutionary theory of economic change*. Cambridge: Harvard University Press.

Nerur, S. P., Rasheed, A. A., & Natarajan, V. (2008). The intellectual structure of the strategic management field: An author co-citation analysis. *Strategic Management Journal, 29*, 319–336.

Nonaka, I. (1994). A dynamic theory of organizational knowledge creation. *Organization Science, 5*(1), 14–37.

Nonaka, I., & Takeuchi, H. (1995). *The knowledge-creating company*. New York: Oxford University Press.

Penrose, E. (1959). *The theory of the growth of the firm*. London: Wiley.

Peteraf, M. A. (1993). The cornerstones of competitive advantage: A resource-based view. *Strategic Management Journal, 14*, 179–191.

Porter, M. E. (1980). *Competitive strategy*. New York: Free Press.

Porter, M. E. (1985). *Competitive advantage*. New York: Free Press.

Porter, M. E. (1991). Towards a dynamic theory of strategy. *Strategic Management Journal, 12*(Special Issue), 95–117.

Prahalad, C. K., & Hamel, G. (1990). The core competence of the corporation. *Harvard Business Review, 68*, 79–93.

Prahalad, C. K., & Hamel, G. (1993). Strategy as stretch and leverage. *Harvard Business Review, 71*, 75–85.

Prévot, F. (2008). The management of competences in the context of inter-organizational relations. In: R. Martens, A. Heene, & R. Sanchez, R. (Eds), *Competence-building and leveraging in interorganizational relations – Advances in applied business strategy* (Vol. 11, Chapter 1, pp. 7–35). Oxford, UK: Elsevier Science.

Ramos-Rodriguez, A.-R., & Ruiz-Navarro, J. (2004). Changes in the intellectual structure of strategic management research: A bibliometric study of the strategic management journal, 1980–2000. *Strategic Management Journal, 25*, 981–1004.

Rumelt, R. P. (1984). Towards a strategic theory of the firm. In: R. B. Lamb (Ed.), *Competitive strategic management* (pp. 556–570). Englewood Cliffs, NJ: Prentice-Hall.

Rumelt, R. P. (1994). Foreword. In: G. Hamel & A. Heene (Eds), *Competence-based competition* (pp. xv–xix). New York: Wiley.

Sanchez, R. (1993). Strategic flexibility, firm organization, and managerial work in dynamic markets: A strategic options perspective. *Advances in Strategic Management, 9*, 251–291.

Sanchez, R. (1995). Strategic flexibility in product competition. *Strategic Management Journal, 16*, 135–159.

Sanchez, R. (1996). Strategic product creation: Managing new interactions of technology, markets, and organizations. *European Management Journal, 14*, 121–138.

Sanchez, R., & Heene, A. (1996). A systems view of the firm in competence-based competition. In: R. Sanchez, A. Heene & H. Thomas (Eds), *Dynamics of competence-based competition: Theory and practice in the new strategic management*. London: Elsevier.

Sanchez, R., & Heene, A. (1997). Competence-based strategic management: Concepts and issues for theory, research and practice. In: R. Sanchez & A. Heene (Eds), *Competence-based strategic management*. New York: Wiley.

Sanchez, R., & Heene, A. (2000). *Theory development for competence-based management – Advances in applied business strategy* (Vol. 6A). Stamford, CT: JAI Press.

Sanchez, R., & Heene, A. (Eds). (2005). *Competence perspectives on managing interfirm interactions – Advances in applied business strategy* (Vol. 8). Oxford: Elsevier.

Sanchez, R., Heene, A., & Thomas, H. (1996). Towards the theory and practice of competence-based competition. In: R. Sanchez, A. Heene & H. Thomas (Eds), *Dynamics of competence-based competition: Theory and practice in the new strategic management*. London: Elsevier.

Teece, D., Pisano, G., & Shuen, A. (1997). Dynamic capabilities and strategic management. *Strategic Management Journal, 18*, 509–533.

Wernerfelt, B. (1984). A resource-based view of the firm. *Strategic Management Journal, 5*, 171–180.

White, D. H., & McCain, K. W. (1998). Visualizing a discipline: An author co-citation analysis of information science 1972–1995. *Journal of the American Society for Information Science, 49*, 327–355.

APPENDIX

1. *Competence-Based Competition*, edited by Gary Hamel and Aimé Heene, published in the Strategic Management Society series by John Wiley & Sons (1994).

2. *Dynamics of Competence-Based Competition*, edited by Ron Sanchez, Aimé Heene, and Howard Thomas, Elsevier Pergamon (1996).

3. *Competence-Based Strategic Management*, edited by Aime Heene and Ron Sanchez, published in the Strategic Management Society series by John Wiley & Sons (1997).
4. *Strategic Learning and Knowledge Management*, edited by Ron Sanchez and Aimé Heene, published in the Strategic Management Society series by John Wiley & Sons (1997).
5. *Knowledge Management and Organizational Competence*, edited by Ron Sanchez, Oxford University Press (2000).
6. *Theory Development for Competence-Based Management*, Volume 6A in Advances in Applied Business Strategy, edited by Ron Sanchez and Aimé Heene, JAI Press (2000).
7. *Research in Competence-Based Management*, Volume 6B in Advances in Applied Business Strategy, edited by Ron Sanchez and Aimé Heene, JAI Press (2000).
8. *Implementing Competence-Based Strategies*, Volume 6C in Advances in Applied Business Strategy, edited by Ron Sanchez and Aimé Heene, JAI Press (2000).
9. *A Systems View of Resources, Capabilities, and Management Processes*, edited by John Morecroft, Ron Sanchez, and Aimé Heene, Elsevier Science Press (2002).
10. *Competence Perspectives on Managing Internal Processes,* Volume 7 in Advances in Applied Business Strategy, edited by Ron Sanchez and Aimé Heene, Elsevier Science (2005).
11. *Competence Perspectives on Managing Interfirm Interactions*, Volume 8 in Advances in Applied Business Strategy, edited by Ron Sanchez and Aimé Heene, Elsevier Science (2005).
12. *Competence Perspectives on Resources, Stakeholders and Renewal*, Volume 9 in Advances in Applied Business Strategy, edited by Ron Sanchez and Aimé Heene, Elsevier Science (2005).
13. *The Marketing Process in Organizational Competence*, Volume 1 in Research in Competence-Based Management, edited by Ron Sanchez and Joerg Freiling, Elsevier Science (2004).
14. *Managing Knowledge Assets and Organizational Learning*, Volume 2 in Research in Competence-Based Management, edited by Ron Sanchez and Aime Heene, Elsevier Science (2005).
15. *Understanding Growth: Entrepreneurship, Innovation, and Diversification*, Volume 3 in Research in Competence-Based Management, edited by Ron Sanchez and Joerg Freiling, Elsevier Science (2005).